Best Hiking Trails
In the United States

edited by Dorothy Deer

Greatlakes Living Press, Publishers, Matteson, Illinois

Best Hiking Trails In the United States
©Greatlakes Living Press 1977
All rights reserved
Printed in the U.S.A.
International Standard Book Number: 0-915498-52-9
Library of Congress Catalog Card No.: 77-71553

Excerpts from:

Hiking Trails in the Midwest© Jerry Sullivan and Glenda Daniel 1974

Hiking Trails in the Northeast© Thomas A. Henley and Neesa Sweet 1976

Hiking Trails in the Pacific Northwest© Amos L. Wood 1977

Hiking Trails in the Southern Mountains© Jerry Sullivan and Glenda Daniel 1975

Reprinted by permission.

Greatlakes Living Press
21750 Main Street
Matteson, IL 60443

Contents

Introduction

U.S. Hiking Trails

Backpacking ranks 18th in popularity among outdoor sports, and it is rapidly gaining in popularity. Within the past five years, some half dozen new backpacking and wilderness camping magazines have hit the newsstands. And more and more stories cater to backpackers' needs. Some are exclusively planned for the wilderness outdoor person; others are sporting goods stores that have greatly expanded their line of hiking and wilderness camping gear.

This book, *Best Hiking Trails in the United States*, is the outgrowth of a number of regional guidebooks published by Greatlakes Living Press. The best trails in each state were selected by the various authors and other avid backpackers to make this a volume of super trails for hikers. It is, of course, impossible to be comprehensive in a national guidebook. If you plan to do a great deal of backpacking in any one region, then we refer you to the guidebook prepared for that specific area of the country.

Two of the regional guidebooks were written by a pair of avid backpackers who, in searching for trails for their own hiking, discovered a lack of printed information and maps. Jerry Sullivan and Glenda Daniel co-authored *Hiking Trails in the Midwest* and *Hiking Trails in the Southern Mountains*. The Chicago-based writers specialize in outdoor and environmental articles for newspapers and magazines. Because of their expertise in the art of backpacking, they are often called upon to conduct seminars.

(The trail numbers we use in the Southern Mountains and Midwestern sections are the Forest Service numbers used on all Forest Service maps.)

Edward B. Garvey authored *Hiking Trails in the Mid Atlantic States* It was a joy for him. As a resident of Virginia, he had already hiked in almost all of the states in the area with the exception of Delaware. He had previously written the book, *Appalachian Hiker*. To complete this Mid-Atlantic guide simply meant more hiking in his beloved Appalachians . . . all under the guise of work.

Following his retirement from government service with the National Science Foundation in 1969 and a couple of years of travel in Europe with his family, Garvey went to work for Appalachian Outfitters, a chain of wilderness outfitting stores in Virginia, Maryland and North Carolina. Here he had a chance to rub shoulders with many other hikers and backpackers, sharing experiences, offering advice and sometimes learning from them.

Amos Wood, author of *Hiking Trails in the Pacific Northwest*, has been hiking with his wife for more than 30 years. Their children are avid hikers and backpackers, and for years the family spent vacation time on hiking and camping trips. Some of these trips were close to home, but others were in British Columbia and as far north as Alaska. They have hiked the sea level beach trails, gone on hiking/fishing trips into the foothills, and covered the alpine trails in the summertime. The Wood family enjoys the outdoors, and they try to get out every weekend, if possible.

Trails were selected by the authors and other hikers familiar with the specific areas, so that only the very best trails are included in this book. But we have also tried to offer a variety of types of trails so that hikers will enjoy varied terrain and points of interest. Some hikes are long to appeal to the overnight backpacker; others are short for day hikers.

As we said before, this book is not designed to be comprehensive. It is planned to introduce you to super hiking trails across our country. And then, once you've caught the hiking bug, you'll build your library of regional guidebooks on the areas you hike in the most.

It is also our hope that beginning hikers will use this book, and choose those hikes that are less arduous. And as they walk the trails, we hope their enjoyment of the outdoors will deepen to the point that they will enjoy hiking and backpacking as much as we, the authors and editors, do.

Preparing for Hiking and Backpacking

The pleasures of tramping in the wilderness are difficult to explain. The freedom you feel walking where and when you choose, the satisfaction of enjoying the wilderness atmosphere without trying to change or conquer it, living with minimal equipment surrounded by nature — these are reasons enough to take to the woods and mountains.

Then there is the physical exertion and mental diversion achieved through hiking. Straining your body by walking with a 40-pound pack on your back is an effort. But when you see things you would never see otherwise, it's worth it.

The little discoveries surprise you. You learn that strawberries growing in the sun are sweeter than those that ripen in the shade, and you find out that an incredible racket in the bushes is more likely to signal the presence of a robin than a bear.

Backpacking is an incredibly exhilarating experience. But you also open yourself up to dangers you wouldn't otherwise face. Dealing with these requires knowledge, experience and common sense.

Experience is something that everyone has to get for himself. And the best way to get it is gradually. Don't start out with a major expedition. Take some one-day hikes, then two-day outings — perhaps on trails that offer developed campgrounds. When you feel comfortable with this sort of trek, then get into real wilderness travel.

Backpacking ranks 18th in popularity among outdoor sports, and it is rapidly gaining in popularity. Within the past five years some half dozen new backpacking and wilderness and camping magazines have hit the newsstands. More and more stores cater to backpackers' needs.

Who should hike?

One of the attractions of hiking is that anyone in reasonably good health can do it. Hiking can be fitted to individual capacities more easily than many other forms of outdoor activity. You can confine yourself to the "turnpikes," broad, level, smoothly surfaced trails, or you can scramble over rocks. You can walk two miles a day or 20.

Children can get into hiking. When they are very small, you can carry them. When they get older, they can help with the hauling. Very young children, obviously, shouldn't carry too much, but they can make a contribution. With young children along, keep the schedule loose. Plan to cover shorter distances with more stops.

1

Older people, too, take up the pastime. The legendary Grandma Gatewood started backpacking at age 65, and hiked the 2,000-mile Appalachian Trail. She did it again at age 67 and again in her early 70's.

What should you take along?

If you are planning on some day hiking, you can get along without anything more than a pair of comfortable shoes. If you intend to wander about in the wilderness for days at a time, you'll probably end up spending hundreds of dollars on sleeping bags, tents, packs, stoves, etc., etc.

If you would like to test the lay of the land before making a large investment, check out the possibilities of renting equipment. Many shops specializing in equipment for backpacking, mountaineering, skiing and related activities will rent you whatever you need. Two places that rent by mail are Eastern Mountain Sports, Inc., 1041 Commonwealth Ave., Boston, Massachusetts. 02215 and Turin Bicycle Co-Op Ltd., 1932 N. Clark St., Chicago, Illinios 60614.

If you have decided that backpacking is your thing and you are prepared to spend some money, read *Backpacking One Step at a Time* by Harvey Manning.

Most of the book is devoted to a thorough discussion of equipment, and once you've read it, you will be more prepared to face the catalogs and store clerks. It is also a good idea to talk to people who have done some backpacking.

If you do not have access to an outdoor store, you can resort to catalogs. Check outdoor magazines at your local library or newsstand and send for catalogs. Some nationally known outdoor catalog merchandisers are: L. L. Bean, Freeport, Maine 04032; Holubars, 6287 Arapahoe Ave., Boulder, Colorado 80302; and the well-known cooperative, Recreational Equipment, Inc., 1525 Eleventh, Seattle, Washington 98122.

Since 1971 Edward Garvey has been affiliated with a small chain of outdoor stores in the Virginia, Maryland and North Carolina area. This permits him to see and examine new products coming into the market. He also gets feedback from both store employees and customers who use the products.

Competition is keen in the manufacture and distribution of backpacking gear, and a variety of competing makes and models are available that will fulfill your needs. Your decision should be based on the advice of the salesman and fellow hikers, your own appraisal of the article being purchased, and that very important consideration — how much you wish to spend.

If you are dealing with a salesman, and if you are green as grass in the knowledge of backpacking gear, inform the salesman of that fact. And if you have a definite limit on how much you can spend for a certain item, inform the salesman of that. also. Any salesman worth his salt will be appreciative of both situations.

Backpacking has its basic four needs, in order of importance: 1) hiking shoes, 2) the backpack, 3) sleeping gear and 4) shelter.

Selection of hiking shoes should be your first concern. Even a one-day hike can be misery without comfortable, good fitting, well broken-in shoes.

Hiking shoes: Today's hikers prefer a shoe that is six inches high, made of leather, and thick sturdy composition soles. Within this framework you could purchase shoes that weigh from 2½ pounds per pair. to over five pounds per pair (for a size 10 shoe). The cost could range from $30 to $80.

If you are just getting into back-packing, he suggests (using size 10 as an indicator again) a pair of shoes that weigh in the three to four pound range and that cost somewhere between $40 and $60.

Take plenty of time in getting your shoes fitted. Wear the type of socks (usually a thin inner pair and a thick outer pair) that you will wear while hiking. Insist on a roomy fit to allow for the swelling that comes from carrying a 30 to 40 pound pack hour after hour. Break the shoes in thoroughly on short walks before going on any extended hike.

Backpack: In purchasing a backpack you will find an almost bewildering array of makes, styles and materials to choose from.

Over the past 20 years, the backpacking fraternity has come to prefer a combination aluminum frame to which is attached a pack of heavy duty nylon taffeta or cordura nylon with various side pockets and compartments to permit quick access to any desired article. The backpacking frame must have both shoulder straps and a waist strap, the latter strap being of such design as to permit much of the weight of the pack to rest on the sturdy hip bones rather than on the more fragile shoulder bones.

When buying a frame, the main thing to be concerned about is fit. Frames come in different sizes for people of different height, so be sure the waist belt fits around your waist and not over your diaphragm.

Backpacks that meet these general requirements can be purchased at costs ranging from $50 to $125. Cubic inch capacity may range from 1,500 to 6,000.

For growing youngsters and for adults who feel they may make only occasional use of their packs, a pack and frame combination should cost in the $30 to $60 range and have a cubic inch capacity of perhaps 2,000 to 2,500.

If you've already had your initiation into backpacking and know that it's going to be your thing, then get a pack and frame combination in the $50 to $90 range with a capacity from 2,500 to 4,000 cubic inches.

Two other items to consider are waterproofing and padded hip belts. There are waterproof backpacks and those made with no waterproofing. You can get valid arguments either way.

If you buy a non-waterproof bag and you are hiking in wet weather areas you will wish to buy a waterproof cover of some type for your pack.

A padded hip belt is a belt approximately one-half inch thick and four inches wide that distributes the weight of your pack more comfortably over a wider area of your hips than does the conventional inch-wide belt. It adds about $10 to the cost of your backpack.

If you are going nothing but day hiking, you can dispense with a pack. But a simple rucksack makes an easy way to carry an extra sweater, picnic lunch or camera gear. There are many inexpensive packs for day hikers. They are just sacks with two fabric straps attached.

Sleeping bag: The sleeping bag can be made or bought in a variety of fabrics and with a variety of filler material.

You can make a simple sleeping bag from a single blanket by sewing it so that it is closed on three sides. The bags that you buy at an outdoor store, however, are generally made with nylon ripstop or taffeta cloth and filled with either goose down, duck down or a synthetic material such as Dacron II.

Goose down is generally considered the warmest ounce for ounce, and duck down is rated as 85 percent as effective as goose down. Down bags compress to a very small package.

Synthetic fills such as Dacron II do not enjoy wide popularity but a small and growing segment of the backpacking fraternity thinks the synthetic fills are superior to anything on the market. For one thing they generally are cheaper than goose and duck down.

Also, the synthetics are bulkier and firmer, the firmness being an asset in that you need less protection between you and the ground than when the highly compressible down filling is used. Bags with synthetic fill are also easier to clean.

In considering how warm a sleeping bag to buy and how much to pay, you first must decide in what months of the year you plan to use it. Perhaps 80 percent of all sleeping bag use in the United States occurs between April 1 and October 31.

If you anticipate that all of your backpacking will be done in temperatures above 20°F you can purchase a lighter weight, less expensive bag than you would otherwise need.

Presuming you are one of the 80 percent hiking in the warmer months, a bag with two pounds of goose down or its equivalent should be more than sufficient. Such a bag may cost from $90 to $150.

If you are buying a bag at an outdoor store, ask to try it on for size. A bag that is two inches too short is *much* too short! When buying a bag costing from $40 to $100 you have every right to try it on for size.

There are mummy type bags, barrel bags and full rectangular bags. The mummy type bag is tapered to fit the body, is the lightest to carry and the easiest to keep warm. But some people find the mummy bag too confining.

Many sleeping bags are made so that two can be zipped together. Whether you need this feature or not depends in part on whom you go backpacking with. Two in a bag provides more body heat, but it also provides a lot of space at the top of the bag for the heat to escape.

Two accessories to the sleeping bag are the ground cloth and mattress. The ground cloth can be an inexpensive piece of clear plastic (costing, say, 80 cents) about 6 feet by 8 feet in size. Or you can buy a piece of waterproof nylon — easier to handle but more expensive — for about $11. A few backpackers require no mattress whatever, but most of us want some type of protection between the sleeping bag and the ground (in addition to the razor thin groundcloth).

Veteran backpackers have progressed from air mattresses to foam pads to the present-day preference for either Valera or Ensolite (trade names of two types of closed cell insulation). The Ensolite is softer and easier to roll up into a small bundle. Ensolite does not absorb water and it provides excellent protection against cold. It comes in various thicknesses and sizes. For warm weather camping I use a piece 20 x 40 inches that is a fourth of an inch thick (cost, $3). For temperatures that are below 30°F, I would use a piece approximately 21 x 56 inches and three-eighths of an inch thick, costing $6.

These pads don't really provide much cushioning. They are designed for warmth, not softness.

Tents: Many books on backpacking treat the tent as an optional article in areas where there are reliable wet and dry seasons. Or along routes such as the Appalachian Trail where there are frequent shelters. But many trails are short on shelters, and rain is unpredictable.

Tents also provide protection against those twin scourges of the wilderness: mosquitoes and black flies.

A very inexpensive shelter is the plastic tube tent. A tube tent for one person costs $1.50. Next on the list of inexpensive shelters is an eight by ten foot waterproof nylon tarp with grommets which costs about $25. This can be used as a tent or a ground cloth or partially as both.

From here we move into bona fide tents, those ingenious little homes on your back that are made from colorful ripstop or taffeta nylon, with sewn-in floors, and mosquito netting. One- and two-man tents weighing from three to five lbs. can be purchased for as low as $40, and they range up to $200.

Tents for backpacking generally are made of nylon, often with a urethane coating on the floor for extra protection against moisture. Nylon is very light, and it does not mildew. It also is much more waterproof than canvas, and that, oddly enough, is its principal drawback.

The average human being releases about a pint of water in a given night, mainly through breathing. In a nylon tent, this moisture is trapped. When the cool of the night arrives, the water can condense on the wall of the tent and falleth as the gentle rain from heaven on the sleeping camper. Good ventilation helps, but it doesn't eliminate the problem.

Many tents now have double walls. The tent proper has walls of nylon taffeta or a similar material that is not an absolute barrier to moisture. However, since this means also that it won't stop a heavy rain, an outer tent is added — a waterproof nylon fly. This stops the rain, and exhaled moisture condenses harmlessly on *its* inner surface.

The double layer principle does create two problems. First it makes the tent heavier. And second, it makes it more expensive.

Check the dimensions of the tent carefully. Make sure it's big enough for your needs.

Food and cooking: With regard to food and cooking, it all depends on your needs and how long you will be on the trail. If you are out for a day's walk, a candy bar and/or a sandwich stuck in a rucksack — or even in your pocket — will do quite well. But if you wish, you could carry an elaborate picnic lunch.

If you are on an overnight hike, almost any kind of food you like can be carried without too much strain. For longer trips, freeze dried foods probably are essential. There are a number of companies making such foods, which can be purchased in stores that sell camping supplies or by mail.

Many of the main courses can be prepared right in the package. Just add boiling water and stir. Jerry Sullivan and Glenda Daniel usually don't eat a lunch on the trail, but take small snacks to munch on whenever they stop to rest or admire the view. Gorp, a mixture of M&M candies, raisins, nuts and granola is a high-energy trail snack.

Trail foods do not provide a balanced diet, but a few days without all your vitamins is not likely to hurt. But the meals are heavy on sugar, providing a source of quick energy.

Remember, whatever you eat, carry out your garbage! Burying it doesn't help, because animals will dig it up.

There is an endless variety of mess kits available for campers. There are kits for one person and for six. There are kits with folding handles and detachable handles. Some kits include silverware, some don't.

The best way to go at this is to determine the minimum that you need. If you are using freeze dried foods exclusively, you can probably get away with one pot for heating water. Put a lid on it and the water will heat faster.

Common practice is to use a cup for everything. Main course, dessert, beverage are all taken in succession from the same cup. If you look enough, you might find a nice large 12 ounce cup ideal for this sort of thing. Avoid plastic cups as they break and also absorb flavors.

A spoon is all you need for silverware. You should have a pocketknife along for other purposes, and this can be employed as cutlery when needed.

There are, of course, lots more things you can carry, if you wish; it's your back.

Cooking instructions for hikers used to center around techniques for building fires. But the campfire these days is going the way of the pine bough bed. There are so many people using the woods that fires are just too obtrusive. They use up dead wood that should be rotting back into the soil. They leave ugly black rings, and they carry the risk of setting the whole countryside ablaze.

What substitutes for the campfire is the lightweight stove — if fuel is available for it. There are basically two kinds, the Primus, Optimus and Svea, which burn white gas, and the Camping Gaz, which burns butane.

The white gas stoves are all made by the same company. They come in a number of shapes and sizes, but the guts are the same in all of them. To prime them, you place a hand on the fuel tank. Body heat creates enough vapor at the burner to allow you to light the stove. Obviously this process takes longer in cold weather than in warm.

The butane stove starts instantly. Just turn the knob and touch a match to the burner.

Some advantages and disadvantages: The fuel for white gas stoves has to be carried in cans or metal bottles, and it has to be poured into the stove's fuel tank. Be sure to start out with a full tank each time the stove is used, because it will get too hot for safe refueling. Butane is sold in cartridges which are simply screwed into the stove. The cartridges are easier to handle, but they are heavier and more costly than white gas with an equal heating capacity. It is impossible to tell how much fuel is left in a cartridge, and the amount of heat produced goes down rather drastically as the fuel level drops. This can lead to endless waits for water to boil, and there is no way to speed up the process, since it is not safe to remove a cartridge until it is empty.

You may wish to carry a cloth and a scouring pad for the dishes. There are a number of bio-degradable detergents specially designed for back-packers, but there seems little need for them. Soap that is free of deodorants, disinfectants or perfumes is acceptable. We use a bar of laundry soap, scraping off a few slivers with the pocket knife for each washing. Remember to dump soapy water on the ground well away from any streams, lakes or other surface water.

Halazone tablets have been a part of the backpacker's equipment for some time, but it seems they are being taken off the market. The FDA asked the manufacturer to provide test information on the safety and effectiveness of these pills, and the manufacturer decided that the market was too small to justify the expense of these tests. You can substitute household bleach, but we don't recommend it. It will kill bacteria, but it won't bother parasite eggs. The National Park Service recommends five minutes of boiling, and we suggest you follow their advice whenever you need to drink any questionable water.

Clothing and personal hygiene: You can wear anything you like on the trail, just so it is comfortable and durable enough to take whatever demands the trip will make on it. Some people like to wear shorts, but the sun can be a problem on bare skin, and of course, the bugs may have a feast. The same problems arise with short-sleeved shirts. Most backpackers take along one change of clothes. And they don't concern themselves much if their clothes look a little lived in, but it is a good idea to have some dry duds in case you get rained on.

For a day hike, you might take along a sweater in case it gest cold. For backpacking trips, you should be prepared for the worst weather possible for that season in that place. A parka would be absurd while hiking in Missouri during August. But in October on Isle Royale, it might be a lifesaver in quite a literal sense.

The subject of rain gear creates controversy. Some people just say forget it. If you put on a poncho that is waterproof, it will stop water from either direction. Hiking on a warm rainy day wearing a moisture-proof poncho is like marching around inside a steam bath. However, there are water-resistant jackets that will keep out all but the most persistent downpour without drowning you in your own sweat. They are made of treated cotton or of a cotton-nylon blend called 60-40 cloth.

Some people never wash on the trail. Some people feel like they are living in a grease trap if they can't scrub their faces every morning. If you want to was, take along a handtowel and soap.

Some other items: A candle lantern. Since the campfire is more or less taboo, these are handy to have around. There are folding types that you can set on a log or a rock or hang it from a tree. Most use ordinary kitchen candles.

Flashlight. There small ones available that will fit in a shirt pocket, and they come with replaceble batteries.

Map and compass. Handy always, and essential in wild country.

Fire starter. This is flammable stuff that is squeezed out of a tube, for emergency use.

Waterproof matches.

Strong but light nylon cord.

A garden trowel and toilet paper. The proper procedure for woodland defecation is to dig a shallow hole away from the trail and away from water. Be sure to cover up the hole.

You might also want to bring along items needed to repair damaged equipment. A sewing kit and safety pins, an awl with heavy thread for fixing tents, wire for reattaching a pack to a frame and a pair of pliers all can be useful.

Hazards of the Trail

Hiking pleasures so outweigh the problems that these hazards and discomforts seem small. Nevertheless, all hikers and backpackers will face some of them and need to know how to cope with them.

Insects: The most common problem insects are mosquitos, black flies and deer flies. By all means carry insect repellant and a large bandana kerchief, the latter for both head and neck protection from the small flies that have pronounced fondness for ears and eyes. Woodticks present a problem in the early spring months. To ward off ticks and chiggers, spread repellant on your calves around the top of your socks. Cutters is one of the most effective brands for repellant. Some stores now carry Jungle Juice, developed for use in Vietnam. It has the same ingredients as Cutters, but in a higher concentration. If ticks do get imbedded in your skin, a drop of alcohol or gasoline will generally cause them to disengage.

Sore feet and blisters: Sore feet should not occur on the hiking trail. But feet do get sore, and much too frequently. The most likely culprit is the owner of a new pair of hiking boots who has failed to either obtain proper fit or to break in the boot properly.

At the first indication of soreness—STOP. Even if you are with a large group of hikers—STOP. A quick first aid remedy now will avoid longer and more frequent pauses later on. Moleskin is the best remedy. Cut a piece of moleskin in the proper size and shape to cover the irritated spot. If you know where your points of irritation will be before starting out, you might put moleskin on those areas before beginning your hike.

Moleskin comes in sheets of adhesive-backed pads available at most drugstores and sporting goods shops.

Sometimes it may be a wrinkle in your sock causing the irritation. If it is not easily straightened, reverse your left and right socks.

Moleskin can also be applied to blisters. In this case, the moleskin should be placed to protect the blister, but not cover it entirely. Then replace your socks and boots, and resume your hike.

Chafing: Chafing is second only to ill fitting shoes as a source of discomfort on long distance hiking. Chafing is primarily a hot weather ailment from skin rubbing against skin with a big assist from perspiration. It occurs chiefly in the crotch and buttock areas but again it can occur any place where skin rubs against skin, or where clothes or equipment rubs against skin. Powders are quite effective in relieving discomfort — corn starch, baby powders, or a medicated powder such as Ammens. One experienced hiker maintains that relief can be obtained from Vaseline. As with sore feet, early treatment is important.

Snakes: The fear of poisonous snakes is one of the principal reasons why many people are reluctant to hike or camp out where such snakes are known to exist. But first let us put the danger of snake bite in its proper prespective. Some 6,680 people are bitten by poisonous snakes each year in the entire United States. Of this number about 14 or 15 die, less than one fourth of one per cent. The authority for these statistics is *Emergency Medicine* magazine, July, 1969. Compare this to the 45,000 or so people who die each year from automobile accidents.

Statistically you are much safer hiking in the woods, even where there are poisonous snakes, than you are driving on the highways. Learn to identify the poisonous snakes which frequent the area in which you are hiking. In the rare, rare event that someone in your party is bitten, the doctor needs to know what type of snake did the biting so that the proper anti-venin can be used. The rattlesnake generally (but not always) assists in the identification by sounding his buzzer. The buzz is an unmistakeable, insistent noise that leaves no doubt as to what will happen if you ignore it.

More and more hikers are not carrying snake bite kits. This is a calculated risk, perhaps, but there is a growing number of people who think that a snake bit kit in the hands of the untrained person is more dangerous than the bite. And how does one get training on cutting through someone's flesh to just the proper depth? *Patient Care* magazine, May, 1972, contains excellent instructions. What follows is a condensed report of the article's instructions on getting the patient to a doctor.

Get the patient to the doctor quickly. Those who obtain treatment within two hours after being bitten stand a very good chance of recovery. If there are enough people in the party, carry the patient out on a litter. If that is not feasible, have the patient walk slowly, but avoid running. Place a tourniquet about two to five inches above the wound. Don't make it so tight that it constricts the blood flow in the arteries. Loosen the tourniquet slightly as swelling appears but do not remove it.

If you carry a snake bite kit, be sure you know how to use it.

Bears: In wilderness area, where hunting is permitted, they will avoid you. In national parks where they are protected, and especially where they have developed the habit of raiding garbage cans and receiving handouts from tourists, they become a menace. In such areas be certain to remove all food from your pack and tent and suspend the food sack by a rope from a tree. Be sure the suspended food is at least eight feet off the ground, preferably a bit higher. Bears are good climbers, so hang the food in such a manner that the bear cannot reach it by climbing the tree.

Domestic Dogs: Each year hikers get bitten by dogs. There seems to be something about a hiker and that pack that infuriates them. In dog territory, carry a staff. If they keep pestering reach for a stone, real or imaginery. That scares most of them. Where dogs are really a problem, carry a small squirt can of "HALT." The stuff doesn't seem to hurt the dogs but they suddenly lose interest in attacking.

Nettles, Poison Ivy, Poison Oak: Learn to identify all of them, but especially the poison ivy. The stinging nettles are irritating and will pierce right through your trousers. Fortunately the sting lasts only a few moments.

Poison ivy is an entirely different matter. Even a mild case can cause much discomfort for about two weeks. And a really bad case can almost totally incapacitate a person for days, though such cases are quite rare. Any part of the plant can do the damage, the leaf, berries, bark, or roots. And unlike stinging nettles, which sting immediately on contact, the poison ivy causes no discomfort upon contact.

In a day or so, if the infection is mild, you will discern a number of tiny pimple-like blisters which will ooze water and can itch furiously. If the infection is a severe one, angry looking red patches will appear; they will slowly become larger blisters from which water will occasionally seep forth.

There are many lotions on the market that alleviate the itching, but only time — ten days to two weeks — really cures it. Learn to recognize poison ivy in all its forms, as a shrub, a trailing vine or as a climber. And it's a terrific climber, very much like a grape vine, only the poison ivy vine, as it matures puts forth dark hair. So if you see a climbing vine, thick as your wrist covered with darkish hair, watch out! It's poison ivy . . . *Rhus.toxicodendron.*

Wearing long trousers can save you from rubbing your skin against poison ivy or poison oak.

Exposure: Hikers sometimes are done in by exposure and heat cramps, exhaustion or sun stroke. The best way to avoid heat related illness is simply to take it easy. If the heat is bothering you, sit down. If the sun troubles you, find some shade.

If you begin to feel giddy and weak, if you turn pale or start vomiting, the answer is gradual cooling. Apply cool, wet clothes to your skin, and have someone fan you gently. Don't drink water in large amounts. The idea is gradually to restore fluid balance. Salt tablets can help fend off heat exhaustion. And they should be taken — again not all at once — if you develop any of these symptoms.

There really is no reason why these things should be problems. They cause trouble mainly because hikers decide that they have to make 20 miles in a day. Then the temperature goes up and the hiker goes down. Give yourself time. Nobody is chasing you.

Hypothermia: Hypothermia is considered to be the only word that accurately describes the rapid collapse of the human body due to the chilling of the inner core. Two aspects of this killer are surprising: (1) It occurs most often in temperatures of 30 to 50 degrees, and (2) it is the number one killer of outdoor recreationists.

Outdoor books are increasingly devoting space to hypothermia; the 20th Appalachian Trail Conference meeting at Boone, North Carolina, in June, 1975 had as one of its workshops "Dangers of Hypothermia and How the Hiker May Protect Himself". Space permits only a brief coverage here.

Principal contributing factors to hypothermia dangers are wind, exhaustion and getting wet. Have rain gear that will keep out water under windy conditions (this eliminates most types of ponchos). When weahter is wet, cold, and windy, wool clothing is your best bet. Carry a tight, storm proof tent. Make camp early in the day. Don't push yourself too

far. In planning your trip, think hypothermia. Let people know where
you're going and when you expect to be back. Three people rescued
from the 4,860 foot Spruce Knob in 1975 were overdue at home. A telephone call to the Forest Service office in Petersburg, West Virginia,
prompted a snowmobile rescue trip. So let family or friends know
where you are going, when you expect to be back, and where to telephone in case you do not return on schedule.

Do some more reading on the subject. A little leaflet given me by the
Forest Service called *Four Lines of Defense Against Hypothermia* is
useful. Single copies may be obtained free by sending stamped self-ad-
dressed envelope to the Appalachian Trail Conference, P.O. Box 236,
Harpers Ferry, West Virginia 25425.

Map and Compass: The most frequent map reference made throughout
this book is the reference to the topographic maps of the U.S. Geological Survey. For simplicity we have referred to these maps as "USGS
Quads." The U.S. Geological Survey (USGS) is an agency of the Federal Government that prepares a variety of maps for many purposes.
We are concerned with topographic maps, which the USGS defines as
"a graphic representation of selected manmade and natural freatures
of a part of the earth's surface plotted to a definite scale. The distin-
guishing characteristic of a topographic map is the portrayal of the
shape and elevation of the terrain."

USGS maps are available from a number of retail outlets throughout
the country. They are also available from USGS itself, both from over-
the-counter sources and by mail from two big central warehouses.
Maps of areas east of the Mississippi River should be ordered from the
U.S. Geological Survey, 1200 South Eads St., Arlington, Virginia
22202. For maps west of the Mississippi, order from USGS, Branch of
Distribution, P.O. Box 25286, Federal Center, Denver, Colorado 80225.
In Washington, D. C. area over-the-counter purchases only may be
made from: 1028 General Services Building, 19th & F Streets, NW,
Washington, D. C. or from Room 1C402, U.S.G.S. National Center, Re-
ston, Virginia. As a first step you might write to the USGS at either Arlington, Virginia, or Denver and ask for the free "Index to Topographic
Maps of ——————— (Name of state)." Also ask for the free
booklet "Topographic Maps." The maps sold for $1.25 as of May
1977.

In addition to the USGS quads, there are many other maps made
reference to in this book, principally U.S. Forest Service maps and
maps issued by hiking organizations. The latter generally show trail
routes and location of trailside shelters in much more prominent fashion than do the general purpose USGS and Forest Service maps. For
most of Ed Garvey's hiking in the Appalachians and in the Alps he has
relied on maps prepared by hiking club organizations and have found
them to be quiet satisfactory.

A convenient way to carry a map is to fold or refold it so that the immediate area in which you are hiking is exposed. Then put the map in a plastic case that has clear see-through plastic. Some of these map cases are designed with cloth carrying straps that permit fastening them to your belt.

To use map and compass together, not that the compass has a moveable needle with one end, generally colored red, that points to magnetic north. Magnetic north is not exactly the same as true north and the difference on the map is referred to as the angle of declination. Just remember that your compass points *generally north*. Many of the hiking club maps do not attempt to make the disction.

Compasses show directions in two ways — by degrees (from 0° to 360°) and by the abbreviations for North, South, East, and West and for the points in between. To orient compass to map, put the map flat on the ground and lay the compass on top of it. Hold the compass firm and keep turning the map around until the North arrow on the compass points in the same direction as the North line on the map. If the map has two North lines, like up your compass with the one labeled "MN" (magnetic north). Once you've done that move the compass over to the exact point where you are at present. Take a reading, either by direction point, e.g., NW, or by degrees, e.g., 315 degrees to the spot on the map that you want to go to. Take compass in hand and sight in that same NW or 315 ° direction and pick out some prominent landmark on that sighting. Upon reaching that landmark, take another reading on your 315 degree course, etc. I've oversimplified somewhat but this is basically the system. Two books on the market that explain this in detail with illustrations are *Be Expert With Map & Compass* (Bjorn Kjellstrom), published by Charles Scribner's Sons and Orienteering (John Disley), published by Stackpole Press. Both books were selling for $3.95 in May, 1977.

Who should carry a compass? Just about anyone who is hiking or vacationing in forested or mountainous areas with which he is not intimately acquainted. In the wooded Appalachians it is amazingly easy to become lost. Once you are out of sight and out of earshot of the familiar landmarks, all the trees and shrubs suddenly look totally unfamiliar. People who most frequently get lost are not the backpackers but those who just wander off from a known spot and cannot find their way back. What makes these cases so tragic is that frequently the person involved may be wearing only light clothes and is ill equipped for the exposure he may face before being found. .

When hiking or camping in unfamiliar areas it is wise to fix firmly in your mind a landmark, a road, or trail that you can always head for in case you do become lost. Suppose that you are walking on a prominent hiking trail that runs north-south and you make a camp at a point 50 yards to the west of that trail. If you stray too far from your camp area and those trees suddenly take on that unfamiliar look, you know that all you need to do is to walk straight east until you pick up that north-south trail. You may not just know whether to go north or south when you reach that trail but you must check it out either way until you are back at your campground.

There is a little known book that came on the market in 1974. It is entitled *Celestial Navigation For The Simpleminded* and has clear simple directions for using the sun, moon, shadows and other objects to ascertain directions without use of the compass. It was written especially for car drivers, hikers, hunters, backpackers, campers and other outdoorsmen. It is at present available only from the author, Bill Thomas, whose experiences as an airplane pilot, avid mountaineer, and amateur astromer (to name a few of his pursuits) make him well qualified to write such a book. Cost is $1.25, available by mail from William C. Thomas, Jr., 5906 North 19th St., Arlington, Virginia. 22205.

Make Your Own 2

Sick of what passes for quality and low price when you browse around the old camping store or catalogue? Have a lot of fun when your super pack *(super cheap)* leaves you 10 miles out with one strap gone and the bottom half missing? Enjoy the ripping seams, after getting ripped off at one of those impossible-to-avoid drooling sessions at a sale?

What's worse than the quality and price of so much of the "great" gotta-have-it stuff laid out to tantalize the backpacker's eye is the simple fact that we aren't likely to need it short of atomic war or landing of the Alpha Centaurians.

Make-it-yourself-itis is a benefical disease. First, you'll never have the time to make all the great stuff you "might" need, so you'll tend to concentrate on the most important things. Then you'll get hooked by the satisfaction of making something yourself and seeing it age on the trail. "Makeitis" disease protects people from the sales, flash ads and "great gimmickery" of the annual catalogues. And it develops self-confidence and an ability to cope that often means more out in the woods than any single item of gear ever will.

Making things requires first that the need be well defined. Having once spent weeks on a beaded belt and then coming back from a trip suffering from poorly designed pack straps that would have saddle-galled a mule, we began to understand the importance of setting priorities. Feathered hats, fringed pack covers and embroidered canteen pouches are fine . . . nice things to do once you're out in the woods and feel a need to tinker while sitting around the fire telling lies. Such adornment, done in the woods, looks and is authentic. Made or purchased at home . . . it usually looks corny.

What you *need* has to be selected, and then really looked at for what you want it to *do*, or *not do*. If an item may or will cause pain, wear, or unneeded weight, stay at the drawing table till the problems are solved, and then, convinced you have a good idea, try imagining every type of strain, field stress, function and even places, that it will have to serve.

We have included things in this chapter that are not absolutely first priority, but everything we mention is useful. A brief word of warning: don't choose a tent or sleeping bag as your first item for do-it-yourself experimentation. You may waste a lot of materials and work hours. Few people have the tools and know-how for high quality tents and bags, though if you do, for heaven's sake take a shot at it. In theory there is nothing a backpacker needs that he can't make or improvise, and nothing to equal the satisfaction the packer gets out of going self-made.

To get started making things, collect all your junk, trash, and defunct goodies·of every conceivable description. He who has the largest heaps will find the most nuggets of gold.

Among the high priority junk to collect as a matter of habit are plastic bottles, wire, aluminum tubing, defunct pots and pans, anything nylon, anything of heavy cloth, old socks, old belts, scraps of leather, nylon cord, hunks of foam and big cardboard boxes (to keep it all in and to use in making patterns.)

Some general tips . . . and old pressure cooker makes a fine tubing bender . . . a hand sewing awl saves buying a new sewing machine . . . soft aluminum, copper, or heavy brass wire makes fine rivets, and wood dowels of various sizes end up consumed in a host of projects. An electric drill can double as a lathe, while nails can make D-rings, belt buckles and assorted odd attachments (later in the chapter you'll see how to case harden soft nails and metal). Stock up on nylon thread (waxed), a good glue (such as Pliobond 20), one inch and ½ inch nylon webbing (tubular), heavy "pack weight" nylon cloth and the lighter polyurethane coated nylon used commonly in stuff bags.

Materials are available from many camping stores . . . Recreational Equipment, Inc. in Seattle being one of the best known. But others locally may have your goodies . . . price them, shop, and plan ahead. Especially plan to keep materials on hand for those quick jobs that always crop up the day before you leave on a trip. (We once made two rock-climbing rucksacks the day we left for a big trip . . . saved $40 and they worked better than the models available).

When beginning a project, after being sure of the need, function, and durability required, try to get the pattern or design laid out and at least placed or glued together all in one session. Every product becomes a matter of plan versus compromise. A basic design that minimizes seams, joints, and parts, will save huge hunks of time and effort during sewing, joining and assembly. Also, the fewer things left in the design that can fail the better.

Seams can be glued 20 times . . . but there's a limit to the amount of.sewing a person can stand. Cloth can be drawn on till it changes color . . . it gets cut once. A dowel or plastic strip will bend to the shape of a metal·tube . . . the tube breaks after a few bends. A strip of plastic will often serve instead of metal until the final design is assured.

Never take a factory kit, pattern or design and try doing it by "a into b, ah, c to . . ." Understanding *why* a thing is such and such a size, or shape is how it gets to be a friend on the trail . . . not just another blight, like bugs, rain and blisters.

Possible Sack
This is a good starting project. It familiarizes a person with the prin-

ciples of seams, straps, getting the right sizes and seeing how the thing will work when put into use. And it's more than likely a badly needed item for most backpackers.

First, why make a shoulder bag? (Frontiersmen called them "possibles sacks" because they popped in everything possible from bullets to scalps.) Ever lose your wallet, or have it wear a hole in your hip pocket? Get annoyed by the rash caused by loose change or freshly fueled lighters? Need string when there ain't none to be had? Matches sweaty? No snack on that "little" stroll three miles from camp? Compass in the bottom of the pack? No toilet paper handy in a hurry? Spare roll of film? Jackknife, pencil, bug dope and adhesive bandages always in the bottom of the pack or in one of those pack side pouches ... somewhere? OK, that's the need and serviced connected with a possibles sack.

How about design? Small enough to stay out of the way, easy to get into, big enough for all miscellaneous gear, durable since it gets a lot of rub and scrape, including a good strap with width designed not to cause a problem even when worn under a main pack strap. Color light or bright enough to help you find the thing in the dark, not so garish it's embarrassing to wear. No sharp edges, maybe no metal so you can toss it in the washing machine after it collects a few melted chocolate bar remains and doses of insect repellent.

Can you think of anything else that might influence design? If so, jot your ideas down right now on the design page and see what happens.

Needed: Heavy Pack Weight Nylon Cloth, approximately 20 x 17 inches, sewing awl or heroic sewing machine, approximately 45 inches of one inch flat or tubular web and a heavy, easy-sliding zipper. (Old Army field jackets have fine zippers for such projects.) And some good scissors, a razor blade (set in a short bit of wood dowel for a handle) and your trusty bottle of glue.

Cut a big cardboard box, both for a surface to work on that you won't have to clean the glue off, and to make a pattern from once the design is cut. After using the bag you can then change the cardboard pattern rather than working out all the lines on fabric again.

Note that the side panels overlap the front panels. It's annoying to get down to sewing a seam and find no material there to make a seam with.

For seams ... there are several simple types, one that might last forever (and might take forever), many that will do. Choose your type of seam *before* cutting anything, and pencil in the type right on the fabric by the seam line. Here's how seams may change your fabric cuts:

Seam "A" is quick and easy — nm glue, and thin enough for even modern sewing machines to survive. The edges are messy, though, and the seam cannot be double-stitched effectively. This is the weakest type of seam. B type works for quick jobs, and is quite strong. Just glue down a ⅜ inch fold to one edge, and sew a ⅜ inch lap from the other edge flat. C is the super seam. Fabric ends are neat, the product tough. But it requires gluing a ⅜ inch lap width. But for your first try, glue everything and use ½ inch lap (or even more). Once you try it, you'll see why D, the easiest seam, is included. With D you don't have to get ulcers figuring out which way what end folds where. Seams get ratty with wear, though, so take a little extra effort for a better seam and stay happy.

One more note on seams. Try to place the external edge or fold *down*. A bag with seams up will work fine . . . and water running down against the seam will tend to soak in a lot better, even though the Pliobond helps waterproof all seams.

Always try to have removable straps on bags and packs. They are easier to adjust, renew, or use for other things if need be. Leave a few extra inches on the strap until you've hiked several days with it, then pare it down to the most comfortable choice of length.

Tent Pole Scabbard
Now that you've got your scraps from the possibles sack, how about a tent pole scabbard? The lack of those on most ready made tents has become a pet peeve of mine after seeing too many good packs and tents chewed from pole ends.

Make a tube with a drawstring top long enough and big enough to hold your poles. But first, head to the junk boxes and find a couple of deodorant can tops or other plastic can tops that will contain the poles in a fairly close fit. Then cut a circle with a three eight inch border bigger than the cap and sew it into the bottom of your scabbard fabric. You'll find this quickly shows you what width to cut the fabric after overlap. Then cut your tube fabric out and do the long seam. Chuck in the tent poles, pop your second cap on top, and pull the draw string. You'll have all ends protected and a rattle proof package for those miserable hole cutters.

Run a coat hanger through an extra wide seam to install the heavy nylon cord in your drawstring bag.

Day Pack
Got some practice now and ready for trouble? Good. A day pack is one of the expensive so-so quality items on the market today. Yet it isn't too tough to make and well worth it.

Requirements: It must hold "day" junk, ride easy, get on and off and open up easily, should fold up and stuff away in a small space. Pick a heavy zipper (to heck with weight, use a monster) and position it so it will not interfere with shoulder slings for camera, possibles sack, etc.

Straps should be usable on your main pack also. Anything else?

Materials: Lots of heavy nylon cloth, sauce pan, soft pencil, sewing awl (no chance on sewing machine here, except for long seams), glue, cardboard (be sure to get a flat pattern of this project), two inch strip of foam (possibly narrow down your ensolite sleeping pad?) from 30 to 36 inches long, four rings (heavy "O" or "D"'s, one inch wide that go on pack bottom) and a half inch x two inch dowel.

Some odd materials here, but have patience.

Begin by measuring from between the top of your shoulder blades to the small of your back, subtract an inch or two (this is your pack height for trial test), then measure the width of the small of your back (elbows should not brush ends of the pack when done) for pack width. Add your seam widths, decide on thickness of the bottom (three or four inches is usual) and add it up, one continuous piece from top front panel to top rear panel. Go in from the edge of your nylon cloth width plus seams and draw the basic rectangle of the pack. Now get the sauce pan and put the edge against the center point of the width and draw a circle at top and bottom. (I used an eight-inch pie plate for my own packs.)

Next, come up to midpoint of the long direction on your cloth: ("A" on diagram) which is the center of the bottom and draw in your bottom lines. Come up from the edge of the bottom about one-third of the height of the front and back panels "B". Draw a line from "B" to the edge of your circle. Now round off the corners at points "B" until they look fairly even. Then cut away.

The sides of the pack (and rounded top) can be made from a single strip as wide as the base, plus width of the seams. A zipper flap, if you want one, can be formed by sewing the inside edge of the strip. This tapers the thickness of the pack from bottom to top, and automatically leaves a protective weather flap over the zipper. (One inch is usually enough, more makes zippering more difficult.)

Cut your side strip at least two inches longer than the edge of the front panel. (Excess ends get sewn to the bottom as wear pads anyway.) Lay it flat and have fun trying to draw a curved line free hand style to guide you in sewing the zipper flap edge. The best bet is to bend a longish dowel to a right looking curve and have somebody else trace the line.

To reinforce the strap attachment points, cut circles or squares from scrap and sew one inside and out to the proper location. (As shown on diagram; debatable. Any location seems detachable. Just try your own logic.)

Straps, even comfortable ones, are easy to make. Sew a tube to contain a two inch wide foam pad out of light nylon cloth, fold the ends over to a wedge shape. On the upper end, fold again to make a loop with a D right in it, or see if your idea works.

For attaching the two straps to the top center of your pack, try inserting a two inch long dowel ⅜ or ½ inch thick, through the loops. On the pack, sew a loop through which the dowel will fit like a button. Drill a hole through each end (or through the center of the dowel and tie it down with nylon cord. Fanatics can make a similar arrangement on the bottom ends of the straps too. A double D ring type buckle makes it a lot easier to adjust length, and the folded ends won't slip easily during a hike. Never bother with a toothed buckle, or most square flat friction buckles.

(Note on dowel attachment: round off the ends well or they may wear against your pack.)

Stuff Sacks and Double Packs

Another of our pet peeves is the racket some people make out of selling stuff sacks made out of remnants of material. You can do just as well at home, and get more utility from the product.

What do stuff sacks do? They compress bulky down items to minimum bulk. They also will hold anything, if reasonably softy, or packed without the corners jamming out. If they are made slightly less long than the back is wide, and are big enough in diameter to hold sleeping bags, if they have loops sewn at each corner (i.e., four per end in a square), with one at opposite sides in the middle then they can be lashed together in an impromptu pack, strapped outside a frame pack much more easily and even hung up out of the way in camp or at home.

Two stuffers units drawstrings shouldn't take more than an hour to make. Get out the sauce pan again, along with a bunch of waterproofed middle weight nylon cloth.

For groups who divide up loads, two or three stuff sacks and a bundle of tent pole scabbards are easy to lash together and put straps on if the day pack straps are dismountable.

Tarp Tent (or Awning at home)

Ever question the wisdom of toting a 10-pound tent over a long single night hike, or worse yet, not bother taking it and ending up needing it on a day trip that didn't quite go as planned? A simple tarp can be quite comfortable for a night, even in a heavy rain, though the old tent is still recommended for lengthy stays.

Try getting six or seven yards of good polyurethane coated nylon (rip stop or plain) 48 to 55 inches wide. Cut it in half, lay the pieces side by side, sew a strong seam down the middle, well glued or sealed, then add strong corner loops of ½ inch flat nylon web. Reinforce the center and put a good loop there, more at the middle points of the side, middle points between edges and top center. You end up using a lot of loops; but the product requires no poles, can be set up in a score of ways (even tied to the pack and held down with rocks if need be), and after a few experiments in the back yard, can prove to be a quick serviceable shelter that could turn out to be preferable to a tent many many times during the year.

Pre-tie long cords to each loop. They're handy to "borrow" for scores of other things and you never need all the cord to set up.

Summer Sleeping Bag

It's probably dumb to add this to a make-it-yourself list, but in going over things people can, but usually don't, make we half-decided that a lightweight summer sleeping bag was one of the things we'd seen the least of.

Nearly every bag on the market is designed to keep a person warm . . . sensible? Yet how about August, 80 degree muggy nights full of bugs? The choice is involuntary blood donation or a very low grade of sweat-soaked doze.

A bed sheet isn't quite enough, unless it's a really hot night, and the next might not be. Still, something around that weight would be useful. My first choice has been a pair of U.S. Army poncho liners. One is fine down to 60 degrees or less, two are good to about 45 degrees, and if it's a sweltering night, just pull it loosely over the top and snicker at the frustrated wing critters. Unfortunately I've no idea where to get the liners now. If you've an Army Surplus store around, check it out. They might prove expensive, but they are light, packable, warm enough for almost all summer camping, and stay warm even when soaked. (They dry very quickly.)

As a second choice, back to the bed sheet. Sew up a body size tube of sheet (it's heavy, may as well not carry extra), then get a length of light nylon and sew a tube of that. This proves usesful for 55 to 60 degrees and up, depending on individual tastes in sleeping heat. It saves expensive bags for weather when they are needed, reduces pack weight, and lets a person adapt a little better to higher summer temperatures.

Pack Frame

Of all the beasts that plague backpackers, none is so intimate and perfidious as the pack itself. Manufacturers have been struggling to find a really great design for years, and packers are still arguing back and forth about wicker or frame, hip extension or plain waistband.

Most of the arguments are great. But changing your mind between seasons get expensive. Half for the fun, and half in hope of maybe coming up with something reasonably kind to the body, why not try making a pack frame? If nothing else, the experience will make the next selection from store stock a lot more critical.

As always, begin by defining your own particular needs, add your gripes against packs in general and try to figure out just what size and arrangement you want to end up with. The frame structure and system for putting it together shown here may not be what you want . . . we're just trying to give some basic ideas and suggestions. Change them if you like.

Find a supplier of ¾ inch aluminum tubing, ⅜ inch tube or ¼ inch aluminum rod, gather some coat hangers or heavy aluminum wire, find some scraps of all that dowel we've been talking about, and get set with the old hack saw blade.

Height of the frame is not critical ... attaching the straps is. So start with a pair of ¾ inch tubes long enough to be at least as long as the largest pack you might want to end up with. Then try a few friends' packs until you know just where the vertical frame tubes go up the back. Then take your tubes, put the ends on a couple of boards or bricks on the floor and sit on them, using hands and backside to spread the weight over the middle third of the length. (If you've got a pipe bender this might be simpler.)

Gradually increase the height of the books, bricks or whatever until you've bent the tubes to a shape that fits the back where and as it seems fit.

Next step is to determine what width feels best. Try out an assortment of packs or adjust from your old one, and cut two slender rods or tubes and one thick one about three inches longer than the pack width will be. (You may want to strengthen these tubes with a flexible dowel inserted through them.)

If you happen to have an old pressure cooker around, put your feet in it and carefully curve your rods by pulling them up arond the side of the cooker. (Clean socks might avoid certain comments during this operation.) Test the heavy tube by fitting to the proper hip area until it fits. The two slender rods need be only slightly more curved, and won't be against the back anyway.

Now measure from tip to tip on the short tubes and cut them to the width you want your pack to be.

Lay your vertical tubes on a sidewalk or flat rough surface and scrape them on one side (mark edge for drilling holes.) After computing where you want your cross bars there are several ways of putting them in place. One is to drill out a hole that fits the small tubes (requires making those tubes longer) and putting a thin pin through the vertical support to hold the cross members. This weakens the frame, but it will work. Just don't expect durability with 100-pound loads.

Another method, much harder to put together but better, is to drill a hole in the end of your rods and find a nail or anything metal that's strong and fits the hole or end of your tubing. Drill the vertical supports to size and stuff in some White Knife Auto Body Filler. (There are plenty of fast-hardening fillers available at an auto store. *Quickly* put your nail or connecting rod into the hole and filler about halfway through the big tube. If the connector is rough it won't pull out after the filler hardens. Under normal conditions, there will never be any pull on the connection anyway.

For the heavy tube at the bottom of the frame, use one of 3/8 inch width instead of 3/4 inch to nail and follow the same procedure outlined above.

With the cross members in place and curves arranged properly, drill *down* through each end, if not through the connector inside the tube then at least through the edge of it. Use a very fine drill that will permit hammer mashing a bit of coat hanger wire through the hole until it's flush with the tubing.

For a top bar on the frame there is a tough choice. Best would be to bend your vertical supports from one tube, leaving the top bar neatly curved and in place. (It's possible to ruin a lot of tubing trying it, though.) As an alternative plug the top ends of your vertical support with auto body filler. Drill your top cross bar for a slender tube or heavy nail and drive a short length through. Drill the filler to fit your cross bar studs, and if desired, pin it in place with coat hanger "rivets."

If solidly done the frame is now ready for straps, bag, waistband and use.

Using heavy cloth, lace a back support between the verticals so that the two middle cross bars will hold it in place and add another band across the bottom of the pack, using the bottom bar and lower center bar to hold that.

Straps made so they can be removed, connect to the bottom bar and upper center bar.

If the counter forces of the structure do not permit attaching the straps to that slender upper bar, then trying adding a wire brace between top and bottom bars, wrapping round the middle bars enroute.

Some ingenuity will overcome the many minor frustrations of the job, and will help in designing a bag to put on the frame. (Hint: My first frame pack bag could have carried the Lewis and Clark provisions.)

Seasoned backpackers may sneer at this whole idea . . . too heavy, probably not all that strong, hard to make fit, lot of time to waste making it . . . and they are probably quite right. But such a frame will be yours, maybe better than what the store offers. And, counting nylon for the bag, straps, etc., your frame pack should cost in the realm of $15 - less if you're a good scounge. As for the time required to make it, if you've a good drill, pressure cooker, and clean socks, it can be done on a winter's day.

So far the "makings" have been of the strictly utilitarian type, but very near to all backpackers' dusty hearts are the little camp luxuries, fiddle stuff and gadgets. Some useful, some just nice, some dubious ideas are tossed in here.

Camp Knife

That pig sticker hip knife ever prove less than handy and need sharpening beyond the edge that's easy to keep doing rough camp chores? A handy little gadget that takes maybe a half hour to produce is the hacksaw blade whittle-eat-saw-and-trim knife. Get an old hacksaw blade and some heavy wire that fits the hole in each end, add a length of ½ or ⅝ inch dowel and some copper wire or rawhide and you can make a very serviceable, fine edge, knife. (Find a length of ½ inch brass tube and you can make a beautiful jackknife.)

For a knife, merely break off between four and six inches of blade

from a hacksaw. Drill a proper size hole two or three inches from the
end of a hand-size length of dowel and cut a slot down to the hole for
the blade. (It helps if the slot isn't quite straight.) Shove the blade in
and hammer your wire down through the holes until it's flush with the
dowel. Then wrap the split section of handle with wire or rawhide.
Hone down the un-toothed edge of blade, and you've got a saw, butter
knife, whittler's tool and fine little thread cutter for ripping out seams.

Note that one end of the blade makes a knife with the saw teeth
pointed forward, the other end back. Best is a knife with the teeth
pointed toward the hilt . . . it cuts a lot easier. Edge the tip for a chisel
if you want one.

To make a jackknife, use a longer dowel slotted far enough past the
rivet hole to accept the blade when folded back. Instead of wrapping
the hilt with wire, find a length of brass (nice shiny stuff that won't rust
in a wet pack) that fits fairly tight over your dowel. Now take some
brass carpet tacks and with the ring on your knife put one in each side
of each end. The brass ring will slide forward to lock the blade open,
then back to lock it closed.

Camp Slippers
One of the many blessings often done without is the chance to get out
of boots after a hard day's hike. Feet need the air, change of pressure
and wear. Getting them out of the business boots after arriving at camp
can keep feet healtheir and happier.

An easy slipper to make is from heavy old socks. Put two together,
one inside another, and stand on a piece of ensolite. Trace the foot,
cut out the ensolite, and glue it to the bottom of the socks. From pack
nylon or leather, trace another foot pattern, angling the marker this
time in order to get a pattern about 1 ½ inches bigger all round. Glue
the sole to the ensolite.

At various points around the sole, slits will have to be made to allow
folding upward over the foam to the sock. Experiment folding and cutting where the material tries to crease. Once the slitting is done stitch
up the sole flat, adding a band over the arch and behind the heel for
strength and shape.

(Known as socks with soul.)

We've used various types even when winter camping in an ingloo.
They work. But practice. Make one out of junk first, and you'll learn
enough to find your first pair turn out quite well. To be fancy and as-
sure durability, add a ginding strip around the top of the sole and sew
a nylon cover to the top of the foot and around the ankle. Lot of trouble, you say . . . check the price and durability of similar products out
of the store shelves.

Belt
Dumb thing to make, but it can improve life for skinny people whose
hip bones love to stick out where they can get galled by a leather belt
or pack waistband.

Make a nylon tube and foam core as described for a pack strap. Two D rings or something similar for a buckle, and the hips are far less threatened then before. (Makes a spare pack strap too.)

It may be wise to stitch down the middle of the belt and zig zag across, too, to prevent the foam from rolling up under use. A little extra effort and the stitching can become a fancy pattern in various colors ... with beads, fringe, six or seven pouches, a scalping knife and sword scabbard.

A wide, fat version can be attached to almost any pack except to the day pack we've described. The day works much better if allowed to hunch down and swing as it wants. The design keeps it out of the way and a band would be too high and constrictive. For frame packs, improve their personality with this waistband, and it takes only an hour or so to make.

Map Cases

Ratty sodden pulp never makes for an easy-reading map. But that's what we've got more often than not on long hikes. Next trip, try stealing some of the golf bag tubes from the family fairway fiend. Those nice long plastic tubes are perfect for a rolled map. Cut the bottom end off to within two inches of the map length, roll and go. Out on the trail, use your hacksaw camp knife to cut and make wooded plugs for each end of the pilfered tube. You can carve a map identification in the plugs. Make the bottom one permanent, the top fancy and easy to get in and out.

By the way, if the family golfer has black tubes in his bag it might be worth going out and buying a few tubes. Black ones have a way of disappearing after sitting around the fire plotting half the night. White ones are easy to locate; some are transparent enough to see black printing through.

I've intended to try using golfer tubes for tent pole and peg containers, but have never gotten around to it yet. It might be worth trying.

3 Northeastern Trails

The mountains of the northeast have been blessed and cursed, sometimes in the same breath, viewed either as lousy little lumps coated with carnivorous scrub or rippled velvet spattered with quicksilver and veined with golden brooks.

Connecticut

Connecticut is rolling hills, covered bridges, country barns, colonial houses — and miles and miles of trails. The hiker can definitely find variety here; everything from a few hours' jaunt to a major backpacking outing, thanks to the combination of an extensive system of state park pathways and a far-flung network of privately maintained trails.

Connecticut's 5,009 square miles may be divided into three main regions: The Western Highlands, the Central Lowlands, and the Eastern Highlands.

The northwest is the most rugged section of the state, although the Appalachians are less impressive here than in other regions of the chain. There are almost no high peaks; Bear Mountain, at 2,316 feet is the highest place in the state. Instead, the mountains take on the appearance of a series of rolling crests.

The mountains of this section are part of the Taconic range that leads directly into the Berkshire area of Massachusetts. The hillsides are covered with timber, and rich farmlands fill the valleys. To the southeast, the country becomes lower but remains wild. This is the Litchfield Hills area.

The Connecticut River Valley forms the Central Lowland. This is basically level farm country with a steep, hilly section near Meriden.

The flat, wooded hills of the Eastern Highlands surround narrow valleys that widen near the Rhode Island border. Although the soil here is not deep, there is some farmland, with forest growing in areas where farms used to be.

In addition to the park trails in Connecticut, the major trail network of the state is the blue-blazed system maintained by the Connecticut Forest and Park Association, which has been creating trails since 1929. They are marked by oval trail signs at state highway crossings

and blue arrows where they cross other roads (on the trails themselves, double blazes indicate turns).
Many of these trails are quite long. These are the so-called "through
trails."
Even on the short trails in Connecticut, rough, rocky terrain may be
encountered. Therefore, good hiking boots should be worn. Water
should be carried, particularly on the rockbound trails of the central
part of the state, and in other areas, to avoid bothering private lan-
downers.
More information: Topo maps or the maps in the Connecticut Forest
and Park Association's "Connecticut Walk Book" (available from them
for $5.00 at 1010 Main Street, East Hartford, CT 06108) would come
in handy on longer trips.

Mattatuck Trail (in the Western Highlands)
Location: Access is at Mad River Road on Route 69 in Wolcott.
Length: 35 miles
Description: The trail is a varied and interesting route, passing water-
falls, lakes, and streams, and crossing two mountains, Mohawk and
Mount Prospect, as well as Black Rock State Park and Mattatuck State
Forest, It also passes a sewage plant and a gravel pit. The trail heads
northwest to end at the Appalachian Trail, just past Mohawk Mountain.
There are several side trails. The section connecting Black Rock State
Park with the Mattatuck State Forest is historically significant. King
Philip, trying to keep the colonists from expanding their territory,
chased settlers along this path to keep them from moving farther into
Indian territory.

Quinnipiac Trail
Location: Starting in North Haven, this trail is reached by going north
on State Street 0.1 mile north of the intersection of Route 22 and Bishop Street. At this point, Banton Street begins on the east. Follow Banton to its end; the trail begins 0.1 mile south of here. It ends on Conn.
Route 68 near the Cheshire Reservoir.
Length: 21 miles
Description: The trail follows a series of trap rock ridges, passes
through the Quinnipiac River and Sleeping Giant State Parks, presents
good views from York Mountain, Mount Sanford, and several parts of
the Sleeping Giant's body, and travels by lovely Roaring Brook Falls.
Aside from the viewing points, most of the trail is wooded.

Paugussett and Pomperaug Trails
Location: Access to the Paugussett is in a grove of hemlock at the Well
in Indian Well State Park on Conn. Route 110. It connects with the
Pomperaug in 4.4 miles. The Pomperaug starts at a point reached by
following East Village Road 0.2 miles west of East Village. (This town is
in the middle of an area bounded by Routes 110, 11, and 134).
Length: 9.7 miles

Description: Travel northward along the east bank of the Housatonic River. There are a few steep climbs with some nice views along the ridges, gorges and brooks. The Paugessett connects with the Pomperaug, M 4.4 miles. The biggest portion of the trails are on wood roads, and there is a campground (inaccessible by car) near the end of the Pomperaug after the two paths combine.

The trail goes north from here, merges with the Paugussett just before crossing the river, and continues north to Kettletown State Park.

Another trail following the Housatonic is the **River Trail,** 0.7 miles. From the junction of the Warren Turnpike (Conn. 341) and U.S. 7, follow the turnpike 0.8 miles to where the trail starts heading west.

Sleeping Giant State Park White Trail

Location: Take Whitney Avenue (Route 10) or the Hartford Turnpike. It is located largely in the town of Hamden.

Description: Sleeping Giant takes its name from the fact that from New Haven Harbor its woods and ridges look like a giant lying on his back. Indian legends say that the giant is an old chief sleeping after stuffing himself with oysters. Another legend says that it is the spirit Hobbamock, under a spell of eternal sleep for changing the course of the Connecticut River.

More important to the hiker than who the giant is, though, are the quiet woods, pine groves, rocky crags and cascading waterfalls among the trails. There are several trails. Next to the blue Quinnipiac Trail already discussed, the White Trail is the roughest. It starts where the Yellow, Orange, Violet and Green trails converge and covers the major heights, traveling over the right slope of the giant's left leg and the right knee, steeply descending to the base of the knee, climbing the right thigh, and crossing the waist and the shoulder to the chin. There are good views along the way and the trail ends at the Picnic Area Road.

The **Tower Path,** 1.6 miles, is an easy, wide trail leading from the park entrance to the Stone Tower via the neck and chest.

The **Green Trail,** two miles, is made up of old woods roads. It travels through the Inner Mountain Valley, and across the waist to join the White Trail on the shoulder. The **Violet, Yellow and Orange Trails** fall somewhere between the White and Blue Trails and the Tower Path in difficulty. All start, as does the Green Trail, at the Picnic Area road. They end at a place two miles east of Mt. Carmel Ave. From Whitney Ave., turn north on Chestnut Lane and follow it to the second sharp turn where the trails converge. The Violet Trail travels through wooded country, passes the remains of an old quarry, and provides good northwest views, (there are north views in fall and winter after the leaves have fallen). 3.2 miles. The Orange Trail travels across the waist and along the right leg. From it you can see the Inner Mountain Valley. 2.4 miles. The Yellow Trail involves some steep switchbacks, is basically shade and has some nice views. 2.2 miles.

There are several trails in the region around Waterbury, many of which intersect the Mattatuck Trail. The **Whitestone Cliffs Trail,** 3.7 miles, climbs the steep side of the cliffs for some excellent views of the Naugatuck Valley. Access is at the intersection of Echo Lake Road and Thomaston Road. (Echo Lake Road runs from Route 63 just south of Watertown to the railroad bed). The trail follows an old trolley bed at first that is picked up on the east side of an iron bridge. The trail returns to the starting point.

The **Jericho Trail,** three miles, begins off Echo Lake Road 0.9 miles west of the Whitestone Cliffs Trail, follows and crosses Jericho Brook, traverses many ravines and hills, and joins the Mattatuck at Crane Lookout ¼ mile south of U.S. 6 on Mattatuck Trail.

The **Lone Pine Trail,** three miles, travels through woods, over a ledge and comes within 100 yards of the Quinnipiac Trail. Access is on Summit Road, 0.3 miles past Route 69 in Prospect. The trail ends at Route 68 near the Quinnipiac.

The **Hancock Brook-Lion Head Trail,** three miles round trip, passes through hemlock woods, climbs to the top of Lion Head, and follows a ridge with some nice views. The trail starts just east of the Hancock Brook bridge in Waterville at the end of Sheffield Street. (Waterville is reached by following Route 13 from Waterbury to Thomaston Road, turning northeast about two miles.) For a time, the trail follows a blue trail.

Nipmuck Trail (in the Eastern region).
Location: Drive to Bigelow Brook on Yale Forest from U.S. 171 at North Ashford.
Length: 21.5 miles plus 5.75 miles of Pudding Lane Branch.
Description: The trail stretches south from Bigelow Brook in Yale Forest (near U.S. 171 at North Ashford) to close to Fenton River, about half a mile northeast of Springhill, where it splits into two southern branches: one 0.8 miles west of Route 195 on Pudding Lane in Mansfield, and the other on a dirt road north of the picnic section of Mansfield Hollow Dam Recreation Area. The trail passes through several different types of terrain. On the Pudding Lane section, be careful not to bother the animals at the University Animal Diseases Farm. If you are coming from the south, after the trails have merged and about 9½ miles from Mansfield Hollow, the trail leads onto private property past a "No Trespassing" sign. This is a fairly recent route, so ignore the sign. About 1 mile farther north, is an area known as "Murder Lane." An old cellar hole is all that is left of the place where the crime was committed.

The **James L. Goodwin State Forest and Conservation Center** is a unique place. Formerly a forestry operation, it now includes several forest demonstration areas, as well as the Conservation Center which shows how land use in Connecticut has changed over the years. Reached off Route 6 just east of Clark's Corners, the center has only camping sites for supervised youth groups, except for one lean-to available to backpackers who have registered at the center. Trails include an old railroad bed **(Airline Hiking Trail)** crossing the grounds for about 3.66 miles; a yellow-marked 1.12-mile trail, a white-marked one-mile trail and a red-marked .86-mile trail. In addition, there are about three miles of the blue-marked **Natchaug** (through) **Trail** here.

The **Natchaug Trail** leaves Goodwin and travels through the **Southern and Northern Natchaug Forests,** stretching from U.S. 6 in Phoenixville — near Pine Acres Lake ¼ mile northeast of Clark's Corners to U.S. 44 in Eastford. Interesting features include some large anthills near Black Spruce Pond, the lean-to at Orchard Hill, a scenic climb up Goodwin Brook Falls, rivers, brooks and a chestnut "skeleton." About 11.6 miles.

Pachaug State Forest Trails
Location: Located just north of Voluntown, is the largest state forest in Connecticut. Take Conn. 138 west to the firetower on Trail Roads or go north on Route 49 to Forest Headquarters.
Length: Total of 56 miles of trails.
Description: Unfortunately, at one time this forest's 24,000 acres were also among the most thoughtlessly lumbered in the New England area, although today, careful management is restoring the growth. White pine, hemlock and coastal white cedar are present, which add to the possibility of improving the forest's condition. About 100 additional acres are being converted to conifer type each year. An interesting feature of the park is the Rhododendron Sanctuary. It usually blossoms around the Fourth of July and is an unusual type of area. The highest point in the park is the Mount Misery Overlook (441 feet) which provides views of the forest and the town. It is reached via the Firetower Road or on the Nehantic Trail. There are 20 campsites in the area, although none are available on the trails.

The park contains two short trails as well as sections of four through trails. The white blazed **Castle Trail,** 1.5 miles, connects the **Quinnebaug Trail** at the Phillips Pond Picnic Area with the **Nehantic Trail,** passing the ruins of an old castle on Stone Hill Road.

The **Canonicus Trail,** 2.5 miles, also white blazed, starts south of the Shetucket Turnpike at the Pachaug Trail and leads into Rhode Island, to the Escoheag Hill Lookout Tower.

The **Nehantic Trail,** 14 miles, starts near the camping area at Green Falls Pond, crosses ledges, climbs Mount Misery and Stone Hill, and ends at the parking area in Hopeville Pond State Park.

The **Narragansett Trail,** (20 miles, 16 in Connecticut), begins at Lantern Hill on Route 2, 2.5 miles east of Route 164. It travels through woods and ravines, and passes several brooks and lakes. From the high points, the Atlantic Ocean is visible. The trail ends near the town of Canonchet in Rhode Island.

The **Pachaug Trail,** about 15 miles, starts one mile into Rhode Island on RI 165 at a beach area on the yellow Tippecansett Trail. The trail passes Beach Pond, Dawley Pond, Mount Misery and ends, after going by Pachaug Pond, at the Pauchaug River near Route 138. There are several good picnic areas along the route.

The **Quinebaug Trail,** 9.7 miles, begins at the Lowden Brook Picnic Area on the Pachaug Trail and follows the Pachaug Trail for 0.4 miles. When the Pachaug turns south, it continues west, intersects the Castle Trail, passes through Hell's Hollow and follows Spaulding Road north to end at Plainfield Pike on Route 14A about ½ mile east of Smith Road.

Maine

Rocky coast, panoramic beaches, a wilderness of forests, islands, jagged peninsulas and mountains. All this is Maine, taking up as much room on a map as the rest of New England combined and offering hikers the biggest and most ecologically varied samples of unspoiled land still left on the East Coast.

Boreal forest stretches across the upper half of the state, its topography punctuated by mountains up to 4,000 feet in elevation and hundreds of clear, glacial lakes. Baxter State Park and the Allagash Wilderness Waterway preserve large parcels of the North Maine Woods for exclusive recreational use, while privately owned timber lands are accessible to backpackers who pay a nominal use fee to tour cross country or camp beside streams or old logging trails.

Mount Katahdin, northern end of the Appalachian Trail, is also in this region. It is said to be the first place in the United States to catch the sun's ray each morning.

The state's rocky coastline and the islands offshore were formed during the Ice Ages when peaks along the coast were pushed down. Coastal Maine in its natural state can best be explored by hikers on the island near Bangor that has been designated Acadia National Park.

Mount Desert Island

Acadia National Park To get there, head southeast from Bangor on U.S. Alternate Route 1 to Ellsworth. Continue southeast on Maine Route 3, across a bridge onto the island. Route 3 circles the island's north half and provides access to trails and campsites.

This heart-shaped island about 18 miles long and 13 miles wide, includes Somes Sound, often called the only true fjord in North America, and Acadia National Park, which some have called the most beautiful of the national parks. There are more than 17 peaks on the island, carved here, as throughout Maine, by glacial action. They were reduced to bare granite by the ice sheets, lakebeds were hollowed out between them, and rocky debris was deposited at the feet of the polished peaks.

To get an overview of the park, follow Maine Route 3 (Ocean Drive) around the park loop. At Anemone Cave, where the water has tunneled 85 feet into the granite cliffs, pools shine amidst the algae, kelp, anemone and rockweed. From the island's highest point, Cadillac Mountain, on a good day, you çan see all the way to Mount Katahdin.

Trails on the island are well maintained and marked and provide an excursion for all types of hikers: from mountain climbing enthusiasts who prefer plenty of exercise to those who want non-strenuous seaside strolls. In addition to trails, there is a system of dirt roads called carriage roads on which motor traffic is not allowed. These are marked where they cross the highway.

Among seaside walks maintained by the National Park Service are the Great Head Circuit, about 3½ miles along the cliffs above the sea; Ocean Drive, 1.8 miles over rock ledges paralleling the State Route 3 to Otter Cliffs; and Hunters Beach, a ¼ mile walk along the surf.

Somes Sound divides Mount Desert Island in two. *Cadillac Mountain,* at 1,530 feet the highest island peak, is on the northern segment, just east of the town of Bar Harbor. It is accessible by car and cog railroad as well as by foot. Trails include the *South Ridge Trail,* a 3½ mile path beginning 50 yards west of the Black Woods Campground on the north side of Maine Route 3. It culminates at the parking lot on the mountain top. The steepest trail up Cadillac is the *West Face Trail,* 2.3 miles, starting at the north end of Bubble Pond and passing through woods and over ledges to the South Ridge Trail and the summit. The *North Ridge Trail,* 1.8 miles, has few trees and therefore offers good views. It starts ½ mile east of Jordan Pond Road on Kebo Mountain Road.

Oxford County

Oxford County in southwestern Maine may be divided into the Grafton Notch area and the Mahoosuc Mountain Range, and the Oxford Hills area which juts into Franklin County.

Grafton Notch State Park is accessible from Maine Route 26 about 15 miles east of the New Hampshire state line.

This 3,132 acre park is a relatively new hiking center with new areas still being opened up. Several parking areas provide access also for short scenic walks.

Old Speck (4,180 feet) provides some of the finest hiking in the state of Maine. In addition to the section of the Appalachian Trail known as the Old Speck Trail, there are numerous other interesting paths to and around this summit.

The *Old Speck Link Trail,* 2.5 miles, and the *East Spur Trail,* one mile, are both offshoots and alternatives to Old Speck. Both may be reached via Maine 26, about 2.6 miles northwest of Screw Auger Falls on the west side, at a place where there is a small waterway and the ground is level. They are marked and follow the Old Speck Trail before turning right.

The blue blazed Old Speck Link Trail is a fairly steep ascent to an open meadow at the top with some spectacular views. The East Spur Trail, also blue blazed, turns left from the Old Speck, and provides good variety and some nice views. This trail becomes difficult when it is icy or wet.

The "Eyebrow" is the name of the cliff forming the summit at the north end of the Notch. The *Eyebrow Trail,* 3.1 miles, together with the *Cascade Brook Trail,* 1.6 miles, form a loop offering some spectacular overviews of the surrounding mountains. Both start from a gravel pit, ⅛ mile north of the start of the Old Speck Trail on Maine 26. Both follow west for 200 yards and then the Eyebrow Trail goes straight and the Cascade Brook Trail forks to the left. The Eyebrow Trail is marked with orange blazes, and provides some spectacular woodland as well as outstanding outlooks. It is recommended that the Cascade Brook Trail be taken up and the Eyebrow Trail down to enjoy the best views. In dry weather, take water with you, particularly on the Eyebrow Trail.

The recently completed *Skyline Trail,* 3.5 miles, is perhaps the best route for backpackers from Grafton Notch to Old Speck. The views are excellent as the trail follows along the ridges, and the grades are never particularly steep. The only disadvantage is that there is no water. Access is from the west side of Maine 26, about 180 yards north of the Appalachian Trail. When you see an orange marker, walk west and climb the ledges to where the orange markers continue. This trail can also be started at the start of the Eyebrow Trail.

Baldpate Mountain (3,812 feet) is east of Grafton Notch and has two summits, the East and the West Peaks. The *Table Rock Trail,* 2.8 miles, is a magnificent climb over switchbacks, ledges, hardwood forest and a large system of slab caves. There is a prominent ledge on the top which affords views of Old Speck, the Notch, the Eyebrow and the surrounding area. Caution should be taken so as not to fall into the caves, which are deep, or to be cut on the sharp rock edges of the ledges. The trail begins on the east opposite the start of the Old Speck Trail off Maine 26.

The *Mahoosuc Mountain Range* runs southwest to northeast in southwestern Maine along the New Hampshire border and Maine's part of the White Mountain National Forest. The Mahoosuc Trail, running nearly 300 miles and largely following the Appalachian Trail from Gorham, N.H. to Old Speck, covers most of the range. Several short spur trails may be reached via the *Success Pond Road,* which is reached by turning right (north) on Hutchins Street in Berlin, N.H., from the east side of the Androscoggin River at the Berlin Mills Bridge. Follow Hutchins for 0.4 miles, turn left, pass through a mill yard, and find the road about 200 yards off the edge of the woods.

The *Goose Eye Trail,* three miles, is an Appalachian Mountain Club Trail heading east from a point 8.4 miles from the beginning of Success Pond Road in Berlin, and intersecting the Mahoosuc Trail. It varies from an old logging road to a fairly steep ledge requiring caution on the summit. The *Carlo Col Trail,* 2.57 miles, follows along with the

Goose Eye for a while before ascending separately to the Mahoosuc Trail. This trail crosses the main brook several times, but the Carlo Col Shelter, on the trail, is the last water for several miles, if you are continuing on in the mountains.

The *Notch Trail* to Mahoosuc Notch, 2.8 miles, begins at a clearing 11.3 miles along the Success Pond Road. It eventually leads to the Mahoosuc Trail at a place where the cliffs, boulders, and rock formations are extraordinary.

Green Mountain (3,300 feet) a very attractive summit, is the highest and westernmost member of the *Bear Mountain* range, which is southeast of the Mahoosucs. Unfortunately, neither it nor its sister *Robinson Peak*, (2,800 feet) have marked trails, but they can be bushwacked to the top.

They and *Sunday River Whitecap* (3,376 feet), *Locke Mountain* (1,880 feet) and *Puzzle Mountain* (3,133 feet) offer several different types of trailless opportunity, ranging from fairly easy going on Locke or old logging roads on Puzzle, to the more difficult Sunday River Whitecap which is advised only for serious climbers. Views from all of these peaks are excellent.

To climb *Bear Mountain* (1,207 feet), for which the range was named, start (with permission from the owner) in a field reached in the following manner: Turn west on Maine 219 from Maine 4 at North Turner. After 0.4 miles, turn right, cross Bear Pond, turn left and follow the gravel road along the north shore of the pond for 2.3 miles. The trail, 2.8 miles, is the road that extends past the farm buildings.

The view from the firetower atop *Mount Zircon* (2,240 feet) near Milton is outstanding. The trail, 2.7 miles, leaves a dirt road that heads south from the highway (U.S. 2) between Abbotts Mill and Rumford. The road comes in west of a bottling plant; drive south two miles where the trail begins on its east side. Water is obtainable at the beginning of the trail, which is open to the summit although steep.

Blueberry Mountain (1,820 feet) offers a top with several open spaces for good views, particularly from the southwest. The *White Cairn Trail*, 2.5 miles, leaves from Shell Pond Road, at a point 1.1 miles west on that road from junction with Route 113, continuing just less than a quarter of a mile beyond a gate. The trail follows old logging roads before climbing to the ridge atop Blueberry. A circuit may be made with this trail and the *Stone House Trail*, 1.5 miles, which starts almost half a mile to the left beyond the gate and meets the White Cairn Trail at the top. A side trail off the Stone House leads to a pretty cascade at Rattlesnake Pool.

Franklin County

This area includes many of Maine's highest mountains, but since it has been heavily developed for skiers, hiking opportunities are few.

The firetower atop *West Kennebago Mountain* (3,705 feet) offers outstanding views from this isolated peak. The top is reached via a firewarden's trail, two miles, off a Brown Company tote road. From Maine 16, turn north 4.9 miles west of the place where Maine Routes 4 and 16 meet the Old Cupsuptic Tote Road. After two miles, bear right at a fork, then bear right again at another fork three miles later. The trail is marked on the left with Maine Forest Service signs. The trail climbs steeply through a ravine for 1¼ miles until you reach a warden's cabin. Water is available between the trailhead and the cabin, but not between the cabin and the firetower at the summit.

Saddleback Mountain (4,116 feet) and its companion peak, *The Horn* (4,023 feet), in the Saddleback Ski Area offer many kinds of experiences for the hiker. The views from the exposed summits are outstanding. The Caves offer hours of exploration, and Piazza Rock is an interesting boulder formation. The ski area is in Franklin County north of Maine Route 4 and south of Maine Route 16. *Saddleback Trail*, 2.5 miles, is reached from the lodge at the Saddleback Ski Area. Leave your car here. The trail begins at the right of the longest chair lift, and follows the route of the lift to a point where the trail splits. The east route (turn left) is a gradual ascent that leads to the firetower at the summit. The other route is longer and ends about ¾ mile from the tower. Both intersect the Appalachian Trail. High winds on the open areas of the mountain make caution advisable.

Benedict Arnold's route to Canada is visible from the trail to the top of *Snow Mountain*, 5.3 miles (3,948 feet). To reach the trail, travel 14.3 miles north on Maine Route 27 from Maine Routes 16 and 27 in Stratton. Turn left (west) on a dirt road, follow it three miles to a fork, then follow the right road as far as it is passable, about four miles. The trail begins at the warden's cabin at Snow Mountain Pond.

The Bigelow Range, running southwest to northeast south of Stratton, offers some of the finest hiking opportunties in Maine. It is a 17-mile range highlighted by the twin "horns" *North Horn* (3,810 feet) and *South Horn* (3,831 feet), and the twin "cones" *Avery Peak* (4,088 feet) and *West Peak* (4,150 feet). East of Avery Peak is the *Little Bigelow Mountain* (3,040 feet) and farther west is *Cranberry Peak* (3,213 feet). The views of the surrounding rugged territory, including Flagstaff Lake, are superb, particularly from Avery, and the area offers not only excellent ridgecrest trail walking but several ponds and other interesting features.

The *Bigelow Range Trail*, connecting to the Appalachian Trail, may be followed for the full length of the range, 11.98 miles (to Appalachian Trail), 22.10 miles (to Avery Peak). It starts on Maine 27, one-half mile southeast of Stratton and about 100 yards northwest of the Eustis-Coplin town line. Take the dirt road east from the highway by automobile as far as possible. The trail starts in about one-half mile through a clearing. It follows a lumber road, travels along the first ledges, and is blue blazed to "The Cave" (a large outcropping of rock). The trail then follows the north edge of the ridge with good views through wooded areas to Cranberry Peak. At times, the trail might be hard to follow here. After you descend, the trail turns right, then left, then right, then left and begins to climb. At 6.4 miles, there is a view of the Horns Pond, and the Horns rock formation itself is about 17 yards to the right. In another quarter mile the Bigelow Trail ends at the Appalachian Trail which continues over the Horns to Avery Peak.

The shortest route to Bigelow's main peaks is the *Firewarden's Trail*, 8.4 miles. The trail can be reached from a dirt road running east from Maine 27 about 3.2 miles west of the Sugarloaf Ski Area access road. The Appalachian Trail access is also here. For the Firewarden's Trail, turn right (east) ⅛ mile north of the second fork on the access road. The trail is very steep for one-half mile, becomes easier, and then steep again. Although it is the shortest route, the Firewarden's Trail is not as scenic as the Appalachian Trail or the Bigelow Range Trail.

Massachusetts

Hiking in Massachusetts means walking through history as well as along the trail. Reminders of its 356 years are strewn throughout the towns and countryside of this 8,257-square-mile commonwealth which separates rural New England from the crowded Greater Northeast Metropolitan Area. Hawthorne's House of the Seven Gables, Revolutionary War battlesites, memories of famous Americans from John Adams to John Kennedy, are just a sample of the literary and political heritage that Massachusetts has given to the country.

The state's terrain is as varied as its history. To many people, Massachusetts is simply Boston and Cape Cod. But the scenery changes from the Cape's summer playground of beaches and bays to what has been called the "Switzerland of America" in the Berkshires, to the lush woodland where Thoreau spent two years contemplating Walden Pond.

Geographically, the state can be divided into four regions. The coastal lowlands, including Cape Cod, Boston, and the primary urban areas, offer sandy beaches, four bays, and a surprising amount of good walks and scenery through woods, fields, and streams. The area is basically flatland with a few rolling hills and an occasional rocky area.

Westward, the plateau or eastern upland area, more than 1,000 feet above sea level, comprises most of the state and is a land of low, rounded hills, valleys, short streams, lakes, and ponds, Thoreau's Walden among them. Mount Wachusett (2,006 feet) is the highest point in this area. It is located in a state reservation of the same name a few miles southwest of Leominster. There are excellent views from its summit, which can be reached either on foot or by car.

The Connecticut Valley area, running parallel to the Connecticut River and Interstate 91, contains the most fertile land in the commonwealth. Here there is rich, red soil and plenty of water from the river.

The most rugged areas of the state are the western uplands. They are dominated by the Taconic Range on the New York border, the Hoosac Range, and the Berkshires, all of which run north-south. Actually, the Berkshires are part of Vermont's Green Mountains. The area is one of clear blue lakes and deep valleys; the mountains themselves are hilly, long ridges. There are no "empty" mountains here — all are forested to the top.

Cape Cod National Seashore

The Cape Cod National Seashore was authorized in 1961 to "keep intact the charm and beauty of the old Cape for future generations." Although it was not able to start with unspoiled wilderness, the project does seek to save as much open space as possible. To date, the government has acquired 24,477.85 acres of a proposed 44,600 total for the completed project.

There are four official areas of the Seashore, open for visitor use: The *Province Lands, Pilgrim Heights, Marconi Station Area,* and the *Nauset* or Coast Guard Beach Section. The *Province Lands,* 4,400 acres at the tip of the Cape, were originally set aside in a conservation act by the Pilgrim fathers. Here are some of the most beautiful sand dunes on the Atlantic. The *Beech Forest Trail,* one mile, made up of the Beech Forest Loop and the Pond Loop is reached by turning right from U.S. 6 toward the Province Lands Visitor Center, at the traffic light on Race Pond Road. The Beech Forest Parking lot is on the left about ½ mile up.

The beginning of the Beech Forest Trail is marked by a box filled (hopefully) with a nature guide and trail map. Although the trail is clearly marked, some less thoughtful hikers have left the beaten path to climb up and down the dunes which surround the pond. The effects of their action and the subsequent erosion are obvious; the moving sand dunes threaten the Beech Forest and parts of the trail. Where the trail itself climbs the dunes, rustic log steps have been installed to minimize the erosion.

Although the forest of Cape Cod are now dominated by pines and oaks, early settlers found extensive beech forests such as the one encountered on the Beech Forest Loop. Forest fires, cutting, and overgrazing destroyed the soil, however, resulting in forest more suited to the dry, sandy environment. Six species of pines may now be found in this forest, two of which, Scotch Pine and Austrian Pine, are not native American species.

At *Pilgrim Heights,* two self-guided trails begin, both of them ½ mile loops. These include the *Pilgrim Spring Trail,* an interpretive path emphasizing natural and political history; and *Small's Swamp Trail,* on which you'll encounter blueberries, beach plum thickets, and bearberry heaths. To reach the trailhead, turn right off U.S. 6 about 1½ miles north of the North Truro turnoff at the Pilgrim Heights Area sign.

The lofty bluffs of the *Marconi Station Area* offer some particularly memorable views as well as a scale model of the first telegraph nearby.

Access to the *Atlantic White Cedar Swamp Trail*, 1.25 miles, is gained by turning right at the light 5.2 miles north of the Salt Pond Visitor Center and following the signs to the Marconi Station parking lot. The trail begins at the observation platform next to the lot where a leaflet may be obtained which describes the plant communities. This is the most interesting and varied of the nature hikes on Cape Cod. After passing through a succession of dry upland communities, the trail leads downslope to the white cedar swamp. A raised boardwalk winds through the cedar grove.

The longer *Great Island Trail*, eight miles round trip, is also in this area. Turn west off Route 6 at the Chequesset Neck Road sign for Wellfleet. Turn south at the Town Pier sign, 0.2 miles farther on. Follow along the harbor coast 3.3 miles to a parking lot.

The box at the starting point may or may not contain a map and trail guide, but before beginning your hike, check the tide schedule as the spit connecting Great Beach Hill with Jeremy Point may be submerged when the tide is high. A canteen on this hike is essential.

The trail leaves the parking lot, dropping through a wooded section to the tidal flat. At high tide, this section of trail may be submerged, forcing you to walk along the bank.

Walking on loose sand is more strenuous than on a firm woodland trail. The impression of slipping back half a step for every one forward can become depressing when the sun is hot and your feet are wet, so be prepared.

At Great Island, the trail divides. A short spur to the left takes you to the site of the 18th century Smith's Tavern. Archeologists from Brown University have excavated this site; do not add your efforts to the project. It is illegal to remove any artifacts from the National Seashore. Return to the main trail via the same spur.

The trail leads across the height of Great Island. The forest is dominated by pitch pine. At one point the trail leaflet reads "note the fine grove of white pine." But white pine has needles in bundles of five, and if you look closely, you will discover that at this point pitch pine is the rule.

The trail then drops to near sea level where a large lush saltwater swamp must be skirted before climbing up Great Beach Hill. From the south end of Great Beach Hill, Jeremy Point is still 1.2 miles away along a narrow spit. This section should be attempted only if you are aware of the condition of the tides. From here it is possible to return the way you came or by walking along the beach on the Cape Cod Bay side of Great Island.

The *Nauset*, or *Coast Guard Beach* section, has four trails. The *Nauset Marsh Trail*, reached from the parking lot at the Salt Pond Visitor Center, is a one mile trail emphasizing salt marsh plant and animal cycles. The *Fort Hill* or *Red Maple Swamp Trail*, ½ mile, is reached by turning right on Governor Prence Road near the Fort Hill sign, and continuing to the parking lot across from the Captain Penniman House.

This trail is designed especially to point out the life cycles of swamp plants.

The *Buttonbush Trail*, 4 miles, begins to the left of the Salt Pond Visitor's Center as you face its front door. It is constructed for the enjoyment of those who are blind. A guide rope follows the trail, not only leading the way, but signaling, through the use of plastic disks or pieces of garden hose, when a trail sign or difficult section of the path occurs. Signs are in both large print and Braille, and visitors are encouraged to touch the various trees and shrubs as well as smell, hear and feel the changes in environment that occur over the course of the trail.

Camping is not allowed within the National Seashore. Numerous private campsites, however, can be found on the length of the Cape. Many of these are open only during the summer and some cater only to enclosed rigs such as travel trailers and pickup campers. Nickerson State Park on Mass. 6A just east of East Brewster is the best bet for Cape Cod, with camping on a first-come, first-served basis.

Access to *Martha's Vineyard* is by daily ferry service during the summer and weekend service November through March from Woods Hole. There is also summer boat service from Hyannis and Falmouth. There is a state forest here where nature trails are still being developed, but the coves, beaches, cliffs, ponds and woods make Martha's a delightful place just to walk without specific guides. Woods people will like the north shore; those looking for more varied ocean scenery should head south.

There is also a quarter mile trail up *Indian Hill* to a firetower from which you can get an excellent view of the whole area. To find the tower, follow Vineyard Haven Road west for 100 yards from Tisbury. Turn right on Indian Hill Road and continue ½ mile to a crossroad. Turn right and go ½ mile to Christiantown, an Indian burial ground. The trail begins at the rear of those grounds.

For the current status of trails in *Martha's Vineyard State Forest*, stop at the office of the forest superintendent.

The *Barnstable County Agricultural Society* maintains about 110 miles of intersecting trails on the Cape. Basically bridle paths, most of these are also suitable for hiking and are marked by paint or plastic streamers. The area is flat, although there are occasional hills, and most trails pass several lakes and ponds.

The trails are long, but broken up by roads and interesting trails so you can plan a trip of almost any length. (Camping on private property is not advised without permission.) Following are the trailheads of the nine primary trails. Maps are available for 50 cents from: The Cape Code Animal Hospital, West Barnstable, Mass.; Govone Grain and Feed, Mass. 130, Forestdale, Mass.; Maushop Farm, Cotuit, Mass.; Flying B Ranch, PIne Lane, Barnstable, Mass.; and Circle B. Ranch, Mass. 28, Hyannis, Mass.

Dopple Bottom Trail, 67 miles. Continue south on Mass. 130 past the junction with U.S. 6. The trail begins on the east side of the road opposite the southeast end of a bypass connecting the two highways in Sandwich. The trail is marked in orange.

Mashpee Pond Trail, 40.1 miles. Marked in red, this is a cutoff of the Dopple Bottom Trail, beginning 2¾ miles east of the Dopple Bottom trailhead.

Hathaway Ponds Trail, 19 miles. Near the Chamber of Commerce Building in Barnstable, the trail begins on Iyannough Road, second road on the right beyond a power line southeast of the junction of that road and U.S. 6. The trail is marked in blue.

Cotuit Highlands Trail, 59 miles. This path leaves the Dopple Bottom trail 5-5/8 mile from its beginning heading southwest. It is blazed in red.

Town Line Trail, 16 miles. Leave the Dopple Bottom trail 5.5 miles from its start. This trail is also marked in red.

Mystic Lake Trail, 14 miles. This trail, marked in red, heads south six miles along the Dopple Bottom Trail.

Race Lane Trail, 12 miles. It begins where the Dopple Bottom Trail ends, near Clay Hill and is also marked in red.

Mill Pond Trail, two miles. From the junction of U.S. 6 and Mass. 130, go east 4 miles to the second cloverleaf. Follow Chase Road, which crosses here, north. The trail starts in the town of Sandwich, on Chase Road, a short distance north of County Road. This is a fairly rugged, wooded, trail, marked in blue.

Wequaquet Lake Trail, 52.8 miles. The trail begins at the northeast corner of Wequaquet Lake in Barnstable. It is marked in red.

Mount Wachusett (2,006 feet) in the Wachusett Mountain State Reservation near Princeton and Westminster, is the highest point in central Massachusetts, with magnificent panoramic views of the surrounding low country from its summit. The *Jack Front Trail* to the summit, 1.08 miles, is reached by driving north 1.3 miles from Princeton Center on Mountain Road and turning left at Westminster Road. Continue for 0.8 miles to Administration Road, turn right, and drive 0.4 miles farther to a wood road on the right which is the beginning of the trail.

The trail name is painted above a brook; from here follow the light blue blazes up steep ledges, through hemlock forest, and up again, to join the Mountain House Trail (turn left) which may be followed to the summit.

The *Mountain House Trail,* one mile, coming from the east, begins close to an old shack on the west side of Mountain Road, 2.4 miles north of Princeton Center. It is unmarked and steep, but easy to follow.

The *Harrington Trail,* 1.5 miles, which joins the Mountain House and Jack Frost Trails at the summit, is reached by driving from Princeton Center 1.4 miles north on Mountain Road. Upon reaching a Y crossing, turn left, and turn left again after 0.8 miles. The Harrington Farm appears in 0.7 more miles. The trail begins near the brook at the back of the house.

This trail is longer than the others and in places involves climbing over rocks. At one point, you have a choice between climbing over rocks or following the *Mountain House Link Trail* for a short distance before rejoining the Harrington.

The Western Uplands

The Berkshire Mountains are the major feature of this area, stretching from Mount Everett at the southern boundary of the state to Mount Greylock on the north, only 40 air miles apart.

Mount Greylock (3,491 feet) is the highest mountain in Massachusetts and the center of the Mount Greylock State Reservation. It is located at the state's extreme northwest corner. Three automobile roads and several trails lead to the war memorial and excellent views on its top. The *Mount Greylock-Mount Prospect Loop*, 12.1 miles, combines part of the Appalachian Trail with parts of three other trails to reach Mount Greylock and Mount Prospect (2,690 feet) plus Mount Williams (2,951 feet) and Mount Fitch (3,110 feet).

Access is from the center of Williamstown where U.S. 7 forks north from Mass. 2. Go east on Mass. 2 for 1.7 miles. Turn right on Luce Road (which becomes Pattison Road) and watch for the Appalachian Trail signs and white blazes on the right between the Williamstown and Mount Williams Reservoirs.

There are three camping areas with lean-tos along this route. Since much of the trail follows ridges, it is advisable to carry water. The trail follows the white blazes of the AT all the way to the summit of Greylock. In the first 1½ miles, it climbs 1,500 vertical feet up the north ridge of Mount Prospect, turning left where it meets the blue blazes of the *Mount Prospect Trail*. The trail then descends slightly, crossing the Notch Road (one of the three auto routes to the top), and climbs over Mount Williams and Mount Fitch to the War Memorial on the summit. On a clear day, it is possible to see Connecticut, New York, Vermont and New Hampshire.

The route continues southwest from the summit down Rockwell Road, leaving the AT where the *Hopper Trail* forks right. The Hopper Trail drops steeply soon after passing Sperry Campground. After about a mile, take the right cutoff to meet *Money Brook Trail*, and, shortly after that, you will reach another lean-to. A few hundred yards beyond the lean-to, turn left on Mount Prospect Trail, which climbs 1,200 feet in about a mile to the summit. The trail then descends to the north and meets the AT before returning to the start.

New Hampshire

Covered bridges and the White Mountains characterize New Hampshire. The bridges are a reminder of a bygone day; the Mountains — named for the snow that blankets them from December to the middle of

April — are the here and now. Originally, they were a barrier to the early settlers who crowded along the coast and only gradually moved back through the passes. Today, the mountains, along with the hundreds of lakes, ponds, rivers, and waterfalls throughout the state, make New Hampshire a center of recreational activity in all seasons.

New Hampshire's 9,304 square miles may be divided into six geographical areas. In the Northern Hill Region, rolling grasslands mesh into wild forests. Farther south are the White Mountains. The Connecticut Valley, bordering Vermont, provides some of the best farmland in the state, while the Hill and Lake region, forming a semi-circle along the Connecticut Valley and the area south of the White Mountains, combines forested hills with hundreds of bodies of inland water. The Merrimack Valley is rolling irregular land, but the soil is deep and fertile.

Mount Cardigan Area

Mount Cardigan (3,121 feet) in Orange and Alexandria, is another relatively easy climb. The easiest route up is the *West Ridge Trail,* 1.3 miles. It is reached from Canaan by taking the highway to Orange, (it begins east of the intersection of U.S. 4 and Canaan Street), crossing Orange Brook, keeping right onto Grafton Road when the road forks the first time, then bearing left and turning right to Hoyt Hill. In ⅛ mile is the State Reservation entrance, from which a road leads one-half mile up past some cabins to a parking area and the start of the trail. The trail is marked on the ledges by white blazes and cairns. It intersects several other trails on the way up and passes one shelter, the Hermitage. The trail goes to the firetower.

The *Hurricane Gap Trail,* 0.9 miles, commemorates the hurricane of September 21, 1938. It starts at the Hermitage on the West Ridge Trail, crossed the col, and merges with the Clark Trail.

The *Clark Trail,* 3.5 miles, marked in green, starts at a point 0.6 miles before the Cardigan Lodge and 0.8 miles past the red school house on the road to the Lodge. From Alexandria, take the road going northwest 4.5 miles. One mile past Knudson is the Lodge. The trail starts off this road. From its starting point on a ridge, the trail is first a side road, but gradually ascends into the State Reservation, goes through open woods, enters the Cathedral Forest, crosses several other trails, passes a brook flowing from a spring which is the last water for more than half a mile, and finally, reaches the firetower at the summit.

The *Skyland Trail,* 4.4 miles, marked in pink, crosses five of the six mountains extending south and southeast from Cardigan. It travels from the bridge about 0.3 miles from the start of the West Ridge Trail, to Alexandria Four Corners; (about 4.5 miles west of Alexandria) and crosses Rimrock (2,900 feet), Mount Gilman (2,620 feet), Crane Mountain (2,400 feet), Grafton Knob (2,300 feet) and Church Mountain (2,280 feet).

The White Mountains

Mount Moosilauke (4,810 feet), in the southwestern area, is not too hard to climb and has one of the best views. It should not be approached lightly, though. Although it is not too high, a large area is above timberline. In the winter, it is possible to be blown off the rocky, craggy peak. The Dartmouth Outing Club used to maintain a cabin with cooking and sleeping gear near the top, but these were removed due to overuse and the cabin is now for emergency use only. There is no camping allowed in the area. (Take Route 112 about five miles northwest past Kinsman Notch to Noxon Road, which ends at Tunnel Brook. Noxon Road is ⅓ mile southeast of Route 116.)

The *Tunnel Brook Trail*, 6.5 miles, runs from Noxon Road at Tunnel Brook to the North and South Road, following Tunnel Brook for most of the way.

The *Benton Trail*, 3.5 miles (past Tunnel Brook Trail), which used to be a bridle path, leaves Tunnel Brook 1.4 miles south of Noxon Road. The trail comes up through the South Wall of Little Tunnel Ravine. It then climbs fairly gradually through evergreen forest, crosses a flat, crosses the treeline 0.3 miles below the top, and finally, reaches the top.

The *Carriage Road*, five miles (a former actual road), starts at Moosilauke Inn 2 miles from NH 118, at a place called Breezy Point. To reach Moosilauke Inn, go northest from Warren on Route 118, take the first turn to the right after the Glencliff cutoff two miles to Breezy Point. The trail ascends to the south ridge, and continues to ascend in easy grades. At 1.6 miles, the trail to the abandoned Ravine Lodge turns right. This is followed by a series of switchbacks and junctions with other trails, including, at about 4.1 miles, a 0.1-mile trail climbing to the top of Moosilauke South (4,560 feet). (The next section, leading to North and South peaks, is a cairn-marked, exposed, ridgewalk. It should not be tried in bad weather.) There are some good views from a point midway between the North and South Peaks, and the ruins of a small house at the top.

The *Franconia Range* includes Mount Lafayette (5,249 feet), Mount Lincoln (5,108 feet), Little Haystack (4,513 feet), Mount Liberty (4,460 feet) and Flume (4,327 feet). This range offers some good views, but can be dangerous, as described below.

The *Greenleaf Trail*, 3.25 miles, leads to the summit of Mount Lafayette. It is reached at the north end of Profile Clearing, on the east side of US 3 as you go north through Franconia Notch. It ascends via switchbacks and zigzags past some nice views and rock formations. As it rises more steeply caution should be observed as loose stones become slippery when the weather is wet. At 2.07 miles, a reservoir is passed, and, at 2.15 miles, the Greenleaf Hut is reached. This hut can house 46 people, is open from the middle of June to the middle of September, and overlooks Eagle Lake. It is 7.75 miles from the Galehead Hut, (the Garfield Ridge Trail leads to Galehead from Greenleaf) which is the next nearest hut. From the hut, the trail first dips, then ascends gradually to the summit.

The *Falling Waters Trail*, 2.8 miles, starts across from the Lafayette Forest Service Campground on the east side of US 3, and climbs Little Haystack. The trail passes four waterfalls — Walker Cascade at 0.3 mile, Stairs Falls at 0.9 miles, Swiftwater Falls at one mile, and Cloudland Falls at 1.4 miles. (There are two additional falls at Cloudland's head.) The trail ascends via switchbacks and then graded sections before Cloudland Falls, comes out for a view, continues to climb, passes under Shining Rock Cliff, enters forestland and passes the timberline about 500 feet from the summit.

The *Franconia Ridge Trail*, five miles, connects the Greenleaf and Falling Waters Trails, and goes on to Mount Liberty and Mount Flume. (Mount Lincoln is halfway between Mount Lafayette — the end of the Greenleaf Trail — and Little Haystack — the end of the Falling Waters Trail.) The ridge between Lincoln and Little Haystack can be treacherous. It is a knife edge with a sheer drop on each side, and, in wet or windy weather it is very dangerous. In addition, the rock cairns above timberline on this trail are frequently hard to follow in bad weather as they are not particularly prominent. From Little Haystack the trail descends into the woods, which are followed to Mount Liberty. The Liberty Spring Shelter may be reached by following a fork to the right before reaching the mountain, for a quarter mile. There is water at this shelter. The trail climbs Liberty, descends slightly, and then climbs Flume. The trail ends .09 miles past the summit of Flume at the Flume Slide Trail.

The *Flume Slide Trail*, 3.45 miles, is reached from a point 150 feet above the head of the Flume, which is a well-known narrow gorge in the Franconia Notch area. Go through the Flume entrance at the south corner of the Flume Store (At the Flume ⅓ of the way north through Franconia Notch.) At this point you will be on the wide, gravel Wildwood Trail. Take this 500 feet, turn right on the Boulder Trail, and continue .07 miles to where both the Flume Slide and Liberty Spring Trails begin. The Flume Trail is on the right. The trail follows logging roads to the slide. Caution is urged on the slide due to the poor footing which becomes even worse in wet weather. The trail is marked in white on the slide. Near the top, the trail enters the woods, continues to climb and emerges at the Franconia Ridge Trail. The only water that can be counted on in this trail is below the slide. Allow extra time either climbing or descending the Flume Slide Trail, since the footing is so poor.

The *Liberty Spring Trail*, 3.45 miles, beginning at the point described above, climbs to the Franconia Ridge Trail just north of Mount Liberty. The Ridge Trail leads to the summit. Liberty Spring Shelter, and water (mentioned above) are on this trail.

Various combinations of hikes can be arranged along Franconia Ridge. Since the best part of the trail is between Lafayette and Liberty, a good one-day trip might involve going up the Liberty Springs Trail and down the Greenleaf. If you have more time, plan on staying at the Greenleaf Hut, go up the Greenleaf Trail, and continue over the ridge to the Flume.

The *Pemigewasset Wilderness Area* is a loosely defined area east of Franconia Ridge. Main automobile access is via the Kancamagus Highway (NH 112) which cuts right through the mountains. There are no huts in this area, but there are six shelters. The main hiking access is via the Wilderness Trail.

The *Wilderness Trail*, 8.7 miles. The trail starts at the junction of the Kancamagus Highway and the East Branch of the Pemigewasset River, at a point just west of the bridge over the river, about 4.7 miles from Lincoln.

The trail follows an old railroad bed. At 2.7 miles from the starting point, a side trail leads to the Franconia Brook Shelter; and, from there, another path leads to the spectacular Franconia Falls. There is another shelter at five miles and several junctions with other trails. The trail ends at Stillwater Junction where it meets the *Carrigain Notch Trail* leading either northwest to *Desolation Shelter* in another one-half mile, or southeast out on the Sawyer River Road.

The *Black Pond Trail*, .83 miles, is a short offshoot of the Wilderness Trail. It leaves it to the left at 2.4 miles, follows a logging trail for a time, then follows the Black Pond outlet to Black Pond itself.

The *Franconia Brook Trail*, 7.2 miles, is a link between Garfield Ridge and the Wilderness Trail. It leads from a point 1.2 miles east of Mount Garfield and 1.3 miles west of the intersection of the Garfield Ridge and Gale River Trails, to a point on the Wilderness Trail 50 yards east of the Franconia Brook bridge. Following logging roads and the railroad grade, the trail at 2.2 miles passes the No. 13 Falls waterfall and the 13 Falls Shelter, and comes within 80 yards (turn right) of the Camp 9 Brook Shelter after 6.9 miles.

Mount Carrigain (4,680 feet) is known for its views. The trail to the summit begins 2.05 miles from Route 302 on the Sawyer River Road.

After about 1⅓ miles the trail joins a logging road, which should be followed straight. After about three miles, the trail rises steeply and turns into zigzags ascending Signal Ridge. The trail enters forestland on the ridge, ascends again and comes out among the trees on the mountain. There is a steel tower on the summit. Water is available at 3.1 and 3.5 miles and at an abandoned fire warden's cabin on the ridge.

Mount Chocorua (3,475 feet) is a cone-shaped rocky mountain south of the Kancamagus Highway (N.H. 112) and southeast of the Pemigewasset Wilderness. It is quite lovely, with a pool at its feet, and is not too difficult to climb. It has several trails.

The *Piper Trail*, 4.1 miles, is an ascent from the east. Access is on N.H. Route 16 at the Piper Trail Cabins and Restaurant. The trail does not begin to really climb for almost two miles. At 3.05 miles, Camp Penacook Shelter is reached. The trail then rises to the ledges which are marked with yellow paint, and to the summit.

The *Brook Trail*, 4.2 miles, an approach from Wonalancet, offers some beautiful scenery. Go to Fowler's Mill road between Route 113 A and Chocorua Lake. The Paugus Mill road runs north of that road and in ⅔ mile, the *Liberty Trail*, 4.5 miles, turns right and the Brook Trail, 300 yards later, branches left. It follows wood roads through fine forestland, ascends gradually, then reaches the steep Farlow Ridge ledge. The trail is marked with yellow paint and cairns on the ledge. Before the summit is reached, it is joined by the Liberty and Piper Trails. (There used to a toll on the Liberty Trail — the Brook Trail was constructed as an alternative.) The Jim Liberty Cabin with stove and beds is 3.97 miles from the trailhead.

The *Presidential Peaks*, the most interesting range in the White Mountains, are a series of eight peaks, all reaching above timberline. They stretch northwest from Crawford Notch. Several of them are named for former presidents. They include Mount Washington (6,288 feet), the highest mountain in the northeast, at the head of the ridge, followed by Mount Clay (5,532 feet), Mount Jefferson (5,715 feet), Mount Adams (5,798 feet), which has two minor peaks: John Quincy Adams (5,470 feet) and Sam Adams (5,585 feet), Mount Madison (5,363 feet) and Pine Mountain (2,404 feet). Just slightly lower than the Smokies, the Presidentials, particularly Mount Washington, offer much more rugged hiking.

There are public campgrounds accessible to these peaks at Dolly Copp Campground and at Gorham. There is parking at Randolph East, Lowe's Store, Appalachia, the Dolly Copp Campground, Pinkham Notch Camp, the Glen House Site and Marshfield. There are also places to leave cars at some of the high points on the highways.

Probably the best way to see the Presidentials is via the *Gulfside Trail*, between the Madison Hut and Mount Washington's summit. With the exception of Mount Washington, it does not touch any peaks, but it does go through all the major cols.

The *Madison Hut* is open from the middle of June to the middle of September and sleeps 76 people. It is reached via the *Valley Way Trail*, 3.47 miles, which starts at the parking space at Appalachia. This is the most direct route to the hut and the best in bad weather. Unfortunately, although the trail used to be nicely graded, much of it has washed away and might be rocky. After the first two miles, the trail becomes fairly steep.

The *Gulfside Trail* is marked so as to be followable in bad weather. There are large stone cairns with a yellow stone on top of each, which can be seen even through snow or fog, showing the way. And snow and fog should be expected on this trail. If you are caught in bad weather, try to make it to a shelter or hut. If this is impossible, just go down into one of the ravines. Exposure has proven fatal many times along these paths and you are much safer off trail in a ravine than on the ledge. It is not advisable to be hiking here without a topo map and compass.

The first section of the Gulfside Trail, 2.25 miles, runs from the col between Mounts Madison and Adams and ends at Edmands Col (4,930 feet) between Adams and Jefferson. There is shelter here for emergencies only. Camping is not permitted.

From Edmands, 3.8 miles, the trail enters a steep climb over rocky terrain, and passes a good view at Dingmaul Rock. There is a loop trail to Mount Jefferson passed shortly thereafter that will only add about 0.4 miles to your total. This section of the trail ends at the Clay-Jefferson col.

From this Col, the rough *Mount Clay Loop* splits from the Gulfside Trail to make its ascent up Mount Clay. Its views are much better, although it adds about 20 minutes to your trip and has no water. The trails reunite behind Mount Clay in the Clay-Washington col. About .12 miles further on, the Westside Path leads to the *Crawford Path* and the Lakes-of-the-Clouds Hut in the Washington-Monroe col. This hut is also open from mid-June to mid-September and can house up to 90 guests. Clay-Washington col: 4.9 miles. Lakes-of-the-Clouds hut: 6.77 miles.

From the Clay-Washington col, the trail ascends Mount Washington, reaching the summit in 6.25 miles.

A good two-night trip can be planned by utilizing both the Madison and Lakes-of-the-Clouds Huts. The Lakes-of-the-Clouds may also be reached from the Marshfield Cog Railway station via the *Ammonoosuc Ravine Trail.* This trail offers magnificent views and fairly safe weather due to being below scrub line to within about 100 yards of the hut. The trail ascends first gradually, then quite steeply with views of two waterfalls coming together in a gorge. (You have to climb out to a ledge to really see this. Be careful, but the view is worth it.) After emerging from the scrub close to the hut, the trail follows a line of cairns right to the hut. 2.46 miles.

There are three ways up Mount Washington: one is by automobile on the toll road, one is via the cog railway, and the third is on foot. It is a good thing to remember that the railway and the road form a basically east-west line across the mountain. If you really think you're lost at point, make your way north or south in as direct a manner as possible, and eventually, you should reach one of these routes.

The *Tuckerman Ravine Trail* follows a glacial path up Mount Washington and is the shortest path from the east. It starts at Pinkham Notch Camp on the west side; and, at first follows the Fire Trail or tractor road. After ⅜ miles, there is an excellent view of the Crystal Cascade. After this, the trail ascends first via two long switchbacks, then by just a steep grade. At 2.4 miles, the Herman Lake Camping Shelters are reached. The Herman Lake Shelters, four of which are around the Lake and six of which are nearby, can sleep about 10 people each. There is also a "cook shack" with coin operated stoves and the possibility of firewood. There is a $1.00 fee for use of the shelters and a 50¢ fee for open camping in the area.

After passing Hermit Lake, the trail begins to rise, and after 3.1 miles reaches the Snow Arch on the left. This arch does not always form, although at times snow remains here until late summer. If the arch has formed, do not go near it or attempt to cross over or under it. At least one person has died in the attempt, and huge pieces of snow weighing tons are apt to break off at any time. If the snow completely covers the trail, take a detour over the Lion Head Trail (go back to 2.3 miles and turn left). Also be careful if you are climbing the headwall not to let loose any rocks as these may cause danger to others.

The trail turns left, goes under a cliff and begins to climb up a grassy ledge. At 3.6 miles Tuckerman Junction is reached. The Tuckerman Crossover leads southwest to the Crawford path near the Lakes-of-the-Clouds Hut and other paths lead to other trails. The trail turns right and climbs the rocks to the auto road on the mountain's top. This last section is marked by cairns and painted rocks. 4.1 miles.

The *Carter-Moriah Range* is east of the Presidentials. The *Carter-Moriah Trail* connects its two namesake peaks, Mount Carter (4,843 feet) and Mount Moriah (4,047 feet). It is reached by traveling east on US 2 from Gorham, until the road ends and the trail begins on the left. The trail follows a path, then logging roads, then climbs gently to a ledge with a view of Mount Madison, and continues on to climb Mount Surprise. From here the trail covers wooded ledges until the summit of Moriah, open, and with panoramic views, is reached. The trail descends, then ascends toward the *Imp Shelter cutoff* which may be taken right a short distance to the *Imp Shelter* (3,500 feet), one mile. The trail continues southwest, making the steep climb to reach North Carter at 7.8 miles. The trail goes south across the ridge from here, passing some good views of Wild River Valley, crossing some boggy depressions that may be wet, and reaching Middle Carter, then South Carter, and descending 500 feet to Zeta Pass. The trail then climbs 700 steep feet to Mount Hight which has some expansive views, and descends, steeply, to the Carter Notch Hut. This hut is open from the middle of June to the middle of September and holds 40 guests. 13.9 miles.

The *Great Gulf* is a glacial valley loosely surrounded by the Presidential Peaks and the line of the Carter-Moriah trail. Leaving your car at the Dolly Copp Campground (just off Route 16), it is a good place to hike into for day trips up to the various Presidential Peaks. The *Great Gulf Trail* extends 7.76 miles through the Gulf, connecting Route 16 at Glen House to the summit of Mount Washington. It provides starting points for other Gulf trails and passes two of the three Gulf Shelters.

The *Six Husbands Trail* connects a point 4.42 miles from Glen House on the Great Gulf Trail to the summit of Mount Jefferson. It was named for the husbands of a Pocasset Queen, Weetamoo, who also has a waterfall named in her honor. The trail descends, crosses the West Branch and climbs the southwest bank of the stream from Jefferson Ravine. This stream is the last sure water. The trail follows the stream a bit, turns west, passes some boulders, and climbs two ladders. It passes a cave which is full of snow in August, and passes under a ledge to climb two more ladders. From here there is a good view, and the trail follows the ridge crest to come out on the North Knee of Jefferson where the ascent becomes easier. At this point, the trail is marked by cairns. It becomes steeper as the Jefferson cone is climbed and a mound of snow is passed, continuing west past the Gulfside Trail to the summit 2.2 miles.

The *Sphinx Trail* is important for anyone planning to climb Mount Clay or the south side of Mount Jefferson, since it is an escape route in case of storms. It leaves the Gulfside Trail north of the Clay-Jefferson Col and descends to the Great Gulf Trail ¾ mile above the numbers 1 and 2 Great Gulf Shelters. One mile (descent 1,400 feet).

The *Mahoosuc Range* runs east of the main White Mountain Range through the Maine-New Hampshire border. These mountains are lower than most of the other ranges, nonetheless they provide some worthwhile hiking experiences. The *Mahoosuc Trail*, 27.24 miles, is a path along the entire length of the range, beginning at Gorham and reaching to Old Speck (see Maine), with many side trails into the range. The trail itself makes a nice three-day trip, although car shuttling involves a fairly lengthy ride.

The *Mahoosuc Notch Trail*, 2.75 miles, leads to very interesting cliffs and boulder formations. It starts at a clearing at the beginning of Success Pond Road, follows a logging road at first, and then a trail through the woods which climbs to a beaver pond. Where the trail meets the Mahoosuc Trail, the valley suddenly changes to one of incredible chamber formations. To fully enjoy the Notch, its high cliffs, and formations, pass through it and travel along the Mahoosuc Trail for a bit.

New York

New York state is riddled with trails. There are three basic geographic zones in New York, with three different types of forest and trail. The western and central parts of the state are·characterized by limestone glens where the trails often follow deep winding gorges cut into shale with hundreds of waterfalls, chutes, pools, and small parks scattered throughout the area. Then, there is the Rip Van Winkle country of the Catskills, where hardwoods dominate the mountains. And finally, there are the mountains of the northern Adirondacks. These are mixed hardwood valleys that change to a birch zone on the slopes and end in alpine tundra on the peaks.

Adirondack Park land fell into private ownership and remains so today. Although it is the largest park in the U.S., 60 per cent of its land is still privately held.

The dominance of private ownership gives the park a different flavor from that found· exclusively in government-owned parks. For instance, it does seem unusual at first to find a whole town, complete with high school, dime store and newspaper office within park boundaries.

The state Department of Environmental Conservation operates 45 campgrounds in the Adirondacks and the Catskills. Permits are issued on arrival and reservations are not accepted in advance. The fee is $2.50 per night per site, but is collected only during busy summer months. The department also maintains 200 "Open Camps" along the 1,000 miles of trail and near canoe routes in the Forest Preserve (state-owned sections) areas. These camps feature "Adirondack Lean-Tos," fireplaces and pit privies. If you plan your hike carefully around use of these sites, you can lighten your backpacking load since you won't need a tent.

Finger Lakes Region

The Finger Lakes are 11 lakes with the long and narrow shape of fingers. The Iroquois Indians believed the five largest were formed by the Great Spirit pressing his hand upon the earth. **Buttermilk Falls** and the **Robert H. Treman State Park** west of Ithaca on N.Y. Route 13 are particularly scenic. The Park includes **Enfield Glen,** whose three miles of hiking trails pass 12 waterfalls; as well as fine walks along gorges cut into interesting shapes. The famous **Watkins Glen** region, at the south end of Seneca Lake (accessible via N.Y. Route 14) also offers rugged rock patterns, glens, waterfalls and gorges in addition to lakes and varied plantlife. There is a three-mile trail running the length of the Glen, and an Indian trail along the rim.

Some 5,300 acres of unspoiled marshland offering several miles of hiking trails can be found in the **Montezuma National Wildlife Refuge** at the northern tip of Cayuga Lake. The area attracts numerous species of waterfowl.

Take the Seneca Falls exit from Interstate 90 about 25 miles west of Syracuse and drive east on Routes 5 and 20 to the refuge entrance. Hiking trails are closed in May and June to protect newly hatched birds.

The 350 mile Finger Lakes Trail, almost complete, connects the Red House in Allegany State Park with the Catskills. Part of the National Scenic Trail, the Long Trail of Vermont, and the Bruce Trail of Canada. It is not a wilderness trail, but it does pass through calm woodlands and fern coated areas, and it passes several spectacular waterfalls. Particularly scenic is the section bordering the Finger Lakes. Although most of the trail is finished, some sections (including a spur north to the Adirondacks) are still under construction, and a few segments still need sponsorship.

Further information on the Finger Lakes Region is available from the Finger Lakes Conference, c/o Frances Jacobi, 71 Superior Road, Rochester, New York 14625, the State Department of Environmental Conservation, Albany, N.Y. 12201, or the State Bureau of Parks and

Recreation.

Interesting walks may also be had at **Letchworth State Park,** which stretches southwest to northeast in a narrow ribbon between Portageville on N.Y. Route 19 and Mount Morris on New York 36. This beautiful area has an unusual tree plantation, lovely bridges and borders on the great gorge of the Genesee River, the "Grand Canyon of the East." Indian traditions, such as archery contests, are kept alive here too.

There are about 20 miles of hiking trails in Allegany State Park, which borders Pennsylvania's Allegheny National Forest and is accessible via N.Y. Route 17 east of Jamestown.

The Catskills

Location: Access to the Catskills is via N.Y. Route 23, 212 and 28 west of Interstate 87 between Athens and Kingston.

Length: 145 miles total.

Description: The Catskills, in the southeastern part of the state, have a gentler quality than the land in the west, although there are steep-sided valleys, rocky glens, ridges and ravines next to the rounded mountain tops. These mountains are part of the same Allegheny plateau that widens throughout Pennsylvania and West Virginia, becoming the Poconos and other ranges.

The Indians called the Catskills the "Land in the Sky," the Dutch "Wildcat Mountain." The Dutch word evolved into "Catskills," but it was not until fairly recently in New York history that the area was fully explored.

The trails of the Catskills are well marked and passable all year. Intersections are indicated by signboards and trail routes by circular markers in red, blue, and yellow. Many of the trails cross private land. When this is indicated, camping, fishing, picnicking and hunting are often prohibited according to the owner's wishes.

The Catskill trails may be divided into those of the northern area and those in the central area. Northern trails include the **Indian Head-Hunter Mountain Range Trail,** 23.19 miles. Access is via N.Y. 23A west of Interstate 87 north of Kingston. Drive ½ mile west of the New York City Police Camp and turn south at Tannersville on Platte Clove Road 0.4 miles. The trailhead is south of a bridge across the East Branch of Echoharie Creek. The trail, heading west, is marked in red with a lean-to at 14.2 miles. It passes over the ridges of Indian Head, Twin, and Sugarloaf Mountains, Plateau and Hunter Mountains. There are several good views as the trail follows these ridges for most of its length. It crosses N.Y. 214 and ends at Spruceton Road. Carry a canteen on this trail during the dry season.

The yellow-blazed **Echo Lake Trail,** 2.8 miles, turns off the Indian Head Trail 1.65 miles west of its eastern terminus and continues to the Echo Lake lean-to, a pretty lake and a clear spring.

At mile 4.2 on the Indian Head Trail (from its eastern end), at Jimmy Dolan Notch, a blue-blazed trail, 2.7 miles long, heads north to Platte Clove Road ½ mile west of the Police Camp. This side trail involved a steep descent and after 2.2 miles turns right to follow red blazes.

A trail to Pecoy Notch begins at Platte Clove Road near the turn to Twin Mountain House. It follows blue markers and may be followed south to Indian Head or to Sugarloaf or Twin Mountains.

Mink Hollow Trail, 11.7 miles, leads from Lake Hill on New York 212 northeast to Tannersville. It is marked with blue blazes and heads northeast three miles to an old mill, past a lean-to in another three miles, then across slopes of Sugarloaf, Twin, Indian Head and Plattkill Mountains.

Hunter Mountain (4,040 feet) is the second highest mountain in the Catskills. There are four trails to the firetower on its top. The blue-marked **Becker Trail,** 2.4 miles, is reached by following Stony Clove Road (New York Route 214) one mile north of the Devil's Tombstone Campsite. There is a spring on the trail. The multi-coded **Spruceton Trail,** 3.7 miles, begins eight miles east of West Kill where Spruceton Road meets a truck trail. Follow a blue-blazed trail to Old Hunter Road, then continue on a red-blazed one. At the Colonel's Chair and Hunter Village, a blue trail branches off to a spring while the yellow trails leads to the observatory. The **Shanty Hollow Trail** starts at the Colonel's Chair but follows the yellow markers to a recrossing of the Spruceton Trail. At that point, you may follow a blue-blazed side trail to a spring, then follow yellow markers past a lean-to and eventually to Devil's Tombstone Public Campsite.

The Phoenicia and Willow Trails provide access to **Mount Tremper** (2,720 feet). The **Phoenicia,** 2.15 miles, is shorter, steeper and easier to reach by car. It starts on N.Y. Route 28 about a mile east of Phoenicia Village, heads south, following red markers, and passes one lean-to. The **Willow,** 4.6 miles, begins west of the Willow Post Office on N.Y. 212 at a cross road. The trail follows the crossroad west, then turns left.

The **Diamond Notch Trail,** 4.5 miles, leads from Lanesville north to the Hunter Mountain Trail. Access is on Stone Clove Road (Route 214) at the Lanesville highway bridge and Hollow Tree Brook. Follow the dirt road on the east side of the brook north, and where the road ends, follow the blue markers. There is a spring and a lean-to on the trail.

The **Escarpment Trail,** 24 miles, in the **North and South Mountain area,** is one of the oldest trails in the Catskills and provides continuous views of the Hudson Valley and Kaaterskill Clove. The North and South Mountains are famous for their rock formations, bear dens, blueberries and a high glacial swamp pothole of black alder, which becomes full of red berries in the fall. They also contain the Sleepy Hollow made famous by Washington Irving. The blue-marked trail begins on the north side of the intersection of Kaaterskill Creek and Route 23A. Several side trails along the route lead to lookouts and waterfalls. Lean-tos may be reached off a side trail at 13.77 miles by turning onto the yellow trail at 23.05 miles.

The **Blackhead Range Trail** climbs four miles to the summit of Blackdome Mountain (3,980 feet) and offers spectacular views at its end. The red-marked trail begins at the intersection of Maple Crest Road and Elmer Barnum Road; it follows east on the road, follows the Old Town Road to the left, and turns left again on a footpath to the summit.

Central area trails include the **Phoenicia-East Branch Trail,** 9.85 miles, which passes through woodland and along streams mostly on wood roads, with no steep climbs. It begins near the Woodland Valley Club, reached by following the macadam Woodland Valley Road south from a point on Route 28 about one mile west of Phoenicia. The trail is marked in yellow and ends on the highway to Claryville.

The **Giant Ledge-Panther Mountain-Fox Hollow Trail,** 8.9 miles, begins at the eight mile point of the Phoenicia-East Branch Trail and climbs to Giant Ledge (3,200 feet) and Panther Mountain (3,710 feet). There is a lean-to 125 feet to the left of the trail at the 6.3 mile point. Follow markers at the trailsite.

The **Wittenberg-Cornell Slide Trail,** 8.9 miles, explored by naturalist John Burroughs, leads to Slide Mountain (4,180 feet), highest peak in the Catskills, as well as to Wittenberg (3,720 feet) and Cornell (3,880 feet). It is a famous trail, with good views, hard climbing and, unfortunately, thousands of travelers every year. Access is at Woodland Valley where the Wittenberg Trail intersects a macadam road. The trail is marked in red; there are lean-tos at 1.45 and 6.05 miles, and there are several springs.

There are two trails to the **Belleayre Mountain Observatory** (3,375 feet). The **Hanley Corners Trail,** 3.55 miles, originally a bridle path, is the easiest. It begins in Hanley Corners, reachable from Fleischmann's on N.Y. Route 28 by turning south on Railroad Avenue, crossing an iron bridge and the railroad tracks and continuing straight ahead. The trail is marked in red. The **Lost Clove Trail,** 3.05 miles, also marked in red, begins at Esopus Creek. To get there drive ½ mile south on the road to Oliverea from Big Indian Village on N.Y. Route 28.

The **Pine Hill-Eagle Mountain-West Branch Trail,** 14.25 miles, crosses not only Belleayre, but also Balsam (3,620 feet), and Big Indian (3,680 feet) Mountains. Access from the east is in Pine Hill Village at the foot of Pine Hill. Access from the west is West Branch Highway. The trail is marked in blue. A yellow blazed side trail at the halfway point directs you to a lean-to.

The **Seager-Big Indian Mountain Trail,** 4.1 miles, starts at the Seager Post Office and heads north to end at the Pine Hill-Eagle Mountain-West Branch Trail, following the valley of the Dry Brook. There is a lean-to at 3.2 miles.

The **Oliverea-Mapledale Trail,** 6.85 miles, travels west from the town of Oliverea to where Mapledale Road intersects the Dry Brook. Access is at the bridge over Esopus Creek in Oliverea. The trail passes between Balsam and Haynes Mountains, intersects the Pine Hill Mountain-West Branch Trail at 2.65 miles, is red-marked and has three lean-tos at 1.3, 3.85, and four miles.

The Delaware Trails are a system of five trails in Delaware County immediately west of Catskills Park. The **Trout Pond Trail,** 5.4 miles, marked in blue, is reached from Route 17, westbound exit 93, or eastbound exit 92. Turn northeasterly on Russell Brook Road and follow it about five miles to the start of the trail. There are two lean-tos, at 0.9 and 1.4 miles. The trail ends at the start of the Campbell Mountain Trail.

The **Campbell Mountain Trail,** 4.1 miles, climbs up Brock Mountain and has a lean-to at 1.1 miles. It is also marked in blue and ends at the beginnings of the **Little Spring Brook** and **Pelnor Hollow Trails.**

The **Little Spring Brook Trail,** marked in yellow, travels 0.6 miles to the end of the state land, but a town road may be followed another 1.1 miles from this point to Cat Hollow Road.

The **Pelnor Hollow Trail** continues four miles before the state land ends. The town road here may be followed 1.5 miles to Berry Brook Road. This trail is blazed in blue and has a lean-to at 3.1 miles.

The **Mary Smith Trail,** 4.5 miles, begins 0.8 miles into the Pelnor Hollow Trail or from the Holiday Brook Road and Parking Area 1.2 miles farther east. It leads to Mary Smith Hill Road.

There are six trails to the **Balsam Lake Mountain Observatory** (3,720 feet). The **Neversink-Hardenburg Trail,** 14.7 miles and marked with yellow blazes, starts at the bridge over the east branch of the Neversink, ½ mile south of Claryville and heads to Hardenburg.

The red-marked **South Approach,** 2.75 miles, starts at the 11.2 mile point on the Neversink-Hardenburg Trail, and leads to the observatory. There is a lean-to at 2.35 miles.

The **North Approach,** 3.05 miles, begins two miles east of the Belleayre Post Office at a point where the Pakatakan-Dry Brook Ridge-Beaverkill Trail meets Millbrook Road. The red-marked trail ends at the 11.2 mile mark on the Neversink-Hardenburg Trail.

The **Long Pond Trail,** 3.9 miles, leaves the Neversink-Hardenburg trail at the 2.1-mile mark and leads to the Long Pond lean-to and lake.

Also intersecting the Neversink-Hardenburg Trail is the **Pakatakan-Dry Brook Ridge-Beaverkill Trail,** 14.1 miles, near Margaretville. It is reached via the new Route 28. Turn left at the Agway Farm Store and take the first left-hand route. The trail starts on the right in ⅛ mile. **Pakatakan Mountain** (3,100 feet) is a landmark along the trail. There are intersections with other trails leading to Balsam Lake Mountain. There is a lean-to at 7.9 miles. The trail ends at the 11.2 mark on the Neversink-Hardenburg Trail.

The Adirondacks

Most of northern New York is included in the Adirondack region. The mountains here are far more rugged than the Catskills, with peaks of open rock to 5,344 feet, hundreds of little lakes, hundreds of miles of trail and many kinds of physical environments. This is the biggest hunk of wild real estate not under restricted access or commercial control in the east. It's still possible to hike, camp, swim, climb and just look around without paying for it here.

Adirondack hikers are faced with a variety of terrain, ranging from sandy hills with conifer cover, to the alpine conditions of the High Peaks region. Typically soggy from early spring until mid-summer, the trails have a lovely black goo between stretches of sand, gravel and boulder.

In the High Peaks region of the Mac Intyre Mountain Range are the open rock summits of the "46." The name refers to the number of peaks over 4,000 feet high, (or at least once thought to be over that height until a resurvey lowered some of them). Most are found in the region south of Lake Placid, with Mount Marcy as the center. Marcy, at 5,344 feet, is both the highest point in the state and the most heavily trafficked. Characteristic of overused trails, there is the "herd" path up Marcy from Heart Lake. It is deeply rutted and widely tromped, with deep holes bypassed by equally muddy bypasses. The northern approaches to the Marcy area are probably the most used. We'd highly suggest any visits to the area be out-of-season.

Since climbing the "46" peaks is an addictive project claiming a goodly number of trail stompers, we should mention the *Adirondack High Peaks* book put together by the Adirondack Forty-Sixers Club. It's a fine collection of advice, and information of practical and historic interest. We'll also add that, given all the people on the trail during those peak user weeks, bushwacking the "46" off-trail has become more and more popular. Thanks to the structure of the peaks, it's fairly easy to navigate. Slide scars, ridges, and streams provide a wealth of navigable routes, with, of course, a few tough tangles of bush to bust here and there.

Many of the "46" peaks are listed as trailless . . . but in fact there are frequent paths to, or to be found at, the summit. Sometimes the path merely means that a lot of people have made the same mistake. Usually some feature of the mountain has forced hikers into the same spot and collectively they've established a route out. But any of the peaks can be climbed off-trail — depending on how serious the climber is. In some cases, it can get to be a highly technical rock climb, in others, a matter of getting all the bush-busting a human body can stand. Add black flies to the project, and peaks like Street and Nye that look like little lumps become something a lot of climbers tend to talk about with red-eyed fervor about conquering. Anyone planning such trailless jaunts to the Peaks area should base his outing on a set of topo maps. And, for the sake of keeping up the blood supply, some good insect repellent.

One fairly unique kind of natural route throughout the Adirondacks is formed from the big slide scars left when the thin soil slips off the steep-sided humps of anorhosite. Mountains like Giant, Gothics, and Big Slide are well noted for their characteristic markings, and the routes up them vary from "better than the scrub" to serious rock climbing challenges. The west face of Giant, the slides of Gothics, and several others are rock climber routes, not hikers' pathways. Marshall, Seward, Colden, and McComb have scars that can be used as routes . . . but with caution. Rain, or snow (which can and has fallen in every month of the year) can make them dangerous.

Streambeds are not normally a good make-do route in this area. They are far too rocky and cluttered to make decent time on. It's often easier to get above the stream a distance to where the ground may be more even. Ridges sometimes work well, but old blowdown can make them rough. Best bet is normally to get away from the rugged little stream and into standing trees on or just under the ridge lines. But there is no real rule of thumb to go by. Movement becomes a matter of finding the least resistance when making your own way.

The Northville Placid Trail

Location: The trail begins at the western end of the bridge over the Sacandaga River in Northville.

Length: 133 miles

Description: This 133-mile, blue-marked trail is destined to be part of the National Scenic Trail cutting across the northern U.S. For now, it connects the lower (southern) Adirondack village of Northville to the High Peak region and Lake Placid.

The first nine miles of the trail follow N.Y. Route 30 from Northville to Benson Center. Since the trail was first laid out in 1922, these miles are preserved as part of the trail for historic purposes, but if you have the time it's a good idea to walk them. The scenery along the Stony Creek Valley is worth lingering over.

These nine miles and the next 24, going on to Piseco, constitute the trail's first section in brochures compiled by the state Department of Environmental Protection. The path is bordered by wild forests. The second section, 17 miles long, follows a logging road north to Spruce Lake, then cuts through country that was not opened until the trail was put through. It still imparts the atmosphere of true wilderness. The third section, about 26 miles, from West Canada Lake to Stephens Pond Junction, is rolling upland. At one time, it was heavily lumbered, but wild growth is returning. The next 17 miles, between Stephens Pond Junction and Long Lake, are wild country with steep ridges. The trail follows streams and around lakes. The next 13 miles, from Long Lake to Shattuck Clearing, is primarily through open woodland. (If you want to avoid some walking here, you can take the mail boat from Long

Lake Village to Plumley's Landing.) The final section, about 25 miles, to Lake Placid, follows old logging roads over a fairly easy grade.

There are no stores selling supplies between Piseco and West Canada Lake or between Long Lake and Lake Placid. Otherwise, accommodations, restaurants, and stores are available at various communities along the way. There are lean-tos and open camps at fairly short intervals, and temporary camping is permitted at undeveloped sites on state-owned land.

Turn-back or alternate routes out are few and far between, on the northernmost portion of the trail and, once Long Lake is left behind, the hiker is committed to keep going — with no civilization except the ranger station at Duck Hole before reaching Lake Placid.

Spring, by the way, is not the finest time to do this trail. Beavers, bogs, and bugs can put some pressure on a hiker's patience. Late summer or autumn gives the feet a more solid trail and a much more kindly population of bugs.

One particularly interesting place should be pointed out: the remains of Noah Rondeau's "town" on the Cold River, right in the middle of a 40-mile stretch of woods. Rondeau, who died in 1967 at the age of 84, was a hermit. He lived at his "Cold River City," complete with a long hut called the "Town Hall," a shorter hut called the "Halls of Records," and three wigwams: his "Wife's Kitchenette," the "Pyramid," and the "Beauty Parlor." This "Mayor of Cold River" would venture out only once each year, at Christmas, to get his mail and to play Santa Claus. Otherwise, his only contacts for years were the growing number of "46ers" and other hikers who "discovered" his city in the woods.

The High Peaks Trails
Giant to Seward: Actually, there is no direct trail between Giant (4,627 feet) and Seward (4,361 feet). Since the main division of the High Peaks is between three passes running north-south, any crossing from east to west is going to run into all kinds of trouble: Up, down, around . . . and over half of the "46." But this is as good a way as any of providing a sequence for describing some of the High Peak Trails, (and a challenge for anyone who wants to try to make the crossing).

Beginning on the east side of Giant, as a warm-up, is the longest ascent in the High Peaks, five miles, going up from about 1,000 feet to over 4,600 by way of Rocky Ridge Peak. The yellow-marked trail begins on the northwest side of Route 9, just outside of New Russia and heads southwest to the summit. Watch for the trail sign. This is a fairly new trail, but not nearly as well kept up as others in the region. There is one lean-to about ¾ mile from the start.

From the summit of Giant, the whole High Peaks region sprawls out to the west. (If you did intend to make the crossing you might reconsider while standing above the first pass through the mountain below Giant.) There are several trails down Giant — one marked in red, along the ridge to the northeast (about 6¾ miles); one to the north and down into Keene, (about 5¼ miles); and one straight down the Slide scar. The ridge trail is a fine one for early spring since the snow melts early. The north trail gets you down but isn't very interesting. And the path down the slide scar is a job of work, recommended to experienced climbers only. It's steep and mossy, wet and dangerous. Once off the bedrock, it's still a long way down a boulder-chocked stream bed to the highway below Roaring Brook Falls. This trail is called the **Roaring Brook Trail,** and is 3.57 miles long.

Chapel Pond, in a mountain pass on Route 73 at the end of the southernmost route down Giant Mountain, is a fine site for rock-climbing and a popular base for heading up Giant or into the Dix Range west of Route 73. Camping is not permitted in the Chapel Pond area, though, so hikers should plan to get well up the **Dix Trail** or otherwise off Giant before nightfall.

The trail up **Mount Dix** (4,857 feet), 6.7 miles, begins at the top of the hill along the southerly approach to the Ausable Club which heads west from Route 73 north of Chapel Pond. A sign indicates the trail and parking area. This trail is very steep and marked in blue.

A popular off-trail route, not marked, but with pathways worn by use descends Mount Dix on the east, turns south, climbs **Hough Peak** (4,300 feet), **South Dix** (4,000 feet), and **McComb Mountain** (4,405 feet), for a magnificent view of Elk Lake and the mountains in back of it. Descent from Dix Mountain to the **Elk-Lake-Dix Trail,** red-marked, is south and west by way of Slide Brook. There is a lean-to on the south slope of the mountain where the trail begins. This trail may be taken south to Elk Lake, a 2.33 mile gradual descent to Elk Lake Road, or it can be followed north, passing a lean-to at Lillian Pond at 1.33 miles, intersecting, at 3.66 miles, a yellow alternate trail access to Dix from Route 73, and continuing north, 6.12 miles past Hunter's Pass and back to Chapel Pond.

The **Trail to Marcy from Elk Lake,** 10.96 miles, is one of the longer approaches to that peak. Camping is not permitted on the first 6.5 miles northeast from Elk Lake; the land is privately owned. The first lean-to on this route is at nine miles, and the trail is marked in blue.

An easy trail up Marcy from the southwest is by way of Calamity Brook from the ghost town where Tahawus used to be. This trail also known as the **Upper Works Trail,** 10.11 miles, is reached by taking N.Y. 28N, 9.1 miles east of Newcomb, turning right, turning right again at the first fork, passing the Sanford Lake bridge and the huge titanium open pit mine on the right, and continuing on to the end of the road where you can park.

The trail begins on red markers, crosses Calamity Brook on a suspension bridge at 1.18 miles, crosses a blue trail from Indian Pass at 1.7 miles, crosses the brook again and follows blue markers to the right as they follow the brook. The trail begins to climb gently, then steeply northeast, then gently before descending to cross the brook again at 2.79 miles. The trail climbs again, goes around Calamity Pond, passes a monument to David Henderson, an iron works manager whose death was the "calamity" after which the stream, mountain, and pond were named, and reaches several lean-tos and the red markers at 4.46 miles. Take the red markers left to pass Lake Colden and climb Marcy. The trail rises 3,600 feet from the ghost town.

The **Van Hoevenberg Trail** up Marcy, seven miles, is the previously mentioned "herd trail" from the Adirondack Lodge at Heart Lake south from N.Y. 73 at North Elba. The trail passes three lean-tos, has some good views and follows Marcy Brook for a time. Markings are in blue. Since the top of the mountain is a rocky cone, watch for rock piles or paint blazes as markers at the summit. (More about Heart Lake below.)

The **Indian Pass Trail,** about seven miles, runs from the Tahawus ghost town north through the cleft between the MacIntyre Range and MacNaughton to Heart Lake.

Another pass, **Avalanche,** is a good route for the return trip. From Tahawus, follow the yellow markers to the first lean-to. Then continue north, following the red. The trail is a gentle, winding trek for almost four miles, passing two lean-tos, with plenty of drinking water available. The last half-mile rises steeply to a lookout rock where most of the mile-long stretch of thousand-foot-high cliffs on the west wall of the Pass can be seen. (There are several rock climbing routes up this face.)

The trail drops down into regions of huge boulders toward the north end of the Pass. Hunt around a little and you'll probably find some ice, even in mid-summer. Cold air running out from under the boulders is refreshing as you walk through. Also at the north end of the pass is a blue-marked trail to the left going to Scott Pond, one of the more remote-feeling sites we've ever been in.

Beyond the boulders of the Pass, the main trail north follows a gentle valley for several miles with a lean-to near an old lumbering operation clearing and dam. This area was a one-time fur trappers' haven.

The last camp south of your destination at Heart Lake is Rocky Falls lean-to, 2.25 miles before the end of the trail.

Heart Lake is owned and operated by the Adirondack Mountain Club. It has many rentable lean-tos, and some foodstuffs and supplies are available at the new Hikers' Center along with showers and phones. It is a starting point for several trails.

Returning to Tahawus is a matter of choosing a trail. You can go over **Algonquin Mountain** (5,110 feet) to Lake Colden and then down, or to Lake Colden via Avalanche Pass. Either is a fine example of Adirondack Trail, but the popularity of Lake Colden might discourage you from planning to camp there. Both trails are marked in yellow. They split just after passing MacIntyre Brook with the Avalanche Pass Trail on the left, and rejoin shortly after the Avalanche Pass Trail passes Avalanche Lake and intersects a blue trail on the right. The blue trail leads into the Algonquin Mountain Trail. Follow this to a red trail on the right, take it around Flowed Land Lake and turn right on the blue trail which follows Calamity Brook. At the junction with the red trail going straight ahead, take the red back to Tahawus.

Tahawus to Indian Pass is a nine mile round trip; to Heart Lake another 10.2 miles; return via Lake Colden is 21 miles for complete circuit.

To go from the **Tahawus ghost town to Duck Hole,** (6.45 miles), follow the yellow markers north from Tahawus 1.59 miles to an intersection with the red markers, just north of Henderson Lake, but south of the Henderson Lake lean-to. Follow the red blazes along an inlet to the lake. The trail does not begin to rise until you've walked a mile and a half and then only gently. The trail turns right to go around Little Hunter Pond and then goes up a short, steep grade. The trail then descends, steeply at first, then more gently onto a level section. The trail continues to rise and fall along easy grades, passing Upper and Lower Pond and skirting an arm of Duck Pond, before ending at the Northville-Placid Trail described above. Turn left on this trail half a mile to reach a lean-to and the Duck Hole Ranger Station.

The route up Seward is not a trail (there aren't any), but there is a popular path that can be followed if you use caution. The hurricanes have made the going in this region difficult; the climb is not for the inexperienced climber without equipment. Sometimes it is hard to predict what areas will be passable from the map, and you may spend hours going around something you didn't know was there. Do not attempt this without maps, plus a compass, food, first-aid kit, and whatever you need to spend an unexpected night in the woods. From Duck Hole, the route follows the light-duty road to the west just over three miles (there are lean-tos about ¾ mile farther along this road), and takes off to the northwest up Mount Seymour (4,120 feet), down to the north, back to the road and another lean-to, and up toward Seward to the southwest. The trail turns south, then southwest again. From Seward, you may wish to continue south for exploration of Mount Donaldson (4,140 feet), and Mount Emmons (4,040 feet). It's 4½ miles from Seward and Donaldson as the crow flies, but plan on covering at least double that amount.

Cranberry Lake Area Trails
Location: The Cranberry Lake Area is southeast of Route 3 in the western Adirondacks. Access points from that highway are at Wanakena and the town of Cranberry Lake.
Length: 50 miles interconnected trails.
Description: The region offers 50 miles of interconnected hiking trails in one of the largest wilderness areas in New York. Three outstanding features of the lake are worth noting: The big swing bridge at Wanakena, some big pine at High Falls, and the old bobcat dens on Cat Mountain off the southeast tip of the lake. (There actually was a bobcat a few years back — it followed one of the authors all the way from Cat

Mountain Ranger Station down to the lakeshore). There has been relatively little civilization buildup here; beyond the trails and canoeable waters, unbroken forestland reaches south past Beaver River. The trails themselves tend to be far less stomped down than those in the High Peaks. Some are even obscure in autumn.

There are 13 lean-tos along the trails, and there is a public campsite just east of Cranberry Lake Village. Permits are not required for stays of less than three nights at undeveloped sites or lean-tos. For longer stays, see the forest rangers in Cranberry Lake or Star Lake.

The Loop, actually a series of truck trails and connecting paths, starts in the village of Wanakena. It forms a 16-mile hub from which several other trails branch out over the region. Follow the red-marked **High Falls Truck Trail** for the first mile and a half south, then fork left to follow the blue **Leary Trail** for 2.7 miles. Rejoin the truck trail and follow it east for another 1.75 miles, at which point there are two lean-tos and the magnificent sight of High Falls. (The blue-marked **Plains Trail** cuts across the Loop here, heading north to Glasby Pond, and shortens the Loop by 2.2 miles). The main trail then becomes red-marked for 4.7 miles east and then north to **Cowhorn Junction.** Just past Cowhorn Junction, follow the yellow trail left 1.5 miles to the red-marked **Cat Mountain Trail.** This will lead west past the edge of Dead Creek Flow and join the **Dead Creek Flow Truck Trail,** also red-marked, back to Wanakena. The yellow-marked **Buck Pond Trail,** three miles, leaves the High Falls Truck Trail on the right, 5.5 miles into the Loop and heads south to Buck Pond. Continue on a yellow-blazed path three miles to Cage Lake where the trail winds east to Muir and Wolf Ponds.

Proceed south from here via the blue-blazed **Five Ponds-Wolf Pond-Sand Lake Trail** two miles to Sand Lake. Or head north five miles past Little Shallow, Washbowl, Big Shallow, Little Five, and Five Ponds. There are two lean-tos along the route. The **Big Deer Pond Trail,** blazed yellow, leaves the Loop at Cowhorn Junction and travels two miles southwest of Big Deer Pond.

The **Cat Mountain Trail,** 2.05 miles, is a short, steep climb to spectacular views from atop Cat Mountain. It begins on the Loop near Dead Creek Flow at the point where the 0.2-mile yellow Janack's Landing Trail cuts off. Follow the red markers right up the hill.

The **Six Mile Creek Trail,** 4.2 miles, joins the South Flow section of Cranberry Lake to the Loop at Cowhorn Junction. It is marked in blue, has a lean-to on the north shore of Cowhorn Pond, and has two side trails: a red-marked one leading right three miles to Ash Pond a mile north of Cowhorn Junction and one leading left to Olmstead Pond (2.2 miles) and a lean-to.

These Cranberry Lake Trails do not connect with the Loop, and the first three are accessible only by water. The **Clear Pond Trail,** ½ mile, starts at Hedgehog Bay on Cranberry Lake and leads to Clear Pond. It is marked in yellow.

The **Curtis Pond Trail,** 1.2 miles, starts at the southeastern end of East Inlet on the lake and is red-marked. It heads southeast to Curtis Pond.

The **Darning Needle Pond Trail,** 2.4 miles, follows Chair Rock Creek south to Darning Needle Pond Trail, 2.4 miles, follows Chair Rock Creek south to Darning Needle Pond, starting at Chair Rock Flow on Cranberry Lake. It is marked in yellow.

The **Bear Mountain Trail,** 2.4 miles, forms a loop, starting at the public campsite near Cranberry Lake Village. It travels over the mountain and has several views of the lake. There is a lean-to 0.6 miles from the public campsite on the red-marked trail.

Moore's Trail, two miles, is a particularly fascinating trail as it follows the Oswegatchie River along a section of waterfalls and rapids, west from Wanakena to Inlet. It is marked in yellow.

Old Forge — Big Moose — Fulton Chain Region

The Old Forge-Big Moose-Fulton Chain region, off New York Route 28 in Herkimer County offers the hiker miles of forestland, large lakes, mountains and streams. Public campsites are scattered through the region, and there are lean-tos on the trails.

In the Old Forge region, the blue-marked **Big Otter Lake Trail,** eight miles, serves as a starting point for several other trails. Basically the fire truck trail from the parking lot ½ mile north of Thendara to Big Otter Lake's southern border, the trail connects to a red trail which goes by a lean-to at Pine Lake before continuing west 9.56 miles to the village of Brantingham. There is also a short (¾ mile) trail to the outlet of Big Otter Lake at the junction of the red and blue trails.

The **Lost Creek Trail,** five miles, marked in red, goes by Big Otter Lake and connects to the East Pond Trail. It starts seven miles from the beginning of the Big Otter Lake Trail, turns northeast, and stops in a dead end.

The yellow **East Pond Trail,** 3.8 miles, passes through sparse forestland and open fields to connect with the Black Foot Pond Trail. It starts 1½ miles east from the beginning of the Big Otter Lake Trail, turns northeast and leads to East Pond, where there is a lean-to.

The **Black Foot Pond Trail,** one mile, another dead-end, leaves the East Pond Trail 3.6 miles east from its beginning. It is marked in red and leads to the Old Mica Mine at Black Foot Pond.

The **Moose River Mountain Trail,** ¾ mile, leaves the Big Otter Pond Trail to the south two miles from its beginning, and climbs up Moose River Mountain for a pleasant view. It is marked in red.

The **Middle Branch Lake-Cedar Pond-Middle Settlement Lake Trail,** 8.8 miles, is marked in yellow and leaves the Big Otter Lake Trail to the south after 6.5 miles. It provides access to the bodies of water for which it was named as well as Lost Lake, Pine Lake and several lean-tos, before leading to Old Browns Road which may be followed left to Route 28.

The **Nicks Lake-Remsen Falls-Nelson Lake Trail** is an 18 mile network of trails reached either one mile south of the Village of Old Forge on Bisby Road or via the Nicks Lake Campsite. It follows Nicks Lake Creek, the Moose River, and Nelson Lake and has a side trail to Bloodsucker Pond. There is a lean-to at Remsen Falls. The trail is marked in blue.

The **Scusa Access Trail,** 3.75 miles, begins on the west side of Route 28, 3½ miles south of Thendara, and follows red markers. It is a short trail, basically providing access to the Brown Tract Road after ¾ mile, the trail to Cedar Pond by way of Grass Pond after one mile, and the way to the parking lot south of Thendara at this last intersection.

The **O'Kara-Cedar Pond Trail,** 1.75 miles, runs from the Old Brown Tract Road to the lean-to at Cedar Pond. It is marked in red, with a short yellow loop trail going to Grass Pond in ½ mile.

The **Woodhull Mountain Trail** leads to the Woodhull Mountain fire-tower after following a truck trail for six miles. It starts east of Mc-Keever at a gate and follows the Moose River's south branch, before climbing the last 2.5 miles to the top.

The Big Moose region is northeast of the Old Forge section, and includes several trails accessible only by boat, or by boat and aircraft. The **Beaver River Flow** area, just north of Big Moose, for example, includes the **Trout Pond-Salmon Lake-Clear Lake Trail,** 5.5 miles, which begins on the north shore of the Big Trout Pond Reservoir. There is a lean-to on this blue-blazed trail at Salmon Lake. The **Norridge Trail,** six miles, also marked in blue, leaves from the south of the hamlet of Beaver River which is a community reachable only by railroad or boat. It ends at Twitchell Lake after passing through three miles of hardwood forest and three miles of low hills.

There are three trails reachable by boat on Big Moose Lake. The **Gull Lakes Trail,** one mile, leaves from the north shore of the inlet and is marked in blue. There is a lean-to between the two Gull Lakes. The **Russian Lake Trail,** ¾ mile, also marked in blue, leads from East Bay to Russian Lake's western shore, where there is a lean-to. The **Andes Creek Trail,** ½ mile, leads from the northeast edge of the lake at Andes Creek Inlet to a lean-to.

These trails are reachable by car: The **Cascade Lake—Queer Lake Trail,** 1.6 miles, begins one mile northwest of Eagle Bay Village on Big Moose Road. The red-marked trail follows the road to Cascade Lake for one mile, then becomes a foot trail going upwards to Queer Lake. The **West Mountain Trail,** 2.5 miles, begins on Higby Road near Big Moose Lake and follows Constable Creek east, intersecting the Hermitage Trail, the Windfall Pond Trail, and an alternate trail around Constable Pond, before reaching the Queer Lake Trail and a yellow trail to Chub Pond. (The trail to Chub Pond is one mile).

The **Hermitage Trail,** marked in red, connects the West Mountain Trail to the Queer Lake Trail. The yellow marked **Windfall Pond Trail** splits after about 1½ miles, with the blue trail reaching Windfall Pond in another ½ mile and Cascade Lake 1½ miles after that. The yellow trail continues on to Queer Lake, reaching it after a total of four miles.

The **Bald Mountain Trail,** one mile, leaves the Rondaxe Road parking lot and climbs to the firetower on Bald Mountain for some magnificent views. It is marked in red. The **Scenic Mountain Trail,** 4.5 miles, also leaving the Rondaxe parking lot, heads northeast past Fly Pond and Carry Pond, climbs to 2,100 feet, descends 95 feet to Mountain Pond, and follows a ridge east to the Bubb Lake Trail and Route 28, with many excellent viewpoints along the way. This trail is marked in blue. The **Bubb Lake Trail,** one mile, starts one mile west of Eagle Bay on Route 28 and leads north to Bubb Lake and Sis Lake, following blue markers.

The blue-marked **Safford Pond Trail,** 3.75 miles, connects the Orvis School parking lot (on Big Moose Road eight miles north of Eagle Bay) to Safford Pond. The **Snake Pond Trail,** one mile, also blue-marked, leaves the Twitchell Lake road one mile north of Big Moose and continues northwest to Snake Pond.

Blue Mountain Lake Trails
Location: Blue Mountain, almost 4,000 feet above sea level, is the dominant feature of the **Blue Mountain Lake Region,** on Routes 28 and 30 in Indian Lake.
Length: Total of 44 miles of trails.
Description: Known to the Indians as the "Hill of Storms," the mountain towers over the east shore of the lake. The region has several lakes, ponds, and mountain summits in addition to 44 miles of trails and 12 lean-tos. There are public campsites at Lake Durant, Forked Lake, and Lake Eaton. The Northville-Lake Placid Trail, which we have already discussed, also passes through this region.

The **Owls Head Mountain Trail,** 3.1 miles, red-marked, leaves Long Lake on the north, near the end of Endion Road. (Turn left after crossing lake — do not go toward Lake Eaton Campsite.) The trail climbs 1,060 feet to the summit.

As you drive north on Route 30, the **Sargent Ponds Trail,** 4.3 miles, is reached via a macadam road on the left as you pass Blue Mountain Lake. The road follows the lake to the beginning of the trail in 1.35 miles. The trail goes around Chubb Pond, goes by Helms Pond, and follows the Helms Pond outlet to Upper Sargent Pond. The trail is marked in red.

The view from **Blue Mountain,** two miles, is a spectacular one of waterways and forestland. The trail to the summit begins near the Adirondack Museum on the east side of Route 30. It is marked in blue and climbs 2,000 feet.

The **Tirrell Pond Trail,** 3.25 miles, goes around Blue Mountain, and connects the hill behind the museum with the Northville-Lake Placid Trail, via red markers. From Blue Mountain Lake Village, the distance around the mountain, ending on Route 28 near Lake Durant, is 8.7 miles.

The **Wilson Pond Trail,** 2.9 miles, connects a parking lot across from Eagle Lake on Route 28 with the lean-to at Wilson Pond and a fine view of Blue Ridge. The red-marked trail passes Grassy Pond and the inlets to Rock Pond and Slim Pond, and includes a climb up a ridge.

The **Cascade Lake Trail** connects the cemetery on the south end of Blue Mountain Lake Village with the Northville-Lake Placid Trail which may be followed to the Lake Durant Public Campsite. It is 2.8 miles to the Cascade Pond lean-to and 3.35 miles to the trail junction.

Rhode Island

In Rhode Island there are 57 parks in the state, only nine of which have hiking trails. You can still find places to walk. With 40 miles of coast (384 miles if you count the land along the bays and the shores of 36 islands), there are plenty of informal beach and shore walks.

Or visit Newport to gape at the mansions of the nineteenth century shipping magnates and industrialists who spent their summers here. Your first walk can be the *Cliff Walk,* a particularly lovely three-mile stretch between the craggy Atlantic Coast and the lush splendor of fine Victorian houses. Cornelius Vanderbilt built his opulent 70-room "Breakers" here, and William Vanderbilt settled nearby at "Marble House," one of the most ornate buildings in America.

You'll find milder weather in Rhode Island than in the rest of New England, partly because of the warm air from Narragansett Bay. There are fewer extreme temperatures. January averages in the 30's, July in the 70's. The coast, though, is vulnerable to hurricanes.

The state contains 1,234 square miles and may be divided geographically into the coastal lowlands and the northern uplands. The coast consists of sandy beached peninsulas almost separated from the mainland by salt marshes and ponds. To the west are rough, tree-covered hills. Roughly two thirds of the state is heavily forested. Much of the southeastern section of the state is actually a series of bridge-connected islands. Here the shores are high, rocky cliffs and inland from the shores are rounded, grassy slopes.

There are many inland waterways in Rhode Island, several small but swift rivers, waterfalls, lakes, ponds, and reservoirs. Many of the so-called rivers are actually saltwater arms of the bays.

Southwest Region Trails

Locations: There are several intersecting trails in three connecting parks in the southwest area, maintained by the Appalachian Mountain Club and the Rhode Island Department of Natural Resources. The parks are the Arcadia State Park, Dawley State Park, and Beach Pond State Park. They are about 30 miles south of Providence via Interstate

95. Dawley is just east of the Interstate and the others are west near the towns of Arcadia and Esoheag.

Length: About 70 miles total.

More Information: Write Rhode Island Dept. of Natural Resources, (check address).

Breakheart Trail, 14.3 miles. The trail starts at the bridge below Fish Ladder Dam at Breakheart Pond in Arcadia State Park. It is marked with yellow blazes and passes through deciduous woods, pine groves, and swamp before ascending Penny Hill (370 feet) for a panoramic view. The trail follows wood roads as well as paths and has at least one side trail. The trail ends at Falls River Bridge, where it connects with the Ben Utter and Escoheag Trails.

Ben Utter Trail, 4.3 miles. Begin at the Falls River Bridge, two miles north of RI 165 on Escoheag Hill Road and the westward extension of Austin Farm Road. This trail, marked with yellow blazes, passes the remains of a vertical sawmill and an old grist mill, goes through the Stepstone Falls picnic area, which has both a spring and toilet facilities, and culminates at Stepstone Falls.

Escoheag Trail, two miles. From the Escoheag Post Office on RI 165, take Escoheag Hill Road north 0.9 miles to the first road on the right. Here a sign directs you to the Ledges picnic area where the trail starts at the south end of the parking place: The white-blazed trail passes through two valleys, some forest area, ledges and open country before ending at Falls River Bridge.

John B. Hudson Trail, 1.6 miles. The trail begins at RI 165 about 2.5 miles west of RI 3 and follows a logging road and a brook south and ends at Breakheart Pond where there is an unusual dam. The trail is marked with yellow paint, and one mile from Appie Crossing a white-blazed side trail leads to two overnight shelters.

Arcadia Trail, 3.4 miles. The trail, marked with yellow blazes, begins at the Tefft Hill Camping Area, one mile east of Arcadia Picnic Area on a dirt road and ends at Appie Crossing. It passes the Arcadia State Park picnic area and bathing beach, so it is not the place to go for solitude. There is, however, an overnight shelter on the trail and another on a side trail going west just north of Arcadia Pond.

Tippecansett Trail, 45.5 miles. The trail starts opposite the shelter near the parking space at the Stepstone Falls Picnic Area, which is 2.5 miles north of RI 165 via Escoheag Road. This trail heads south, passing through several types of woods and sections of mountain laurel. The yellow-blazed trail intersects several other trails, including some that began in Connecticut and three highways before ending at Narragansett Trail just south of Yawgoo Pond.

The Rhode Island Recreation Map, published by the Rhode Island Department of Natural Resources, shows hiking trails in the state parks as well as on other property. State game and other natural areas with hiking trails include the **Carolina, Great Swamp,** and **Burlingame Man-**

agement Areas, George Washington Management Area, and the **Kimball Bird Sanctuary.**

State parks with hiking trails include **Colt, Diamond Hill, Goddard, Lincoln Woods** and the **Ninigret Conservation Area.**

Vermont

Vermont's summits offer the hiker great variety in walking opportunities. Vermont covers an area of 9,609 square miles. The Green Mountains split the state down the middle from north to south. The Hogback Range north of Bristol and the Granite Mountain ranges near Barre are considered a part of the Green Mountain group. The Taconic Mountains extend into the southwestern corner of the state, and the White Mountains of New Hampshire reach into Vermont in the northeast.

Other sections of the state include the Champlain Valley along Lake Champlain, the Connecticut River Valley, and the Vermont Valley in the west which includes several river beds.

New England atmosphere surrounds you in Vermont, but with a difference. Industrial development has not left a heavy mark on the state. People are much more bound to agriculture and logging than to factory schedules and the hustle of city life, and this has been true throughout the history of the state.

There are over 700 miles of hiking trails in Vermont, ranging from short walks in the valleys to major backpacking routes. Two hundred and fifty miles of trails are located in state and national forests, although most of these are constructed and maintained by private groups.

Most of the high mountains in the southern half of the state are within the boundaries of the Green Mountain National Forest, which was formed in 1932. The Forest is divided into two large parcels, one north, and the other, south, of Rutland. Many of the trails in the forest were built by the CCC.

The Vermont Agency of Environmental Conservation maintains 41 parks throughout the state, with 29 of them having hiking or nature trails. There are 36 state campgrounds with 2,100 sites ranging from facilities for trailers to primitive campsites. Only two state forests — Groton and Coolidge — have backpacking campsites accessible only on foot. Since camping is prohibited on state land other than in campsites most state lands can be used only for day hikes.

Long Trail

The major trail in Vermont is the famed Long Trail stretching from North Troy near the Canadian border to Blackinton, Massachusetts. The trail traverses the higher summits of the middle ridge of the Green Mountains.

Conceived in 1910 by James Taylor and the newly formed Green Mountain Club, the trail was completed in 1931. The main trail is 262 miles long, but 98 side trails add 174 miles, creating a system of 436 miles of trails. The main trail is blazed with white markers while the access routes are blazed in blue. There are 71 Shelters — an average of one every four miles — with bunks for six to eight people. The Green Mountain Club maintains most of the trail and 49 of the shelters. The Forest Service, the Middlebury Mountain Club, and others maintain the rest.

The Long Trail has been described in detail in the GMC guide book, "The Long Trail — A Footpath in the Wilderness," available from the Green Mountain Club, Inc., P.O. Box 94, Rutland, Vermont 05701. Since this book is readily available, we will describe only the particularly noteworthy areas and those sections which are used in conjunction with other routes.

All of the trails we describe in Vermont are in the Green Mountains. Loosely, they are described from south to north.

Mount Equinox Trail
Location: Head north on U.S. 7 from Manchester, Vermont. Take Seminary Road (the first left) around the Burr and Burton Seminary. Then take the first right into a driveway leading behind the school. Leave your car in the parking area.
Length: Three miles round trip.
Description: Walk up to the athletic field and cross it to the far left corner. The trail is unsigned but well traveled, with blue blazes apparent as you enter the woods.

At 3,816 feet, Mt. Equinox is the highest peak in Vermont not on or connecting to the Long Trail. In the 19th century, many trails covered its slopes, linking settlers' homesteads. But as the settlers returned to the easier life of the lowlands, the unattended trails grew over and became not readily passable. Only the Burr and Burton Trail leading to the summit is easy to follow.

Gradually meandering upward from the athletic field, you will begin to follow an old road that will straighten out. Soon, a yellow-blazed path goes off toward the left. Staying on the blue-blazed road, you will encounter a fork at approximately 0.4 miles. Bear left and cross an intersecting road at 0.6 miles. At 0.7 miles, bear left at a fork and right at the next fork. This is the last decision that you will have to make for a while, the trail being quite obvious from here. It is also your last rest, since the trail continues persistently upward to the two-mile mark.

"No Trespassing" signs are soon encountered, but these do not pertain to individuals without firearms. At 2.5 miles, a red-blazed trail intersects; pass it, following the yellow blazes. Very soon bear right onto the trail to the summit. At 2.6 miles, the Lookout Rock Trail exits right. Go left across open rock, to the top.

The summit is rather developed. The Equinox Skyline Inn and accompanying road to it are situated nearby. Various radio towers also share the advantage of this high overlook. However, the view is beautiful. Massachusetts, New Hampshire, and New York are readily visible. With excellent eyesight (and/or binoculars) Mount Royal near Montreal is faintly visible to the north.

A loop on your return trip to Lookout Rock offers a good view of the Vermont Valley and Equinox Pond. Follow the Lookout Rock Trail from the summit for 0.4 miles to Lookout Rock. This is a fairly simple walk. On the way, you will encounter a small memorial erected in honor of Mr. Barbo, the dog of a former owner of Mt. Equinox, Dr. J.G. Davidson.

Your descent continues via yellow blazes to the Burr and Burton Trail junction (unsigned). Turn left onto it and go back the way you came up.

Lye Brook Wilderness Trail
Location: Take Vermont Route 11 east from Manchester Center. After one-half mile, turn right onto Richville Road. Follow this for 1.4 miles to the intersection of Lye Brook Road. Go left on Lye Brook Road for 0.2 miles and park on the side of the road.
Length: 15.4 miles round trip via North Bourn Pond Shelter.
Description: Lye Brook is one of the two designated wilderness areas in Vermont. It contains 14,300 acres of woodland. As a wilderness, it is closed to motor vehicles. There are no developed facilities of any kind except for the shelters on the section of the Long Trail that passes through the area.

A free permit must be obtained before entering the area. The permit is primarily used as an information gathering device for management and planning purposes. It may be obtained from the U.S. Forest Service, Catamount National Bank Building, Manchester Center, Vermont 05255.

The blue-blazed Lye Brook Trail starts on a dirt road on your left. Soon Lye Brook will appear on the right side of the trail. The road will begin to swing widely to the right. Follow blue blazes at all intersections. The trail follows the left side of the Lye Brook Hollow, tending gradually upward for the next 3.5 miles. Several small streams will be crossed. In wet seasons, the sound of rushing water will accompany you most of the way.

After the 3.5 miles, the trail tends to become almost flat. At 6.2 miles, the trail skirts to the left of a swamp; and, if much rain has fallen recently, the going can get rather muddy. Keep faith, because the South Bourn shelter, home for the night, is an easy two miles away.

The Lye Brook Trail intersects the Long Trail at the South Bourn shelter. There is pure drinking water here from a mountain spring. This structure and the North Bourn Pond shelter are located on Bourn Pond, a rather large body of clear water. The shelters are supplied with a caretaker from the Green Mountain Club in the summer season and a modest fee is charged for camping.

To walk to the North Bourn Pond Shelter, follow the Long Trail north around the shore of the pond for 0.4 miles. From the shore of the pond near here, one can get an excellent view of Stratton Mountain. Camping the night at either shelter is quite pleasant, but keep in mind that drinking water is conveniently available at the South Bourn Shelter.

Lye Brook Trail to Waterfalls
Location: This is a side trail off the main Lye Brook Trail. It can be either an addition to the Lye Brook Trail backpacking trip or a scenic day's excursion in itself. Remember that even when you enter the Lye Brook Wilderness for a day hike, you need a free permit from the USFS.
Length: 4.6 miles round trip.
Description: Follow the Lye Brook Trail from the road for two miles. Here you will see the diagonal crossing of an old railroad bed. Directly on your left will be a rock wall which was part of the railroad bed. As the bed crosses the trail, follow it to the right. This is not a cleared trail and, consequently, you will be climbing over and under logs. Follow the bed for about ⅓ mile and you will hear and see the falls. Pass through a thicket of small spruce to a deep gorge. The remains of an old trestle can be seen and to the left, the waterfalls.

Trainloads of logs crossed this trestle on their way to sawmills in the valley. On the return trip, keep your eyes open for other remnants of this industry that once flourished here. Other railroad beds can be seen at various places along the trail. Old skidways intersect your path and meander back into the hills where they aided in transporting the forest's harvest.

Mount Mansfield

The Abnaki Indians who lived in the valleys near Mount Mansfield spoke of it as "Mose-O-Be-Wadso," an Algonquin name meaning "mountain like the head of a moose." Indeed, the naming of the several peaks follows this anatomical suggestion. From south to north there is the Forehead at 3,940 feet, the Nose at 4,062 feet, the Upper and Lower Lips at 3,964 and 4,030 feet respectively, the Chin at 4,393 feet and the Adam's Apple at 4,060 feet. The Chin is the highest point in the Green Mountains.

Many trails of varying difficulty cover this fascinating mountain. Most lead to or include spectacular panoramic views.

Bear Pond Trail
Location: Take Vermont Route 108 northwest from Stowe to Smuggler's Notch.
Length: 2.3 miles.
Description: The trail heads west off the road at Smuggler's Notch. It is

said to contain the steepest half-mile of trail in Vermont and should only be attempted by very experienced and surefooted hikers.

Hell Brook Trail

Location: Take Vermont Route 108 northwest from Stowe to the Big Spring parking area near Smuggler's Notch. The trailhead is across the road from the north end of the parking area.

Length: Four miles round trip.

Description: If you're in bad shape, or out for an easy day, this is not the trail for you. If, however, you want to clear our your lungs, tone up your leg muscles, and get a real workout, then this, the second steepest trail in Vermont, is where you should head.

Follow the blue blazes up, up, and up. If you're hoping for a break in your ascent, forget it until you reach the top of the ridge about 1.3 miles away. Hell Brook plunges to the left of the trail for most of the ascent. Frequently you can catch glimpses of waterfalls and cascades as the noisy water makes its way over outcroppings and ledges.

Several small tributaries of Hell Brook must be crossed, offering a good excuse for a rest and drink of cold, clear water. Because of these stream crossings, the trail often becomes quite muddy, making waterproof and sturdy hiking boots a necessity.

At several points along the trail outcroppings of rock are undercut to form natural shelters for hapless hikers caught by a surprise rainstorm. At one point, the trail leads under such an overhang and makes the going difficult over large boulders that litter its entrance.

After 0.9 miles, a junction with Hell Brook Trail Cutoff to Taft Lodge (also blue-blazed) is encountered. Stay to the right on the Hell Brook Trail and in 0.4 miles you will meet a triple trail junction. The Bear Pond Trail heads off to the right, while the Hell Brook Trail goes ahead and then west around the summit of Adam's Apple. Go left onto the Adam's Apple Trail. The 0.1 mile ascent to the summit of Adam's Apple is steep but not as taxing as the previous trail was. Soon the forest gives away to low shrubs and finally the round bare summit.

The view is splendid to the north and east, but the summit of the Chin blocks the view to the west and southwest for the most part. Lake of the Clouds lies just below you to the north. A few feet deep, this lake is trapped on the very top of the Mansfield ridge.

After a rest, head toward the Chin by going down into Eagle Pass between Adam's Apple and the Chin. Rock cairns guide your way into the low shrubs and soon you follow blue blazes again to the junction of the Long and Hell Brook Trails. Follow the white-blazed Long Trail now, upward to the Chin. The going soon becomes very steep and tricky, requiring you to climb over many ledges. In 0.2 miles, all the misery pays off as you come out in the Arctic-Alpine environment of the Chin's summit. Please stay on the trail here, since this flora is rare for the Green Mountains and its delicate roots cannot withstand the boots of the many hikers visiting it.

Look around you in any direction at the breath-taking panorama. Northward, all the Green Mountains are clearly visible to Big Jay and Jay Peak. Especially clear weather even allows Montreal's Mount Royal to be seen. To the west, all of Lake Champlain is visible, framing the Adirondacks behind it. To the east, the Worcester Mountains are clearly seen and Mount Washington and the White Mountains lie in the southeast. The Green Mountains as far as Killington lie in sight to the south. Closer up, Smuggler's Notch lies in the valley at the base of Spruce Peak, the nearest mountain to the west.

The return trip can be made via a seldom-used trail that cuts off some of the steepness of the Hell Brook Trail. Follow the Long Trail back down the way you came and stay on it past the Hell Brook and Adam's Apple Trail junction in Eagle Pass. In 0.6 miles from the summit, you will come upon the Taft Lodge. Take the Hell Brook Cutoff Trail to the right of the Lodge for 0.7 miles to the junction with the Hell Brook Trail. This footpath is blue-blazed but not always obvious, so you'll have to keep alert for markers. It is also partially overgrown, but its very gradual descent is a welcome relief from the steep ups and downs encountered since the beginning of the hike. At the end of this trail, follow the Hell Brook Trail downward.

The going will be just as miserable as when you came up. In 0.9 miles from this junction, you're back to the Big Spring.

Sunset Ridge — Laura Cowles Trail Loop (to Cantilever Rock and the Chin)
Location: Take Vermont Route 15 east from Burlington to Underhill Flats. From there, go east on a paved road for 2.8 miles to Underhill Center. Go another mile to a right turn to the Mount Mansfield-Underhill State Recreation Center and Camping Area. Leave your car at the camping area parking lot and proceed along the old road for one mile. At a sharp turn in the road, the Sunset Ridge Trail — blue blazes — is seen going off to the left.
Length: 5.7 miles round trip.
Description: This footpath is a very common westward approach to the summit of Mt. Mansfield. It offers challenging hiking with good views and some astounding sights along the way. Novice hikers should beware, though. This is not a simple trail. Steep ascents and descents on often slippery ground are the name of the game.

One-tenth of a mile from the trailhead, the junction of the Laura Cowles Trail appears. Bear left onto the Sunset Ridge Trail and begin a climb to Lookout Rock, 0.3 miles away. In 0.1 mile, you come across the Cantilever Rock Trail heading off to the left.

Take the Cantilever Rock Trail 0.2 miles to its end at the base of a cliff. Above you, you will see a strange geological phenomenon indeed. A horizontal needle of stone extends 40 feet from the cliff without support. Discovered in 1960 by Clyde H. and Clyde F. Smith, this rock has an estimated weight of 75 tons. It extends straight out 60 feet above the base of the cliff. A wooden ladder provides access for closer inspection.

Follow the Cantilever Rock Trail back to the Sunset Ridge Trail. Go left and upward. The going now becomes wet, steep, and slippery. The path begins to wind up and across exposed ledges. Great care is needed not to slide, and often, hiking the side of the trail with the support of nearby trees is necessary.

At 1.6 miles, you come to the junction of the Story Trail on the left. Stay right on the Sunset Ridge Trail and soon you will intersect the Laura Cowles Trail again at its upper end. Bear left, and at the 1.8-mile point, meet the Long Trail. Bear left on this white-blazed trail and in 0.2 miles, you will reach the summit of the Chin.

The return route takes you back down to the junction of the Sunset Ridge Trail and the upper end of the Laura Cowles Trail. Now follow the Laura Cowles Trail downward to the left. The trail is very steep and care is advised to avoid hazardous spills. Open ledges are crossed,but soon the trail takes refuge in the forest again. Small stands of trees decorate the way as you continue your steep descent. In a little while you will encounter a small brook that meanders and crisscrosses the trail. Do not, by the way, let the occasional orange blazes fool you. Stay on the blue-blazed trail to the junction of the Sunset Ridge Trail, and return to your car the same way you came up.

 **Mid-Atlantic Trails**

The mid-Atlantic section of the United States is a beautiful part of the country, with wide sandy ocean beaches, rolling Piedmont, the great agricultural valleys between the mountains and the Appalachians—"the friendly mountains"—as they are often called, with their tremendous acreages of hardwood timber, clear cold water gushing from thousands of springs and mountain streams.

Delaware

Delaware, our first state, is also one of our smallest and hiking trails here are almost non-existent. The only one of note is the Brandywine Trail and even there, more than half the mileage lies in Pennsylvania. There are two other trails in the offing. One of them, the Brandywine Battlefield Trail, approximately five miles long, will begin at the Brandywine River Museum. The other projected trail, the Brandywine-Susquehanna Trail, will be approximately 205 miles long. The completion of this trail is the pet project of Bob Yost, the energetic president of the 400-member Wilmington Trail Club. For information, write the Wilmington Trail Club, P.O. Box 1184, Wilmington, Delaware 19803.

More information: Copies of the Official Map of Delaware and maps and information on state parks, state forests and recreation may be obtained by writing or visiting Division of Parks and Recreation, Edward Tatnall Building, Dover, Delaware 19901; telephone 302/678-4401.

Brandywine Trail
Location: This trail begins .5 miles east of State Route 100, near the intersection with Birch Run Road approximately 15 miles south of Pottstown, Pennsylvania. It ends near the Hagley Museum in Wilmington. The trail is maintained by the Wilmington Trail Club. Edward Garvey visited the area in early October, 1975, and hiked the last 15 miles in an all-day steady rain with three active members of the Club: Turner Darden, Mary King and her sister Maggi Donovan.
Length: 37.5 miles
USGS Quads: 7½ minute, Pottstown, Downingtown, Unionville, West Chester, Pennsylvania; Wilmington, North, Delaware.

Description: The trail is marked with the conventional A.T. two x six inch white paint blazes. It begins at Horse-Shoe Trail Road near the village of Ludwigs Corner on State Route 100 some 15 miles south of Pottstown, Pennsylvania. From there it goes generally south over country roads and wooded trails until nearing the village of Lenape. From Lenape, the point where Garvey was introduced to the trail, it follows paved roads for two miles and railroad tracks for perhaps another two miles. Near the end of the tracks is a blue blazed trail to the left leading for approximately .3 mile to the Brandywine River Museum, with its collections of Wyeth paintings.

After the railroad walking, the trail swerves over to the banks of the Brandywine River, where the hiker passes under towering sycamore trees, goes by a number of impressive estate homes, and eventually reaches a point directly across from the first stone buildings used in the powder-making activities of the early DuPont enterprises. Garvey found the trail generally in excellent shape and extremely well marked. The one exception was a half-mile stretch near the end where paint blazes were sparse and the trail was a tangled mass of waist-high grass and weeds.

One should not plan a hike on the Brandywine Trail without allowing sufficient time to visit many points of interest close by. The Hagley Foundation and the Eleutherian Mills have walking and bus excursions which show the DuPont's early powder plants, plus dioramas and models of early flour mills, textile mills and iron ore industries. One can visit the 200 room Winterthur Mureum, which is a former DuPont home on nine levels with many exquisite examples of early United States furniture. There is also a restored Town Hall, the downtown Brandywine Village restoration, and the Longwood Gardens.

One important restriction applies to the Brandywine Trail. The Pennsylvania part of it is open to all. South of Chadds Ford, however, the trail goes through many private estates and permission for use is to members of the Wilmington Trail Club only, or to groups or individuals escorted by members of the Club. If you wish to hike on the Delaware section of the trail, you need to make advance arrangements with the Wilmington Trail Club, P.O. Box 1183, Wilmington, Delaware 19803.

Maryland

More information: To obtain the Maryland Highway and Natural Resources Map and other information on attractions and events, visit, write or call the Maryland Division of Tourist Development, 1748 Forest Drive, Annapolis, Maryland 21401; telephone 301/267-1686.

For information on state parks write to Maryland Park Service, Tawes State Office Building, Annapolis, Maryland 21401; telephone 301/267-5771.

For information on state forests, write to Maryland Forest Service,
Tawes State Office Building, Annapolis, Maryland 21401; telephone
301/267-5776.

Chesapeake and Ohio Canal Towpath Trail
Length: 184 miles
Location: Entrance to the trail can be made from scores of places on
the Maryland side of the Potomac River. Consult road map or one of
the C&O guides mentioned in trail writeup. To begin hike from Washington, D.C., proceed to intersection of Virginia Avenue and Rock
Creek Parkway, turn right on Rock Creek bikepath, past Thompson's
Boathouse, proceed under bridge and enter the towpath at a point
marked by an historical marker.
Description: This canal and towpath begins in the District of Columbia
and follows the east side of the Potomac River for 184 miles, all the
way to Cumberland, Maryland. It has been owned by the U.S. Government since 1938 and is now a National Historical Park. It provides a
hiking and biking path along its entire length with hiker-biker campgrounds located about every five miles. Some 22 miles of the canal
and locks have been restored. This part of the trail extends from Washington, D.C., to Seneca, Maryland, and is the most widely used area of
the canal. In this span the canal offers not just hiking and biking, but
boating, canoeing, and occasionally in winter, ice skating.

Construction on the canal began on July 4, 1828, with President
John Quincy Adams turning over the first spadeful of dirt. A director of
the canal company predicted that the canal would be completed all the
way to the Ohio River in three years. It actually took 22 years to reach
Cumberland, Maryland, and it never did reach the Ohio River at Pitts-
burgh as had been originally planned. Still, the canal is an engineering
marvel. It has 74 lift locks, all built of stone, each having the capacity
to lift or lower a boat about 8 feet. Elevation of the canal at Cumberland is 615 feet; at Washington it reaches tidewater. In addition to the
locks, the canal has 11 aqueducts that permit the flow of water and
canal barges across the tributaries of the Potomac. Of these the Monocacy Aqueduct, at milepoint 42, is the most impressive and is the most
greatly admired structure on the canal. It is built of white granite, is
438 feet long and has seven arches, each with a span of 54 feet. Unfortunately, the aqueduct was badly damaged by Hurricane Agnes in
1972. The Paw Paw Tunnel, at milepoint 155, goes through 3118 feet
of rock and saved six miles of canal construction.

Edward Garvey had largely ignored the canal for almost 20 years,
even though he lived within six miles of it, but, in 1968 he began making a number of Sunday hikes on the canal, going a bit further north
each time until, by the end of the year, he reached Monocacy Aqueduct at milepoint 42. There are many access points by car throughout
the entire length of the canal. He recorded on each map the day he

had hiked, the total mileage, and the hours required. There are mile markers on the canal making it possible to compute hiking speed. In reviewing his map notes, he found that he averaged about four miles per hour, his best effort being a 4.2 mile rate for one 6-mile stretch.

The canal is a great place for observing bird and animal life, trees, flowers, and other plants. Garvey observed both raccoon and opossum on the canal and was surprised on one occasion to scare up a small white-tailed deer at milepoint 32.

The walkway-bikeway is an elevated trail varying in width to 12 feet. Bikeway detours have been provided at a few points where the going is unusually rough, but hikers can traverse the entire route on the towpath. The overnight accommodation — "biker-hiker overnighters" — provide water (generally from a pump), cleared areas for tents, picnic tables, and fireplaces. There are American Youth Hostels at Seneca, Sandyhook, and Cumberland (milepoints 23, 59, and 184 respectively) with a fourth, at Williamsport, milepoint 100, due to open in the spring of 1976.

More information: The current edition of the *American Youth Hostel C & O Canal Guidebook* can be purchased from bookstores or from the American Youth Hostel, 1520 16th Street, N.W., Washington, D.C. 20036; cost: $1.75.

Another excellent guidebook, which comes in a more convenient carrying size, is the *184 Miles of Adventure — Hiker's Guide to the C & O Canal* issued jointly by five Council offices of the Boy Scouts of America. This 50-page book has a map on one page and an opposite page narrative for each 10-mile segment of the canal. It has a listing of the exact location of every hiker-biker campsite and conveniences the camper will find there. This book also contains the requirements for obtaining the BSA medals and patches for hiking all or parts of the 184 mile trail. The book costs $1 and may be purchased from book stores, outdoor stores, and from BSA Trading Posts.

An 11 x 26-inch folder issued by the C. & O. National Historical Park is quite useful; it has a good map on one side and much explanatory information on the other. Available from C & O Canal Association, Box 66, Glen Echo, Maryland 20768.

Assateague Island National Seashore Trail

Length: 29 miles
Map: National Park Service map "Assateague Island"
Location: The village of Chincoteague is 190 miles from Washington, D.C., via U.S. 50 east to Salisbury, Maryland, south on U.S. 13, cross Virginia state line and within three miles turn left (east) on State Route 175 to Chincoteague. From the village go east across bridge to Assateague Island and continue on a macadam road to the bath house maintained by the National Park Service.

Description: A delightful variation from mountain hiking is the 29-mile beach trail hike along the east coast of the Assateague Island National Seashore; administered by the National Park Service. The island also includes the Chincoteague National Wildlife Refuge, administered by the Bureau of Sport Fisheries and Wildlife of the U.S. Department of the Interior. The island is the home of the famous Chincoteague ponies, and each year during the last week in July all the ponies are rounded up and herded into Assateague channel where they swim to Chincoteague Island for the annual auction. Those not sold are returned to Assateague for release.

There are but three walk-in campgrounds on Assateague Island, plus one youth group campground near the National Park Service ranger station in Virginia. There are a number of motels, cottages, and campgrounds in nearby Chincoteague. There is also a campground in the Maryland Assateague State Park, which is an enclave within the National Seashore at its northern end. The Park Service also maintains a campground adjacent to the state park on the north end of the island.

There is no marked trail, as such, but the hiker walks along the beach being forced to walk on higher ground near the sand dunes at high tide; but most of the time one is able to walk on the hard-packed sand. Mileage markers (the National Park Service ranger station at Chincoteague is the zero point) are posted just above high tide line.

There are two recommended ways of negotiating the 29-mile beach trail. One is to headquarter either in the town of Chincoteague or at one of the campgrounds at the north end of the island and hike a different section of the island each day — alternating the hiking with other activities such as swimming, fishing, crabbing, or whatever.

For those who wish to backpack straight through, a camping permit is required for overnight stops at any of the three walk-in campsites.

More information: Permits, maps, the Assateague Island National Seashore leaflet, and other information may be obtained by writing to either the Superintendent, Assateague Island National Seashore, Route #2, Box 294, Berlin, Md. 21811; or to Virginia District Ranger, Assateague Island National Seashore, P.O. Box 38, Chincoteague, Virginia 23336.

The three walk-in camp sites are just that, no buildings except toilets and no water. From May 15 until the first frost in the fall, there is an insect problem. Hikers should bring insect repellent. For overnight camping, a tent with mosquito netting is advised.

The prevailing winds are from the sea, and the insect problem is minimal when walking directly beside the ocean. Walking even in the hard-packed sand is somewhat tiring. The wind blows almost constantly and conversation is difficult. Nevertheless, hiking along the National Seashore can be very pleasant. The sight, sound, and smell of the wind and water combine to make one feel invigorated and relaxed. The hiker will suffer no ill effects from high altitude on this hike, for the highest elevation on the island is only 47 feet above sea level. But watch for severe sun and windburn. Hikers should wear hats and be especially careful not to invite sunburn by over exposure. It is easy to forget about the sun when one is cooled by a constant breeze.

The island is actually 35 miles long but hiking is generally confined to the lower 29 miles. The upper six miles is partly on private property and the northern tip is reachable only by boat.

New Jersey

Batona Trail
Length: 29.8 miles
USGS Quads: 7½ Minutes; Medford Lakes, Indian Mills Chatsworth, Hammonton, Atsion, Jenkins, Green Bank, and Oswego. All these cover the Wharton State Forest area to the south; 15 minutes: Pemberton, Egg Harbor.
More information: An 8 x 16-inch map containing mileage table and particulars is available for 35 cents from Morris Bardock, 1233 Princess Avenue, Camden, New Jersey 08103; telephone 609-964-5089.

Maps and folders of the two state forests may be obtained by writing to: Bureau of Parks, P.O. Box 1420, Trenton, N.J. 08625. Or, by writing to or visiting, Lebanon State Forest, New Lisbon, N.J. 08064 (office located on State Route 72 approximately .5 mile south of intersection with State Route 70); and Wharton State Forest, Batsto R.D. 1, Hammonton New Jersey 08037 (office located at Batsto Village).

Those wishing to hike with members of the Batona Club may obtain the club's six-month schedule of hiking, camping and canoeing trips by writing to: Laura Cramer,˙ 6244-A Mulberry Street, Philadelphia, Pennsylvania 19135.
Location: Begins on State Route 542 at the Batsto Fire Tower near Mansion in the Wharton State Forest. Terminates some 30 miles to the north in Lebanon State Forest two miles north of Route 70.

Description: This trail begins in Wharton State Forest and ends in Lebanon State Forest to the north. It goes over a sizeable stretch of private land and has a public campground at roughly the midpoint and another about 7 miles from the northern end. The Carranza monument, also near midpoint, was erected in memory of Emilie Carranza, a Mexican pilot, whose plane crashed at that point in 1928.

The trail goes over land that is rather flat but extremely interesting. Elevation averages 50 to 60 feet. The people in south Jersey take some kidding about the lack of elevation. The fire tower is located on the high point - Apple Pie Hill, with a dizzying elevation of 205 feet. On the extreme northern end of the trail, the forest growth is young oak, 15 to 20 feet high. In the pine barrens it is almost all pine, again mostly 15 to 20 feet high. Here the hiker may encounter deer, beaver, squirrels and an abundance of bird life. The streams, being cedar water, appear to be brown in color. The trees do not provide too much shade and hiking in mid-day in the summer could be on the warm side and somewhat buggy. Insect repellent is advised.

Several paved roads cross the trail, and it could be day-hiked by starting in various points. Backpackers should allow at least two days for hiking and exploring. Plan to spend a few hours for exploring the historic Batsto village at the southern end of the trail. Now a museum, it was once a thriving industrial community of a thousand people. Restored buildings include the grist mill, saw mill, iron furnace site and the town mansion, among many others. Admission: $1 for adults. Open year round.

Camping facilities are available at both Lebanon and Wharton State Forests. Primitive camping permits are required, which may be obtained at the State Forest offices. There are water pumps at the campsites, but water should be carried. The trail is blazed in pale pink.

Hewitt-Butler Trail

Location: At Hewitt, drive on Route 511 (Greenwood Lake Road) to the · junction with East Shore Road.

Length: 18 miles

Description: Marked with 2 x 3 inch blue blazers, this trail extends the entire length of the Wyanokie region from Hewitt south to the village of Butler. At its northern terminus the trail begins on Route 511 (Greenwood Lake Road) at the junction with East Shore Road.

From Hewitt the trail proceeds southwest, crossing the Horse Pond Mountain Trail and then the Burnt Meadow Road. It ascends to the top of and then follows the top of Long Hill for some 2 miles. After leaving Long Hill it ascends to Tip-Top Point, and shortly thereafter to Manaticut Point, with fine views. It then descends steeply, and crosses West Brook Road, after which it ascends to an easterly view which includes the New York City skyline. Next, the trail crosses the three Pine Paddies from which there are excellent views of the Wanaque Reservoir and Wyanokie High Point. From here it proceeds past a brook onto the Snake Den Road in vicinity of the AEU (American Ethical Union) Camp. The trail can be reached by car at this point.

Leaving the Snake Den Road and entering Norvin Green State Forest, the trail proceeds south near the crest of Wyanokie High Point, and after leaving the Forest, it goes west before crossing Otter Hole Road (limited parking) and entering the woods to pick up the Torne Trail and make a steep ascent of Torne Mountain. In the 4 miles between Snake Den Road and Torne Mountain the Hewitt-Butler Trail intersects seven other trails.

Leaving the summit of Torne, the trail goes past the upper end of Torne Trail and proceeds to South Torne and Osio Rock. It then descends steeply and follows an old road through the valley before arriving at Star Lake. The trail continues past Cold Spring Lake to Macopin Road and from there continues on auto roads for an additional mile to the center of Butler

Stonetown Circular Trail

Location: To reach the trail, cross the Wanaque Reservoir from east to west and take the first road right, Stonetown Road. Proceed north for a scant mile and park on the left at a fire station.

Length: 9.5 miles

Description: Blazers: red triangle on white. This trail goes over a number of peaks involving the equivalent of a 2500-foot climb which is considered strenuous. Driving time at each end of the hike plus the 9.5 miles of up and down hiking makes a full day's activity.

From fire station, retrace the route south on the road for .5 mile and turn left into the woods. The trail begins immediately ascending Windbeam Mountain, a climb of about 600 feet. It proceeds on a counter clockwise direction for its entire length. Fine views are visible from a lookout point on the way up and from a fire tower on top (elevation 1026 feet).

The trail proceeds north, climbing Bear Mountain and Board Mountain with beautiful views of the Wanaque reservoir. Next it turns left (west), descends, and follows White Road reaching Stonetown Road at a point 2 miles north of a fire station. Turning south, it follows Stonetown Road for .3 mile before turning right off the southern terminus of Horse Pond Mountain Trail.

Turning south it descends, crossing Sawmill Brook on a bridge on Burnt Meadows Road (6.2 miles from starting point). It then follows the road south for .3 mile before turning left to climb Tory Rocks. From here the trail winds south and ascends Signal Rock with view of the Ramapos, Windbeam, and Bear mountains. Descending and continuing south, the trail parallels Stonetown Road to Magee Road and turns left to the fire station on Stonetown Road.

Pennsylvania

With some 4700 miles of developed hiking trails, the state and federal agencies and the hiking organizations have done a particularly good job of getting their trails signed and paint blazed. They have developed maps, handout sheets, pocketsize guide books and other materials which make it easy for the hiker to ascertain what hiking trails are available and precisely where he should go to get on them.

More Information: A copy of Pennsylvania Hiking Trails may be obtained from: Appalachian Trail Conference, P.O. Box 236, Harper's Ferry, West Virginia 25425. Retail price of the book in 1975 was $2.50.

To obtain copies of the official map of Pennsylvania and to obtain information on attractions, points of interest, resort areas, etc., write to Travel Development Bureau, Pennsylvania Department of Commerce Harrisburg, Pennsylvania 17120.

For information on Pennsylvania's game lands and maps for same, write to: Pennsylvania Game Commission P.O. Box 1567 Harrisburg, Pennsylvania 17120.

For information on state parks, write to Bureau of State Parks 3rd and Reily Streets Harrisburg, Pennsylvania 17120.

For information on state forests, write to Office of Public Information Harrisburg, Pennsylvania 17120.

Allegheny National Forest

The Allegheny, a forest of some half million acres, is located in the northwestern part of Pennsylvania and touches New York State and New York's Allegany State Park on its northern boundary. The northern part of the forest surrounds Allegheny Reservoir, with its 12,000 acres of water surface and 91 miles of shoreline. A number of the recreation sites are accessible only by boat.

There are no trailside shelters, and backpackers are urged to arrange their hiking schedules so that nightfall will find them at a point where it will be convenient to use one of the 18 designated campsites in the forest. Where this is not feasible, so-called "throw down" camping is permissible — *i.e.*, camping directly beside the trail. Wood fires are permitted. No overnight camping is permitted within 1500 feet of either the scenic drives or the Allegheny Reservoir.

The Allegheny has hiking for everyone, from short family day hikes to longer day hikes, to a five to seven day backpacking trip on the North Country Trail.

More Information: There is an excellent map available which shows all of the hiking trails and campgrounds. Write to Allegheny National Forest, P.O. Box 847, Warren, Pennsylvania 16365, and ask for the map of the Forest, plus the narrative description of each of the marked trails and the names and descriptions of the campgrounds. The reverse side of the map has a listing of the 32 recreation sites, with an indicator showing which of these also has camping facilities. Don't assume that each of those red tee-pee pictures on the map indicates a campsite. Furthermore, even when you have ascertained which of the recreation sites has a campground you can't be sure when the campgrounds are open. All of them are open in the summer months, but only a few stay open year round. Therefore, when you first arrive in the forest it is wise to visit the nearest of the four district offices (located at Sheffield, Marshburg, Marienville, and Ridgway) and obtain up-to-date information as to campsites, trails, and roads.

North Country Trail
Length: 78 miles in May, 1975
Location: To reach beginning of trail, proceed west on State Route 346 from town of Bradford (McKean County) for 17 miles to the Willow Bay

Campground. Trail can be picked up in campground area or one mile east of campground on Route 346.

Description: National Trails System Act of 1968 established two long-distance scenic trails — the Appalachian in the east and the Pacific Crest in the west, as initial components of a nationwide system of long-distance trails. Some 12 to 14 other trails were placed in a study category with the proviso that they might later, by act of Congress, be moved into an operations category. One of these study trails was the North Country Trail, which would tie into the A.T. in the northeastern United States, go across the northern states, and join the Lewis and Clark Trail in the west. In the Allegheny National Forest, some 78 miles of the North Country Trail has already been established.

Garvey hiked bits and pieces of this trail as it winds its way south from the Willow Bay Recreation Area, located one mile south of the New York-Pennsylvania state line on the eastern shore of the Allegheny Reservoir. It follows a route south and west to a point 2 miles southeast of Guitonville, near the southern tip of the forest. The trail takes one through the oil well area of Pennsylvania. He followed the trail part way into the Tionesta Scenic Area, 2,000-acre remnant of the original forest that once covered six million acres on the Allegheny Plateau of New York and Pennsylvania. The trail is marked with double white paint blazes.

A detailed guidebook entitled Big Susque Country has a comprehensive topographic map, on which appears the location of springs (W) and telephones (T). This map as well as those described above, is obtainable from Potter County Recreation, Inc. The same organization will, on request, furnish a folder listing some two dozen inns, motels, cabins, campgrounds, and restaurants in the area. The guidebook described the trail in a clockwise direction beginning at the Northern Gateway, but the hiking can begin at any convenient spot and proceed in either direction.

From the Gateway the trail goes east and south passing near Lyman Run State Park, then south to Cherry Springs Fire Tower, and through Ole Bull State Park, which is an excellent overnight camping spot. Approximately 4 miles south of Ole Bull the North Link (2x6 inch blue blazes) connects in 8 miles with the 42-mile Black Forest Trail. Another 4 miles south of the North Link there is the 6 mile long South Link connection with the Black Forest Trail, marked with 3 inch solid blue circles. These two links open up a variety of circuit hikes into the Black Forest Trail area. Shortly after the varietry of circuit hikes into the Black Forest Trail area. Shortly after the South Link intersection, the Susquehannock Trail turns west and in 10 miles reaches the village of Cross Forks (Southern Gateway). From there the trail bears generally north going through the Hammersley Run Wild Area, crossing the East Fork Road and reaching Patterson Park Picnic Area at State Route 44 before making the final leg north to the Lyman Run area and back to the Northern Gateway. The new Donut Hole Trail System connects with the Susquehannock about 4 miles east of Cross Fork. From this trail connection, the hiker can go southwest through Kettle Creek State Park, cross Kettle Creek at that point and proceed south to State Route 120.

Susquehannock Trail System — Potter County

Location: To get to the Northern Gateway, drive to Susquehannock Lodge which is about 10 miles east of Coudersport and 3 miles east of the Denton Hill Susquehannock Trail sign on U.S. 6. The Southern Gateway is at Cross Ford on State Route 144. Both Gateways are marked with 10-foot-high wooden signs.

Length: Circuit trail of 85 miles

Maps: A set of 19 reproduced USGS Quad maps with the trail route shown in heavy black lines is available from the Potter County Recreation, Inc., P.O. Box 245, Coudersport, 16915. The price for the entire set in 1975 was $1.50 plus 25-cents postage. An 8½x13 inch reduced scale map of the entire trail system is also available from the same source. One can also obtain a 20x40 inch map of the STS available from Susquehannock Trail System, Secretary Betty Ahn, Route 6, Ulysses, R.D. 1, Pennsylvania. 16948. Cost: $1.50 Postpaid.

Description: The Susquehannock Trail Club constructed and now maintains an 85-mile loop trail in north central Pennsylvania about 10 miles east of Coudersport. The loop trail links many old CCC fire trails, old logging roads, and railroad grades. Cross Fork is the only village crossed in the 85 miles loop; it has a motel, restaurant and grocery store.

Loyalsock

Location: The trail is in Rothrock & Bald Eagle State Forests in Huntingdon, Centre, and Mifflin Counties (Near Pennsylvania State University). The entrance to the trail is at Colerain Picnic Area, 1.9 miles northeast of Spruce Creek village on State Route 45. Turn across Spruce Creek at Kerm's Spruce Creek Inn and Mobile Station. The sign for the picnic area is visible once you have crossed the creek, but is not visible from State Route 45.

Length: 57 miles

USGS Quads: Montoursville, Huntersville, Picture Rocks, Hillsgrove, Eagles Mere, and Laporte, Pennsylvania. 7½ minute maps. For those hiking the Loyalsock Trail (LT) a better arrangement is to buy the excellent 24 page Guide to the Loyalsock Trail and Side Trails, with the three Loyalsock maps included. Total price for guide and maps: $2.00 in 1975.

Description: Loyalsock—derived from an Indian word that means middle creek—is the name of one of the most beautiful trails in Pennsylvania. The Loyalsock has elevations from a low of 665 feet to a high of 2140 feet, with most of the trail being at the 1700 to 1900 foot elevation. The trail was laid out to take advantage of as many vista points, waterfalls, and other beauty spots as possible. There are eight main sections on the LT, each accessible from either end by automobile, a situation which makes day hiking and car shuttling very convenient. Side trails, loop trails, and lead-in trails are all identified by different colored metal disks. The total length, 57 miles, makes it especially suitable for Boy Scout groups working on their 50 Miler hikes. Distances in the Guide are in hundredths of a mile, and measuring was done with a 52.8 foot chain. Even without benefit of the "new math" I was able to figure out that 100 such chains would equal exactly 5280 feet or one mile.

More Information: The guidebook and maps, the patch, and information on the Loyalsock Trail may be obtained by writing to the LT Chairman, Williamsport Alpine Club, P.O. Box 501, Williamsport, Pennsylvania. 17701.

Mid-State Trail — "Metric System Trail"
Length: 89 kilometers (55 miles)
USGS Quad: 7½ minute, Alexandria, Franklinville, Pine Grove Mills, McAlevy's Fort, State College, Barrville, Centre Hall, Burnham Spring Mills, and Coburn: Mid-State Trail Maps 1-12. Note: The USGS maps do not show the route of the Mid-State Trail. *The Mid-State Trail* guidebook maps do show the route of the MST and of prominent side trails. The 35-page pocket size guide and set of 12 maps cost $1.25 postpaid in 1975. A best buy!

Description: Guidebook distances for most hiking trails in the United States are still expressed in miles. A few show metric conversions but generally less prominently than the mileage information. The MST completed in 1972, went the kilometer route with the publication of its second guidebook. Even in the description of its trail markings the MST guidebook sticks to the metric. A.T. guidebooks will say that the A.T. is marked with paint blazes that are 2 inches wide and 6 inches high. The MST guidebook states that "The main trail is paint blazed with orange rectangles of 5 cmx15 cm (2"x6")." See what I mean?" (By pure serendipity the letters MST also stand for Metric System Trail.)

The MST is narrated in its guide book in a southwest to northeast direction. A special feature of the trail is its many overlooks. The views are varied with farms and woods on one side and heavily wooded ridges and valleys on the other.

At the Colerain Picnic Area sign, the water pump marking the start of the MST is visible to the left near a picnic shelter. From this starting point, the trail proceeds generally northeast and for its entire length of 89 kilometers it runs parallel to and anywhere from five to 15 kilometers south of State Route 45.

Throughout its length the trail leads through or near a number of state parks (blue blazed side-trails provide access to the parks), across streams, across two major highways (State Route 26 and U.S. 322), to campsites and springs, and eventually to the end of the trail at Poe Paddy Picnic Area. There are no shelters on the trail, but public campground facilities are available at the four state parks on or near the trail. The guidebook indicates other points where campsites are available. Fires are permitted except during the high fire danger months of April, May, October and November.

This rather newly completed trail was built by the Penn State Outing Club and is maintained by the same organization. The guidebook (Fourth Edition 1975/1976) lists a number of planned changes in the route and extensions of the trail scheduled for the future. Those planning to do extensive hiking on this trail are advised to contact the maintaining organization for information on changes that have taken place since the issuance of the guidebook and maps.

More Information: To purchase guidebook and maps, the MST patch (available after hiking 20 kilometers), contact: Hiking Division Penn State Outing Club, 4 Intramural Building, University Park, Pennsylvania. 16802.

Southern Mountain Trails

To most people, hiking in the southern Appalachians means the Smokies and the Appalachian Trail. Because there are already so many excellent guides to trails, Jerry Sullivan and Glenda Daniel decided to concentrate in this book on other areas which they felt were quite attractive but not so well known.

Another reason for devoting more space to lesser known trails is the heavy traffic on the Smokies and the Appalachian trails. Each year, approximately 300,000 people hike on the trails of the Smokies. Traffic on the Appalachian Trail through the park has become so heavy that the park service has had to ration use of the trail. The primitive sanitary facilities near the trail shelters have been severly overtaxed. Foragers for wood have picked clean large areas around the more popular campsites. Erosion problems on the steeper grades have become quite severe.

Arkansas

Stand on top of a ridge in northwest Arkansas' Boston Mountains, and you will inevitably notice, in the grandeur spread out before you, that most of the other ridges within sight are rather flat-topped and almost the same elevation as the spot where you are standing. The sharply upthrust peak standing above low gaps on either side that is so prominent a part of the landscape of the Appalchians is absent.

The rocks of these ridges were not spewed out of a volcano. They were not faulted, folded, compressed or twisted by mountain building movements of the earth. Indeed, strictly speaking, the Ozarks are not mountains at all. The Ozark Highlands is a plateau, an area of 55,000 square miles that was lifted as a unit above the surrounding country. The layers of rocks in its bluffs lie flat, except for a slight southward tilt of the entire plateau.

The geologic history of the Ozarks begins with a spate of volcanic activity that occurred between 1.2 and 1.5 billion years ago. Several different outbursts produced masses of rhyolite, granite, and basalt. This activity ceased about a billion years ago, and the entire area was uplifted and faulted again. The result was a series of low hills where the difference between the highest peaks and the deepest valleys was nowhere more than about 1000 feet.

The present landscape of the Ozarks was created by the rivers. They cut the narrow, meandering, steep-sided valleys. They sculpted the spectacular bluffs that wall in the valleys. In places, they cut through the sedimentary rock down to the basalt and granite that underlay the plateau.

The waters also created the caves that honeycomb the Ozarks. Some of these have been decked out with largely spurious legends of Jesse James and opened to the public at so much a head. But the majority are known only to spelunkers — if they are known at all.

With so much water underground, springs — some producing an enormous amount of water — are common. Creeks and rivers sometimes simply disappear into the porous rock, only to reappear downstream. Natural bridges have been formed over many streams by water eroding away underlying strata.

Ozark rivers and caves harbor a number of species of amphibians and fish found nowhere else. Reptiles include the timber rattlesnake, the western cottonmouth, and the northern copperhead. Scorpions and tarantulas, animals usually associated with the southwest, are also found in the Ozarks.

A substantial number of archeological sites have been excavated in caves and rock shelters in the area.

The first settlers came after 1810. The terrain dictated a pattern of settlement that saw farms spread out along the narrow valleys and on the flat ridge tops. The slopes were often too steep for settlement, and disastrous erosion often followed attempts to farm it.

This settlement pattern still exists in many areas, and it is important to hikers. Many streams running through wild land contain unsafe water because of cow pastures on the ridge top above the stream.

The timber of the Ozarks included many extremely valuable species such as white oak and black walnut. Except for isolated patches, the virgin timber was pretty well cut over by the 1930s.

The Ozarks cannot support a large population on a sustained basis. In the Boston Mountains, the most rugged area in the Ozarks, the road maps show numerous communities that no longer exist. As the people left, the Forest Service bought up the land, and the trees began to come back. Today, the Boston Mountains doubtlessly have more wild land than they did in 1925.

Ozark Hikes

There are few established trails in the Ozarks, either within or outside the Ozark National Forest boundaries. Local people out for a weekend trek through the woods tend to follow the banks of streams. It is still possible, on a hike up one of these creeks, to discover a spectacular waterfall or rock formation that nobody has ever seen, or at least recorded.

There are remnants of old pioneer wagon trails in the mountains, but these are likely to peter out in some particularly inconvenient spot. Try to find them if you like; old geological survey maps occasionally show some of them. But be sure to take a compass along, and some means of boiling or purifying water. If you are planning an exploring trip of some duration, take an extra day's food along.

More information: The Forest Supervisor, Ozark National Forest, Box 340, Russellville, Arkanasas 72801, can supply maps and other information on the Ozark National Forest.

Richland Creek Hikes

Location: Take Arkansas Route 16 east from Sand Gap (known as Pelsor on some maps) about eight miles to Ben Hur. Continue east another 2½ miles to Upper Falling Water Creek Road (Forest Road 1205). Turn north on 1205 for eight miles to a small Forest Service campground near the confluence of Richland and Falling Water creeks. This campground makes an ideal base for several hikes. Two hikes are: (1) a single-day trip upstream to land Falls and to Twin Falls at the confluence of Big Devils Fork and Long Devils Fork, and (2) an overnight hike downstream past the Wasson School to the south end of Forest Road 1220 near Stack Rock Mountain.

Length: Upstream trip about 3 miles (but plan 5 or 6 hours to do it). Downstream trip about 9 miles with Wasson School roughly marking the halfway point.

USGS Quad: Snowball, Arkansas

Description: Richland Creek, longest of the scenic Buffalo River's tributaries, winds for 32 miles from its beginning deep in the mountains of southern Newton County north to the junction with the Buffalo. Some 2,100 acres of the lands surrounding it have been designated as a study area to determine their wilderness potential.

The hike upstream from Richland Creek campground is more heavily traveled because of the waterfalls.

Upstream Trip — Walk east from the campground along wide, flat banks of the creek for about ¼ mile to the point where Falling Water Creek flows in from the south. Continue west along Richland Creek at an elevation of about 1,000 feet.

Cliffs, towering two or three hundred feet above you, begin to edge closer to the stream, and soon you are proceeding through a deep, narrow gorge.

At the end of the first mile, you will notice a small stream, full in wet weather, coming downhill from the north. In another mile and a half you will come upon Richland Falls, only about six feet high but an impressive 100 feet wide.

There's a fork in the river nearby and if you bear right (north), you will soon come to the confluence of Big Devils Fork (the stream on the north side) and Long Devils Fork. Both of these empty into Richland Creek with major waterfalls situated within a few yards of each other. Long Devils Fall is about 16 feet high and Big Devils Fall is about 18 feet high. Both are deeply undercut. The cliff walls are dark shale with layers of fossil-laden limestone near the top.

Downstream Trip — If you are hiking with a group and have access to extra cars, it is suggested that you shuttle some of your cars to the trail's other end. Here's how. Drive north from the campground on Forest Road 1208 about five miles to Dickey Junction, then east on Forest Road 1201 about six miles to Forest Road 1220, then sharply right on 1220 across a ford of Richland Creek and the planned end of the hike.

For the first part of your trip north from the campground, you can walk along Drury Road on the creek's west bank or along an old logging road that follows the east bank.

Bobtail Creek flows into Richland Creek in a small flat area about a mile north of the campground. An old homesite being used as a feed lot can be seen on the west side of the creek.

After passing through an old field, the logging road leads across the creek to the east side, traveling through woods for half a mile to within sight of an old tin-roofed house on the creek's west side. If you cross the creek and explore, you'll find a curbed spring under the bluff downstream from the house about halfway to the horselot. The water in Ozark springs is almost *always* safe to drink; the water in Ozark creeks almost *never* is, unfortunately, because of the cow pastures located along the banks of those creeks and on mountaintops near their sources.

From this old house, the road leads through bottomland woods on the east side of the creek for about a mile to another field. Rock formations on the creek at this point are smooth and almost level, and the creek is only a small trickle in all but the wettest seasons. You may decide, therefore, to walk downstream in the creekbed for awhile. You will notice some limestone mixed in with the sandstone boulders.

If you return to the road at the southern end of the field, it will take you up over a hill through a woods to intersect another road descending the hill from the east and leading to the hamlet of Magic Springs.

The road along the creek continues north past a cow pasture where Sulphur Creek pours into Richland Creek from the east. Just past this is another old homestead in a clearing. There's a spring flowing out of a rusty old pipe about 75 yards uphill behind the house.

The road branches past the homestead with the east fork continuing along Richland and the other heading northward up the mountain. Take the hilltop route; the other comes to an end rather soon at a sawdust pile. In another quarter mile, you will reach the Wasson School, where a broad grassy yard makes an ideal place to set up camp for the night.

The school is a single-room frame building, no longer in use, with rock veneer facing, about 30 feet wide and 60 feet long, and a small bell steeple on the gable facing the road. The place is fast falling into disrepair.

Your path downstream next morning will take you through woods to an old field dotted with persimmon trees, then through a gap in a rock fence at the north end of the field. There's a small stream, sometimes dry, to cross, then another wooded area and yet another old homestead, this one fairly large with the traditional dogtrot in the middle. There's an old cemetery at the edge of the woods north of this old ruined homestead.

In the second field past this old house is another house and a large pear tree bulging with delicious fruit in season.

The road past this homestead climbs a hill and overlooks the creek from 100 to 200 feet. In the next open field, there's yet another old homestead, but there's also a modern house nearby complete with TV antenna and the most modern farm equipment. You are approaching civilization. Within the next half mile you will reach Forest Road 1220 and the automobile ford across Richland Creek. In the distance to your west you will be able to see the peak of Stack Rock Mountain, rising some 1800 feet above sea level.

Georgia

In northern Georgia, the mountains of the Appalachian chain gradually give way to rolling hills. Most of the rugged high country lies within the boundaries of the Chattahoochee National Forest which stretches across the north end of the state from the South Carolina border on the east to U.S. 411 on the west.

The Blue Ridge and Cohutta Ranges come together here, forming a large "V" with the Blue Ridge as eastern arm and the Cohutta as western. The highest point in Georgia lies along the Blue Ridge at Brasstown Bald with its elevation of 4784 feet.

The Appalachian Trail follows the Blue Ridge for 78 miles from Bly Gap at the North Carolina border southwestward to the southern terminus of the trail at Springer Mountain, elevation 3782. A six-mile approach trail runs from Amicalola Falls to Springer Mountain, providing access to the A.T.

More Information: For a map and general information about the Chattahoochee National Forest, contact the Supervisor's Office, U.S. Forest Service, P.O. Box 1437, Gainesville, Georgia 30501; telephone 404-532-6366.

Cohutta Wildlife Management Area

The Cohutta district contains some of the wildest and most rugged country in the Georgia mountains. Forest Service gravel roads skirt the edges of the Wildlife Management Area, but only a few dirt roads cross through it. Now that 34,000 acres of these mountains have been set aside as a wilderness area, these roads will presumably be graded and seeded, and the land will be left alone for people to enjoy.

One of the roads that will probably be closed is Georgia Route 2, which crosses the Cohutta from east to west. However, the road will continue to provide access to the edges of the wilderness area.

Current Information: The Cohutta District Ranger Office, Chatsworth, Georgia 30705

Jack's River Trail

Location: This trail is shown on the Forest Service tourist map following the course of the Jack's River across the Cohutta for about 11 miles. It is mainly on the bed of the narrow gauge railroad that was built into these mountains when the area was logged off.

This trail crosses the river about 40 times all told, and the crossings can be difficult. In low water, you would have to wade in knee deep water at times, and at high water, you could find yourself waist deep in a very fast moving current. There are better ways to drown yourself. However, Jack's River is a good trout stream, if you are into fishing, you might want to take Georgia Route 2 east from Cisco, Georgia, about 10 miles to the Shedd's Creek Rd., and then north for a short distance to the Jack's River Bridge. From there, you could follow the trail upstream to a good fishing spot.

12 — Rough Ridge Trail

Location: The south end of the trail leaves Georgia 2 about one mile north of the junction with Forest Road 64 and goes about one mile north of the junction with Forest Road 64 and goes north to Jack's River. Across the river. Hikers can connect with an old logging road between Rock Wall and Penitentiary Creeks. This road leads up to Hemp Top tower and Forest Road 73.

Length: 7.5 miles (to the river)

USGS Quad: Hemp Top, Georgia

Description: The trail leaves the road just south of Cowpen Mountain at an elevation of 3700 feet, following Rough Ridge north. The ridge is narrow and steep sided, but the top is relatively level. As the trail nears the river, at 2800 feet elevation, the downslope becomes quite steep for a little less than a mile, dropping to the river at 1700 feet.

9 — Tearbritches Trail

Location: Take Forest Road 18 north from U.S. 76 about 20 miles east of Chatsworth, Ga. Then go right on Forest Road 68 and left on Forest Road 64. The trail head is about two miles from the 68-64 junction. The trail ends at the confluence of Tearbritches Creek and The Conasauga River.

Length: 3.5 miles

USGS Quad: The northern portion of the trail is on the Hemp Top, Ga. quad. The southern portion is in an area which has been surveyed but which is without a published map.

Description: See following.

90 — Chestnut Creek Trail
Location: Goes north from Forest Road 64 between the 64-68 junction and the Tearbritches Trail. North end is at the confluence of the Conasauga River and Chestnut Creek.
Length: Two miles
USGS Quad: Hemp Top, Georgia
Description: See following.

11 — Conasauga River Trail
Location: Coming north from U.S. route 76 on Forest Road 18, go right on Forest Road 68, and then right again on Forest Road 64. The trailhead is about one mile north of the 68-64 junction.
Length: 4.5 miles
USGS Quad: Dyer Gap and Hemp Top, Georgia
Description: Jerry Sullivan and Glenda Daniel made an overnight trip on the Conasauga, Chestnut Creek, and Tearbritches Trails, so it is convenient to describe them together. They started on the Chestnut Creek Trail, going north from Forest Road 64. They turned northeast on the Conasauga River Trail, and then returned south on the Tearbritches Trail.

The road up to the trail was one of the more hair raising they encountered in the mountains. It was with a long steep drop to one side, and a washboard surface rough enough to send the rear wheels of their car skittering.

The Chestnut Creek Trail was well marked, with a sign visible from the road. If the sign hadn't been there, they still could have seen the area provided for parking cars along the north side of the road.

The trail is well marked with paint blazes, and it gets enough traffic to be easy to follow even without the blazes. It heads northeast from the trail head in a series of short switchbacks downhill, and then turns northwest down a long draw filled with tall, straight yellow poplars until it reaches Chestnut Creek. The elevation change in the first half mile or so is 600 feet: 3200 feet at the road and 2600 at the creek. However, the grades are not very steep.

The USGS quad shows three streams coming into the Conasauga River from the south in this area. None of these streams is named on the map, but Chestnut Creek is apparently the middle one.

The trail follows the creek to the Conasauga, crossing it five times. The trail was easy to follow, and they made all the crossings without getting their feet wet. However, they were there in a very dry autumn. The area had been without rain for weeks. But Jerry and Glenda believe Chestnut Creek would not be too formidable even in spring time.

Chestnut Creek joins the Conasauga at about 2300 feet elevation. A large, flat, relatively open area where the two streams come together would make an excellent campsite. Families with small children could handle the Chestnut Creek trail for an overnight outing. It is only two miles from the road to the river, and the slopes are not very steep along the way.

Taking the Conasauga River Trail from Forest Road 64 to this junction would be an even easier walk, according to the map. They did not walk this portion of the trail, but it should be not much more than a mile in length.

The Conasauga River Trail ends at the junction with the Tearbritches Trail. This junction is on an island of private land in the midst of the forest. A small metal sign tacked to a tree along the trail marks the forest boundary. If you miss that, note that the river turns from northwest to west and the trail climbs steeply up the spur of a hill on the south bank. About 100 feet above the river, the trail drops back down the other side of the hill and crosses a small creek that flows north into the Conasauga. This is Tearbritches Creek, and here the Tearbritches Trail begins.

The trail turns south along the creek for perhaps 50 yards before turning east, crossing the creek again, and starting uphill. Signs made all this clear when they were there, but it is unwise to count on the durability of signs.

The Tearbritches Trail climbs up on a ridge immediately east of the creek that gives it its name. It follows this ridge all the way to the trailhead at Forest Road 64. The first part of the climb is steep and long. With only one switchback to ease the grade, the trail goes from about 2000 feet at the creek to 3200 feet in less than one mile. The first half of this distance is the most difficult. Take it slow, because most of this trail is uphill. Once you hit 3200 feet, you keep going up at a somewhat slower rate until you reach the top of Bald Mountain, 4010 feet. From there, you follow a gentle downslope to the road.

Less than a mile from the trail's beginning, they crossed a tiny rivulet. It held perhaps an inch of water virtually standing still, the only water along Tearbritches Trail.

When Glenda and Jerry reached the road, they were about 1½ mile, from where they had left their car at the Chestnut Creek trailhead. It is downhill most of the way, so it wouldn't have been a difficult walk. However, they caught a ride in the back of a pickup truck, and that made it even easier.

North Carolina

Nantahala National Forest

Nantahala is a Cherokee Indian word meaning "land of the noonday sun." It was given to this steep mountain area of northwestern North Carolina because its valleys are said to be so narrow and deep they receive the direct rays of the sun only at midday. Veteran hikers of the Appalachian Trail tell us there is more up-and-down climbing through

the Nantahalas than anywhere else on the A.T. route from Kt. Katahdin
in Maine to the trail's southern end in Georgia.

Hiking trails in the 420,000-acre Nantahala National Forest are not
numerous, but those that do exist are invariably located in beautiful
and interesting country.

Trails Around Slickrock Creek
Location: West of U.S. 129 south of Tapoco on the Little Tennessee
River and east of the Unicoi Mountains on the Tennessee-North Caroli-
na border.
Length: The network of trails in this area totals about 24 miles. USGS
Quads: Tapoco, N.C.; Santeetlah Creek, N.C.

45 — Ike Branch Trail — 2¾ miles. This trail provides as good an
entrance as any to the network of trails around Slickrock Creek. It begins at the U.S. 129 bridge over Lake Calderwood in Tapoco and runs
south on a logging road to Yellowhammer Branch. From there it runs
west to connect with Hangover Lead Trail (#43) heading south and
then with Slickrock Creek Trail (#42) and Nichols Cove Branch Trail
(#44) at the state border.

42 — Slickrock Creek Trail — 8¼ miles. This trail begins at the
mouth of Slickrock Creek where it flows into the Little Tennessee River
and runs south, following the creek, along the border between North
Carolina and Tennessee. After about 2½ miles it meets the Stiff Knee
Trail (#106), a Tennessee trail that follows Little Slickrock Creek east
to its mouth at Slickrock Creek and the state border. (See Cherokee
National Forest section in Tennessee chapter for details of Trail #106.
In North Carolina that trail deadends into the Ike Branch Trail.)

Slickrock Creek Trail continues south on the creek along the border,
passing Nichols Cove Branch Trail just south of Little Slickrock Creek.

When the trail reaches Big Fat Branch, it leaves the state border and
curves east to meet Big Fat Branch Trail (#41) at a back country
campsite. Slickrock Creek Trail continues south about three more miles
to end at a point just east of Glen Gap. The mountains that rise so
spectacularly to your west on this trail are the Unicoi Mountains. A trail
in the Cherokee National Forest (Fodderstack Trail) follows the ridge of
the Unicois parallel to Slickrock Creek.

43 — Hangover Lead Trail — 5½ miles. This trail can be reached at
its northern end via the Ike Branch Trail from Tapoco. It runs south
from an elevation of 1900 feet at Yellowhammer Gap, up to 2800 feet
on a mountain peak, along Caney Ridge and then up to 3400 feet at
Cold Spring Knob. It descends to Big Fat Gap (2500 feet) and then
south another two miles to Hangover Mountain (5249 feet).

44 — Nichols Cove Branch Trail — 2 miles. This trail branches east
and south from Slickrock Creek Trail just south of the mouth of Little
Slickrock Creek. It runs south along Nichols Cove Branch to a back

country campsite at a junction with Big Fat Branch Trail.

41 — Big Fat Branch Trail — 1.5 miles. Runs west from Trail #43 at Big Fat Gap along Big Fat Branch to its mouth at Slickrock Creek. There's a back country campsite here at the junction of Big Fat Branch Trail with Nichols Cove Branch Trail and Slickrock Creek Trail.

Deep Creek Trail — 3 miles. Runs northeast from Saddle Tree Gap just south of Hangover Mountain along deep Creek to the south end of a forest road. The road leads north to Indian Grave campground and junction with U.S. 129.

Trails in the Upper Nantahala River Country
Location: To reach this area, take old U.S. Route 64 west from Franklin to Wallace Gap where the Appalachian Trail crosses the road. There will be a forest service sign directing you south to Standing Indian Campground.
USGS Quads: Rainbow Springs, N.C.; Prentiss, N.C.
Description: The Nantahala Mountains form a huge horseshoe in this area to make a beautiful, unpolluted watershed for the Upper Nantahala River which runs north and south through the center of the basin. The Appalachian Trail follows the ridgeline around the horseshoe and a number of newly-blazed, well-maintained side trails lead down the creeks and side ridges to the Nantahala River and the forest road that parallels it. At the north end of the basin is Standing Indian Campground. There are enough good trails in this region to occupy your attention for an entire two-week vacation using the campground as a base for exploration.

Just south of the highway on the forest road, you will note a short spur trail leading half a mile east to the John Wasilik Memorial Poplar. This yellow poplar or tulip tree is the second largest of its species on record in the United States. It was the largest on record until 1972 when a bigger one was discovered in Virginia. The tree is named for Ranger John Wasilik, an early ranger on the Wayah District.

The campground is about a mile south. Four trails originate from its southern boundary in Whiteoak Bottoms. Jerry Sullivan and Glenda Daniel investigated two of them, the Kimsey Creek Trail (3.7 miles) and the Lower Trail Ridge Trail (3.5 miles) in one leisurely overnight hike that also took us along a short stretch of the A.T. to Standing Indian Mountain, noted for its spectacular views.

The forest along these trails is made up of fairly young second-growth timber, but the appearance of the woods is still rather park-like because of the Forest Service has spaced the trees for maximum growth and the understory is not dense.

The Kimsey Creek Trail is not as steep as the Lower Trail Ridge Trail. A sign at the southeast end of the campground (across the river) identifies it, and the route is marked with bright and frequent blue blazes. Two blazes signal changes in direction.

The trail follows an old road along the creek. Crossings are bridged. About two miles (1 hour's hiking time) from the beginning, two creeks join. There's a clearing that would make a good campsite. Apple trees, planted by the forest service as part of the game habitat improvement program, border this meadow.

The trail south of the creek heads up over a low ridge and then back down to the stream. The second time it climbs, it leaves the creek for good (about 1½ hours from the campground). In another 15 minutes, it hits a forest road and follows it uphill to a junction with the A.T. at Deep Gap.

Turning left (east) on the A.T., it follows a jeep road for a few hundred feet, then branches right to head uphill on another road. Numerous switchbacks ease the climb. After about 15 minutes, you will reach a sign pointing to a shelter visible from the trail on the left. The wooden-floored shelter is very pleasant, watertight, and contains a rock fireplace. There's a picnic table in front and a small creek flowing by.

The trail continues uphill with many more switchbacks to Standing Indian. The trail follows the west edge of the ridge. A wooden sign on a blue-blazed side trail points .01 miles (right) to the summit. This side trail passes through a stand of rhododendron, a few fir trees (planted), a grassy bald with remains of old campsites to the summit at 5399 feet. This is a good spot for spreading a picnic lunch or just sitting for several hours to watch the clouds drift by.

Back on the A.T., another side trail goes steeply downhill (left) to a spring. There's a sign. Within 50 yards of the spring-summit intersection, a blue-blazed trail (no sign) leads steeply down to the left. This is the Trail Ridge Trail and follows that ridge back to the campground. It stays on the crest of the ridge to within a couple of miles of the campground, above White Oak Bottoms. Then switchbacks take you down a very steep hillside. The forest cover on the ridge crest is almost entirely hardwoods. When you reach Whiteoak Bottoms, however, the timber changes to hemlock mixed with rhododendron, yellow birch and poplar. The trail crosses a game meadow where an old road goes right and the trail goes left across two bridges into the campground. The sign at this end of the trail doesn't give its name but merely says "Foot Trail."

Whiteoak Bottoms, by the way, is reputed to shelter a number of rare and unusual wildflowers and other plants in its boggy areas. Among them are cotton grass and grass of parnassus.

The other trails that originate at Standing Indian Campground are the Park Gap Trail, 4 miles, and the Long Branch Trail, 2.3 miles.
To reach Park Gap Trail, walk north from the campground on the west side of the Nantahala River along an old railroad bed about ¼ mile to the trailhead. It, too, is well marked with blue blazes. Proceed west, uphill to Bee Tree Knob (a climb of one mile and about 500 feet in elevation). Then turn south along Middle Ridge. The trail follows the crest of that ridge south and then west to Pentland Gap and a forest road that heads west and north to U.S. Route 64 at Chunky Gal Mountain.

Long Branch Trail — 2.3 miles, heads east across the road from the campground up that creek just north of Blackwell Ridge to the Appalachian Trail just south of Glassmine Gap. (Elevation change is from 3500 to 4200 feet.)

To reach the other trails in the Nantahala River basin, drive — or walk — south on the old logging road, now a forest road, from Standing Indian Campground. The first one you will come to is Hurricane Creek Trail (No. 36 on Forest Service inventories), 2 miles. It also leads east uphill to the Appalachian Trail along Hurricane Creek. It reaches the A.T. south of Sassafras Ridge and just north of the trail shelter at Bigspring Gap.

At this point another trail (we don't know its name) leads west from the A.T. three miles past Pinnacle Mountain and Little Pinnacle Mountain into the Coweeta Experimental Forest.

Just over a mile south of the Hurricane Creek Trail on the Nantahala River road, you will reach Big Indian Trail (No. 34), 3.7 miles, on your right (west of the river). It climbs in classic serpentine fashion, up the mountain, past Nichols Branch in the first mile and onto Upper Trail Ridge, it crosses Big Shoal Branch at its headwaters, then turns south to follow the slopes of the mountain range parallel with the A.T. about two miles to Kilby Gap. A spur heads left here about 1½ miles back down the road just north of Big Laurel Falls. The right fork joins the Appalachian Trail at Beech Gap.

22 — Bearpen Gap Trail — 2.7 miles, runs east from the road just south of the eastern terminus of Big Indian Trail. It follows Bearpen Creek for the first ¾ mile, then leaves it and turns north for a mile-long climb to Yellow Bald at elevation of 4040 feet. It turns west here to reach a road on Albert Mountain (excellent views) that heads both east and west to join the Appalachian Trail south of Bigspring Gap Shelter and north of Bearpen Gap.

Back on the main road, if you continue south on it, past the spur from Big Indian Trail to a sharp curve in the road, you will see signs directing you south to Big Laurel Falls. The falls is just half a mile from the road and is accessible by a circular trail. You can continue south from the falls, however, along Laurel Branch Trail 1½ miles, along Timber Ridge to the Appalachian Trail just east of Carter Gap shelter.

If you stayed on the main road around the big curve past the trail to Big Laurel Falls, you would soon reach the end of the road's auto-navigable part. You can continue walking along the road about ¼ mile to Mooney Falls, and then, still along the road, parallel Hemp Patch Branch and Mooney Branch to junctions with the Appalachian Trail at Betty Creek Gap, Mooney Gap and Bearpen Gap.

You will be able to see from the map accompanying this section that trails in the Upper Nantahala River Country lend themself to a variety of loop hikes.

Trails Around Apple Tree Group Camp

Location: Apple Tree Group Camp is located 24 miles west of Franklin,

N.C. From Franklin take U.S. 64 west to the Wayah Bald Road. Follow this paved road north over Wayah Gap and past Nantahala Lake to the Junaluska Road. Turn left on the Junaluska Road; the Group Camp is about three miles.

Length: There are eight signed trails in this area with a total length of 32 miles.

USGS Quad: Topton, North Carolina

Description: The use of Apple Tree Group Camp is limited to organized groups and on a reservation basis. However, individuals may use the trails, but you should first contact the District Ranger, U.S. Forest Service, P.O. Box 469, Franklin, North Carolina 28734

Appletree Trail — 2 miles. This trail is a well-worn one. Early pioneers used it because it was already there when they arrived; it was used by the Cherokees who preceded them in this fertile terrain on the banks of the Nantahala River. It begins at the group camp where Appletree Branch flows into the Nantahala River. It heads west up the creek and after 1½ miles it crosses Piercy Creek and a junction with the Laurel Creek Trail and Diamond Valley Trail. It continues west uphill (gaining about 600 feet in elevation) for half a mile to end on the slopes of London Bald and intersect the London Bald Trail.

Nantahala Trail — Six miles, runs north from the campground along the Nantahala River for two miles, then turns west at Poplar Cove just north of a small stream and proceeds past Turkey Pen Cove to join Piercy Creek near its headwaters. It follows the creek about half a mile to a junction with Laurel Creek Trail, where Piercy Creek turns south. The Nantahala Trail continues west another mile to end at the northern terminus of the London Bald Trail. (Nantahala, London Bald, and Junaluska Trails combine to make a 19 mile loop that circles the entire area and connects with all the other trails.)

London Bald Trail — Nine miles, begins at Southerland Gap, at the eastern end of the Nantahala Trail. It runs south along a low ridge, passing Piercy Bald and London Bald on their western slopes. Apple Tree Trail heads east from the London Bald Trail about two miles south of Southerland Gap.

The trail continues south along the ridge, passing Hickory Knob in another mile, then a junction with the Hickory Branch Trail, 1½ miles. (This short spur trail leads southeast along Hickory Branch to Dicks Creek and a junction with the Junaluska Trail.)

About two miles southwest from Hickory Branch, the London Bald Trail turns southeast to cross Pine Branch and end at Junaluska Gap. The Junaluska Trail goes north from this gap and the Choga Trail goes south.

Junaluska Trail — Four miles. This trail follows Dicks Creek north from Junaluska Gap to the campground. It crosses three small streams along the way, all bridged. (They are, from south to north, Matherson Branch, Hickory Branch —where the Hickory Branch Trail comes in — and Youngs Camp Branch.) After the third creek crossing, you will reach a junction with the Diamond Valley Trail. Continue northeast another mile to the campground.

Diamond Valley Trail — One mile. This trail, combined with the Laurel Creek Trail, makes a north-south axis through the center of this recreation area. It runs north along a stream from Dicks Creek through a valley to dead-end at a crossing with the Appletree Trail.

Laurel Creek Trail — Two miles, continues north from the end of Diamond Valley Trail along the banks of Piercy Creek (nobody seems to know why this trail is called Laurel Creek Trail) to a junction with the Nantahala Trail.

Choga Trail — Six miles, makes a wide circle around Rich Knob and ends where it began, at Junaluska Gap. Southeast from the gap it touches the headwaters of two forks of Laurel Branch, then continues downhill gently to join Ingram Branch and follow it to Nantahala Lake.

It follows the borders of the lake around to the mouth of Wolf Creek where it turns northwest along the bed of an old dismantled railroad and follows that to Wolf Creek Gap. A short spur trail (about half a mile long) leads south to Forest Road 1311 and a link with the Tusquitee Loop Trail.

From Wolf Creek Gap, the Choga Trail turns north, joining the Junaluska Creek and proceeding northeast, partly along an old road, back to Junaluska Gap.

Tusquitee Loop Trail — 8½ miles. The western end of this loop is on F.R. 1311 at Old Road Gap, about half a mile west of the spur trail that comes south from the Choga Trail on Wolf Creek. It runs south along the Cherokee-Macon County line uphill from an elevation of 3600 feet to 4794 feet in the first mile to reach Shinbone Ridge. It curves southeast along a ridge top of the Valley River Mountains about half a mile to a fork. The left fork will take you back to the road about a mile east of Old Road Gap. The right fork continues southeast another mile past Signal Bald to to Tusquitee Bald (elevation about 5100 feet). You can continue south from Tusquitee Bald as far as Potrock Bald (2½ miles), but there may be some downed timber to climb over.

Retrace your steps northwest past Signal Bald to the east half of the Tusquitee Loop Trail heading back downhill. It soon reaches the headwaters of Big Choga Creek and follows that stream all the way back to F.R. 1311 at the west end of Nantahala Lake. Walk west on the Forest Road half a mile to the spur trail that will take you back to the Choga Trail and eventually to the Apple Tree Group Camp.

Pisgah National Forest

This 478,000-acre forest contains two National Wilderness Areas, Shining Rock and Linville Gorge, and a mountain range with 18 peaks rising over 6,000 feet in elevation. One of these, Mount Mitchell (elevation 6,684 feet), is the highest mountain in eastern North America.

The Carolina Mountain Club sells a well-researched guide to area trails written by one of its members, Bernard Elias of Asheville, called "100 Favorite Trails of the Great Smokies and Carolina Blue Ridge" and selling for $1.

Address of the club is P.O. Box 68, Asheville, North Carolina 28802. Individual dues for membership are $3.00 per year; family memberships are $3.50.

Shining Rock Wilderness, Pisgah District

Location: Southeast of Asheville, bordered by the Blue Ridge Parkway on the south and Interstate 40 on the north. Entrance from the Parkway is at Milepost 420.2 where Forest Road 816 runs 1½ miles north to a dead-end at a parking lot. Another entrance is near the Daniel Boone Boy Scout Camp, located off N.C. Route 215 near Sunburst. A third way in is from off U.S. Route 276 where it crosses the East Fork of the Pigeon River, about three miles northeast of the Blue Ridge Parkway.

Access to the Wilderness interior is by footpath only. Camping permits can be obtained and reservations made by writing the District Ranger, U.S. Forest Service, P.O. Box 8, Pisgah Forest, North Carolina 28768.

Length: The network of trails in Shining Rock Wilderness totals 25 miles.

USGS Quad: Shining Rock, North Carolina

Description: This 13,600-acre preserve is named for the massive, snow-white quartz rock outcrops that occur within it. The largest and most visible of these is Shining Rock itself, located roughly at the center of the area. Elevations vary from 3,500 feet near the mouth of Dry Branch to 6,030 feet on Cold Mountain, an unusual-looking cone-shaped peak at the north end of the Wilderness. The Pigeon River, a major tributary of the Tennessee, has its headwaters in Shining Rock.

This wilderness has very little dense woods. It is dominated rather by flowering trees, shrubs, heath meadows, and scattered trees, particularly at higher elevations. Waterfalls are frequent along the creeks and rivers. Shining Rock is very different in appearance from the other National Wilderness in this district, though they're only a few miles aparts.

139 — Sorrell Creek Trail, 2½ miles. This trail begins on private land at the mouth of Sorrell Creek where it flows into the East Fork of the Pigeon River. It runs east along the creek, climbing gradually from an elevation of 3200 feet at the road to 3600 feet at the western boundary of Shining Rock Wilderness. Continue along the creek and when it forks again, take the left fork. When it forks once more, take the left fork again. Follow that steeply uphill to the stream's headwaters, then continue by a series of switchbacks to the ridgecrest of Cold Mountain at an elevation of almost 5700 feet. Turn sharply east and proceed half a mile along the ridge to the summit of Cold Mountain at an elevation of 6030 feet. The Art Loeb Trail, No. 141, has its northern terminus on the Cold Mountain summit.

141 — Art Loeb Trail. The total length of this trail is 32 miles; 8.7 miles are within the Shining Rock Wilderness.

If you're going to pick one trail to take in Shining Rock, this one will give you the best and most typical look at the terrain. The Art Loeb's northern terminus is on Cold Mountain. It descends from there 0.8 miles to Deep Gap at an elevation of 5000 feet. (A spur trail, Crawford Trail, No. 101, runs east two miles from this point down the east slopes of the mountain by a series of switchbacks to a road that leads east along Crawford Creek 2½ miles to U.S. 276).

The Art Loeb Trail continues south along the cliffs, known as the Narrows, then up to the peak of Stairs Mountain (elevation 5869 feet). Distance from Deep Gap to Stairs Mountain is 2.5 miles. It reaches Shining Rock itself in another half mile. This white bare quartz outcrop has long been a landmark for airplane pilots. It can also be seen for some distance on the ground. You can circle Shining Rock by forking left (southeast) here and walking half a mile to Beech Spring Gap (and junction with Old Butt Knob Trail heading east), then turning right another half mile down to Shining Rock Gap. Or you can continue directly south along the Art Loeb Trail along the western side of the rock to Shining Rock Gap.

Several trails intersect here. One branch of the Art Loeb Trail turns east and descends by a series of sharp switchbacks to the headwaters of the North Prong of Shining Creek.

The main trail continues south, however, along the east side of Shining Rock Ledge 1.5 miles past Flower Knob, Flower Gap and Grassy Cove Top to Ivestor Gap and the southern boundary of the Wilderness. It continues south 2.6 miles across a jeep road, up Tennent Mountain, a grassy bald with an elevation of about 6000 feet, along a ridge to Black Balsam Knob and downhill to the Blue Ridge Parkway at Milepost 420.

The east fork of Art Loeb runs east from Shining Rock, follows the North Prong and then the main part of Shining Creek east to Shining Creek Gap and a junction with the Old Butt Knob trail.

The distance from Shining Rock Gap to Shining Creek Gap is 3.5 miles. Average elevation along the creek is 3800 feet. From Shining Creek Gap this branch of the Art Loeb Trail turns north to reach the Pigeon River at U.S. Route 276 and the eastern boundary of Shining Rock Wilderness.

332 — Old Butt Knob Trail — 3 miles. This trail has its western terminus at Beech Spring Gap, just east of Shining Rock. It runs east up to Dog Loser Knob (elevation 5720 feet), then down to Spanish Oak Gap and back up to Old Butt Knob (elevation about 5560 feet). It turns southeast downhill from the knob, losing some 1700 feet of elevation in two miles to reach Shining Creek Gap and the junction with the Art Loeb Trail.

107 — Little East Fork Trail — 5.8 miles. This trail begins at the south end of a road at the western wilderness boundary that parallels the East Fork of the Pigeon River about a mile south of the mouth of Sorrell Creek.

It follows the river south about 3½ miles. When the river forks, the trail follows the left (northernmost) fork 1½ miles east to its headwaters at Shining Rock Ledge. A short spur trail leads left (north) 0.2 miles to the Art Loeb Trail, then another half mile to Shining Rock Gap.

The Little East Fork Trail turns south along the west side of Shining Rock Ledge paralleling the Art Loeb Trail south 1.3 miles to Ivestor Gap at the southern boundary of the wilderness.

The Art Loeb Trail runs straight south from Ivestor Gap. Another trail heads east and then south on the east slopes of Tennent Mountain on an old logging road. This trail is called Graveyard Fields, 4.5 miles. It proceeds across open fields on Graveyard Ridge. The trail crosses Yellowstone Prong Creek just downstream from a waterfall called Second Falls and upstream from another one called Yellowstone Falls. A few hundred yards south, it reaches the Blue Ridge Parkway just west of Oaklog Gap.

357 — Big East Fork of Pigeon River Trail — 4 miles. This trail leaves the Blue Ridge Parkway at Bridges Camp Gap and runs north to join the East Fork of Pigeon River near its headwaters. It follows the river north into the Wilderness, turns east, still along the river, at the mouth of Greasy Cove Prong. It skirts Nobreeches Ridge on its south side and curves north along the river past the mouth of Little Buckeye Cove on the left. Bennett Branch on the right, and the Rocky Cove on the right to reach U.S. 276 and the eastern boundary of the Wilderness at Big East Fork.

109 — Fork Mountain Trail — 6 miles. This trail runs west along the southern boundary of the Wilderness from a point on the Art Loeb Trail just south of Ivestor Gap. It follows the ridge of Fork Mountain at an elevation of 5400 feet down gradually to 4800 feet — 6 miles to the park's western boundary.

Trails in the Toecane District

Location: In Yancey County north of the towns of Black Mountain and Old Fort, north and west of the Blue Ridge Parkway between Blackstock Knob and Little Switzerland.

Length: The trails in this area around Mt. Mitchell total 43 miles.

USGS Quads: Mt. Mitchell, North Carolina; Montreat, North Carolina

Description: The South Toe River has its beginnings in this district. The river's tributaries flow down from the Black Mountains, highest range in eastern North America. These mountains have 18 peaks over 6,300 feet in elevation.

The Black Mountains get their name from the evergreen forest of spruce and fir that mantle the top of the range. Along the crest of the mountains grows the largest remaining stand of Fraser fir in the United States.

In 1913 the National Forest Service began buying lands that now make up 'the South Toe River basin on the Pisgah National Forest. These lands, comprising about 25,000 acres, were purchased to protect the watershed and to help maintain a continuing supply of timber for a rapidly growing nation.

In 1915, the Mount Mitchell State Park was established on the crest of the range. More than 1450 acres were purchased by the state and set aside to honor Dr. Mitchell for his work and to preserve the natural beauty of the highest peaks in eastern North America.

190 — Mount Mitchell Trail — 5.6 miles. Beginning at Black Mountain Campground, (elevation 3200 feet), this trail climbs through virgin stands of hardwood, crossing numerous lively streams and seeps. Above 4500 feet the trail enters old growth stands of red spruce and Fraser fir. At 3.9 miles the trail intersects with the Maple Camp Bald .Trail, and at 4 miles the trail reaches the Camp Alice trail shelter.

This shelter contains 10 wire bunks and a fireplace. There are pit toilets, a horse corral, and a small separate shelter for cooking nearby. Water is available at the intersection of the Maple Camp Bald Trail.

From the shelter the trail leaves the old roadway and enters the woods, climbing through young stands of spruce, fir and yellow birch. The dead trees you will notice as the trail nears the mountaintop result from a balsam wooly aphid epidemic. At 5.2 miles a trail intersects from the right. It leads to a parking lot in Mt. Mitchell State Park. At 5.4 miles the trail intersects the Mt. Mitchell tower trail. At this point the blue blazes end and the trail descends 0.2 miles to the parking lot on Mount Mitchell.

179 — Black Mountain Trail — 6.5 miles. The southern half of this trail begins at the parking lot on top of Mt. Mitchell and runs north to the Deep Gap Trail Shelter. The northern half begins at Deep Gap and runs north, still along the mountain crest, to Celo Knob. Elevation varies from 6550 to 6645 feet.

This trail is an ungraded one that offers the hiker spectacular views as it crosses Mount Craig (elevation 6645 feet), Big Tom Mountain (elevation 6558 feet), Balsam Cone (elevation 6611 feet), and skirts along the rim of the Middle Creek Natural Area.

At 3.0 miles the trail crosses Potato Hill (elevation 6440) and descends steeply into Deep Gap. At 3.5 miles the trail reaches the Deep Gap Trail shelter. The shelter has four wood bunks and floor space that will sleep six. There's a spring 400 feet down the mountain on a blue blaze spur trail.

From Deep Gap the trail continues north along the mountain crest at the border between national forest land (east of you) and private land (west). In one mile you will reach Winter Star Mountain (elevation 6203) at the top of Colberts Ridge. Two miles farther north you will pass over Gibbs Mountain, then continue ¼ mile to Horse Rock. In another half mile you will reach Celo Knob (elevation 6327 feet).

178 — Colberts Ridge Trail — 3.7 miles. This trail begins on the Colberts Creek Road and terminates in Deep Gap at the trail shelter. To reach the trail head, take Colberts Creek Road west from Ballew's Store on N.C. Route 80 just north of the Carolina Hemlocks Recreation Area. Proceed 0.6 miles along the road to a sign on the right that says "Colberts Creek Trail — Deep Gap 3 miles." There is a place to park your car on the left just before you get to the trail.

The trail ascends gently for the first half mile, and then more steeply as it climbs slowly toward Deep Gap. There are occasional rock outcrops that give the hiker good view of the crest of the Black Mountain Range and the South Toe River Valley. On clear days you can even see such faraway peaks as Roan Mountain, Grandfather Mountain and Table Rock.

At 3.6 miles the trail reaches Deep Gap and intersects the Celo Knob Trail. At 4.7 miles it reaches the Deep Gap Trail Shelter. It continues four miles to reach the entrance to Mt. Mitchell State Park.

Bald Knob Ridge Trail — 2.8 miles. This trail begins on Forest Road 472 about three miles south of Black Mountain Campground and climbs west to the Blue Ridge Parkway at Bald Knob. It ascends steeply for the first mile, then more gently through stands of virgin spruce and Fraser fir. Some water is available along the upper reaches of the trail.

This trail is considered one of the most scenic along the Black Mountain range because of the park-like appearance as you pass through the virgin stands of conifers. About eight hours' hiking time should be planned for the trip up and back to the South Toe River Road (F.R. 472).

Buncombe Horse Range Trail — 8 miles. This trail, white blazed, also begins on F.R. 472 south of Black Mountain campground. It terminates at the Camp Alice trail shelter. As it leaves the road, it ascends on an old logging road for two miles on a moderate grade. Here the trail leaves the old logging road and passes along the side of a field and enters the woods. It passes through open glades and spruce-fir forest as it winds up the mountain. At 4.2 miles it reaches an old railroad tramway. For the next 3.8 miles the trail follows the path of this old tramway. At 7.4 miles a dirt road comes in from the left. This road leads to the entrance of Mount Mitchell State Park, a distance of 1.5 miles. At 8 miles the trail reaches the Camp Alice trail shelter.

182 — Lost Cove Ridge Trail — 3.1 miles. This trail begins at Black Mountain Campground and runs east to terminate at the Green Knob lookout tower on the Blue Ridge Parkway. Elevation at the campground is 3200 feet. Elevation at Green Knob Tower is 5070 feet. No water is available on this trail.

It climbs steeply from Black Mountain Campground for 0.6 miles and more moderately following a ridge line to Green Knob Lookout Tower at 2.8 miles. From there it descends for 3 miles to the parkway. About 10 hours' hiking time should be allowed for a round trip.

Trail 211 continues south from Green Knob across the Parkway to connect with a network of trails in the Grandfather District.

Maple Camp Bald Trail — 7 miles. This trail begins on the Colberts Creek Road (about ¼ mile west of the Colberts Ridge Trail head) and terminates at the Camp Alice trail shelter. It is white blazed. Average hiking time is 6 hours up, 4½ hours down. Elevation is 2920 on the Colberts Creek Road, 5782 at the Camp Alice Shelter. Horseback travel is permitted.

The trail ascends moderately to steeply, following an old logging road for two miles where it enters a graded trail. For the next two miles the trail climbs through old bald areas that afford excellent views of the Middle Creek Natural Area and the South Toe River Valley. At 3.5 miles the trail enters a burned-over area, burned by the Forest Service for eagle habitat improvement.

At 4 miles the trail reaches an old railroad tramway. For the next 3 miles it follows this old railroad right-of-way to the Camp Alice Trail shelter. At 4.9 miles it passes through a small grassy opening on a ridge line. This opening was constructed as an emergency helicopter landing pad by the Forest Service. From this point you look into the south fork of Rock Creek where two natural landslides occurred during the fall of 1973 following heavy rainfalls. As the trail traverses the Rock Creek drainage, one is afforded good views from several rock outcrops.

At 6.5 miles the trail passes directly above one fork of the 1973 landslide. At 6.9 miles the Mt. MItchell Trail comes in from the left, and at 7 miles the trail reaches the Camp Alice shelter. The shelter is 200 feet to the left of the old railroad tramway. Water is available along most of this trail.

161 — Big Butt Trail — 7 miles. This trail follows the crest of Brush Fence Ridge west of Mt. Mitchell and the valley of the Cane River. Its southern terminus is at Balsam Gap on the Blue Ridge Parkway and its northern end is on North Carolina Route 197 at Coxcomb Mountain.

About halfway, you will pass Flat Springs Gap, where a stream provides a water source. This is also a good camping spot. The trail climbs steeply from Balsam Gap to the ridge crest, then continues on more or less level ground.

There are several more primitive trails in this district. They are not maintained, signed, or blazed, and they are recommended only for experienced woodsmen. One of these lies in the newly-designated Craggy Mountain Wilderness Study Area. If you're interested in trying any of these, visit the ranger office in Burnsville for directions.

South Carolina

South Carolina's mountains run along the state's common boundary with North Carolina from King's Mountain State Park and National Military Park westward to the point where South Carolina, North Carolina, and Georgia meet on the shores of the swift-running Chattooga River, a distance of some 100 miles. The state's highest peak, Sassafras Mountain, is in this area, and rises to an elevation of 3550 feet.

Sumter National Forest

Foothills Trail

Location: Andrew Pickens Ranger District, Sumter National Forest. The trail's northern end is at Ellicott's Rock, a scenic point where the Nantahala National Forest of North Carolina, the Chattahoochee National Forest of Georgia, and the Sumter National Forest of South Carolina share a common boundary. The southern terminus is at Long Mountain Lookout Tower just west of Carolina Route 107 near Oconee State Park.

Length: 18 miles including a 2.5 mile spur trail from the Chattooga River to the Chattooga Recreation area.

USGS Quad: Tamassee, South Carolina.

Description: Oconee State Park makes a good overnight stop before embarking on this backpack trip. There's even a grocery store there in case you've forgotten something crucial. The park's 1165 acres lie entirely within the Sumter National Forest today. They were acquired by the state in 1935, primarily to preserve the stands of champion-size virgin hardwood trees. There are 140 campsites and 18 cabins. For further information, write: Oconee State Park, Walhalla, South Carolina 29691.

To reach the beginning point for your hike, drive east from the park to South Carolina Route 107. Continue east across that road, then north to the Long Mountain Lookout Tower. There's a designated campsite at the foot of the tower, too, in case you prefer it to the more civilized state park. Elevation on the mountain is about 2000 feet.

For the first half mile north you will stay on top of Long Mountain. Then there's a gentle drop down to an elevation of about 1600 feet and another designated campsite just south of the trail's crossing of Tamassee Creek near its headwaters.

The entire length of this trail runs through wild, unsettled country, almost entirely wooded and continuously mountainous. It seems appropriate that the area in general, and particularly that portion of the trail which follows the Chattooga River, was chosen for filming part of the movie *Deliverance.*

From Tamassee Creek, the trail climbs gently again to 2000 feet and closely parallels the state highway for about a mile. A short footpath leads west to the highway about a mile north of the creek.

The trail turns east then, heading uphill quickly to Dodge Mountain (elevation 2400 feet) and proceeding parallel to and about a half a mile south of, Tamassee Road, downhill very slowly for two miles to an elevation of 1200 feet at Townes Creek and another designated campsite. Tamassee Road, providing good trail access from highway 107, crosses the trail near this campsite.

The path from Townes Creek north to the next campground at Cherry Hill (and another junction with South Carolina Route 107) is 3.41 miles. For the first three miles you will be following the old Winding Stair Road steadily uphill to about 2300 feet. At the end of the first mile you should have a good view to the east of Towne's Creek Falls. There's another designated back country campsite at the end of the second mile.

Cherry Hill Campground is located at the junction of the trail with highway 107, Big Bend Road and Burrell's Ford Road. The trail leads north and west from here to reach the Chattooga River and state line at Big Bend in just over two miles.

The trail parallels Big Bend Road for the first half mile, then crosses it and heads north along Burrell's Ford Road for just under a mile. It turns west then and follows an old logging road to the base of Big Bend Mountain and another designated campsite.

The trail west continues to climb up Big Bend Mountain, passing beneath its crest at an elevation of about 2700 feet. Eight-tenths of a mile from the campground on the Big Bend Mountain, you will reach the spectacular Chattooga River at Big Bend (about ¼ mile north from Big Bend Falls). The trail follows the river and state line north from here all the way to Ellicott's Rock (about 5½ miles).

Four miles north of Big Bend along the river you will reach Burrell's Ford Campsite in a rare wide grassy expanse of riverbottom land. Half a mile north is Burrell's Ford across the river into Georgia.

The trail parallels Burrell's Ford Road north a short distance, then leaves it to follow the river (at an elevation of about 2100) about half a mile to a designated campsite. Another campsite is located half a mile farther on where East Fork Creek flows into the Chattooga.

A side trail from this creek confluence leads east 2.5 miles to the Chattooga Recreation Area. For the first mile, this side trail follows cliffs above the East Fork. These cliffs are approximately 70 feet high and are continuously wet with ground water seepage. The trail leaves the cliffs and joins an old logging road for about a mile, then continues cross country to the Recreation Area and Walhalla Fish Hatchery. Car access to the Recreation Area is about two miles of very curvy road from state route 107.

Back on the main trail, the path leads north along the Chattooga from the mouth of East Fork Creek about 1.7 miles to Ellicott's Rock and the state line. There's a designated campsite in the first half mile north of East Fork Creek.

West Virginia

Monongahela National Forest

The best hiking in this state, and from a naturalist's point of view some of the most interesting hiking in the entire southern mountains, is in the Monongahela National Forest.

The forest stretches over 820,000 acres of the Allegheny Mountain Range of the Appalachian System, extending from near Eglon in Preston County southwest for about 100 miles to within six miles of White Sulphur Springs in Greenbrier County. From east to west it extends from near Petersburg in Grant County to the junction of the Cherry River with the Gauley River in Nicholas County, or about 80 miles.

The topography, like that of the national forest lands in Virginia, consists of long narrow valleys interspersed with mostly longitudinal ridges. The difference in elevation between the ridges and valleys often is close to a thousand feet.

The forest lying west of the Allegheny Front is included in the Allegheny Plateau. This portion is characterized by high altitude plateaus interspersed with scores of rugged peaks that rise to elevations of more than 4000 feet.

The broad expanses of level land in the Plateau Province provide little protection from wind. The huge numbers of treeless areas can partly be explained by the effects of widespread fires and the low temperatures and frequent winter ice storms that keep vegetation stunted.

The soil in many areas is highly acidic, which also discourages growth of trees. The heath meadows in West Virginia's highlands are comparable to the heath balds on the Appalachian peaks farther south.

More information: From the West Virginia Highlands Conservancy, c/o Carolyn Killoran, 6202 Division Road, Huntington, West Virginia 25705, order Hiking Guide to the Mongahela National Forest and Vicinty ($3.00), Dolly Sods book ($1.25), Otter Creek book (75 cents), Cranberry Back Country book (50 cents).

Information on a new Allegheny Trail can be obtained from the West Virginia Scenic Trails Association, P.O. Box 4042, Charleston, West Virginia 25304. Another group that has done much trail work in the Monongahela National Forest is the Potomac Appalachian Mountain Club, 1718 N. Street, N.W., Washington, D.C. 20036; telephone 202-638-5306.

Detailed hiking trail information is available by sending $1 for two

maps of the forest, North Half and South Half, on a scale where ½"
equals 1 mile. Send for this and other park and forest information, reservations, hunting and fishing information, other data on outdoor recreation, to: West Virginia Department of Natural Resources, Division of
Parks and Recreation, State Capitol, Charleston, W.V. 25305. Local information and maps are available from the Monongahela National Forest, Federal Building, Elkins, West Viriginia 26241; telephone 304-636-
1800.

Trails in the Dolly Sods Scenic Area

Location: Red Creek Campground, which makes a good base camp for
exploration in this area, can be reached by driving east from Laneville
on Forest Road 19 about five miles, then north on Forest Road 75 for
five more miles. The official Scenic Area comprises 10,500 acres located north of Highway 19 and east of Highway 75.

Length: The 10 trails within the Scenic Area total 27 miles

USGS Quads: Laneville, Blackbird Knob, Hopeville, Blackwater Falls,
W. Va.

Description: The Dolly Sods Scenic Area is located in the highlands of
the Allegheny Plateau. It is bordered on the east by Allegheny Front
Mountain and on the west by Cabin Mountain. The area is drained by
Red Creek and its tributaries.

The region that can be identified geographically as Dolly Sods actually includes more than 32,000 acres, much of it in private land. In
1975, a portion of this that overlaps but does not duplicate the Scenic
Area was named one of 16 new National Wilderness Areas by the U.S.
Congress.

511 — Blackbird Knob Trail — 2 miles. This trail runs west from Red
Creek Campground on Forest Road 75 to Blackbird Knob (elevation
3950 feet). The area is mainly open country, with occasional clumps of
red spruce. There are beaver ponds near the point where you cross
Alder Creek, about half a mile from the campground. At the trail crossing of Red Creek, a jeep trail cuts off to the right.

The east side of Blackbird Knob is partially wooded. The trail does
not actually climb to the top of this mountain but skirts its southern
slopes to join the northern end of Red Creek Trail.

The U.S. Geological Survey map shows Blackbird Knob Trail continuing west across the left fork of Red Creek and on to Cabin Mountain, but Forest Service maps show it stopping at the Knob. The West
Virginia Highlands Conservancy people say the portion of the trail west
of the Knob is "essentially nonexistent."

514 — Red Creek Trail — 6¾ miles. Runs south from Blackbird Knob
gently downhill to Red Creek at the point where it forks. (Another trail
goes west here — #553, Breathed Mountain Trail).

Red Creek Trail follows the stream for which it was named its entire
length. The water in Red Creek is an unusual color, a mixture of

brown, red, and yellow that results, according to the Highlands Conservancy booklet, "from tannic acid derived from spruce needles, and from the numerous spaghnum bogs."

From the fork in the creek, the trail continues south down the west banks on steep slopes above the creek at elevations between 3500 and 3600 feet. The area along the creek is wooded.

Soon after you pass a junction with Rocky Point Trail (#554), the Red Creek Trail will cross the creek — just south of the mouth of Fisher Springs. Another trail goes east up Fisher Springs Run.

Red Creek Trail continues south along an old railroad grade above the creek past the official Scenic Area Boundary at the mouth of Big Stonecoal Run. (Stonecoal Trail, #513, branches northwest here across Red Creek on a footbridge.)

Red Creek Trail angles west, still along the creek at an elevation of about 3100 feet, and comes to another trail (#552) at the mouth of Little Stonecoal Run. The trail ends at Laneville Cabin on Forest Road 19 — four miles east of Route 32 and 2½ miles west of Dolly Sods Picnic Area.

553 — Breathed Mountain Trail — 2½ miles, heads west uphill quickly about 300 feet to an elevation of 3800. It turns southwest then across a wide flat treeless area before turning northwest through a forested section, past a stream blocked by beaver dams, and uphill gently west to a junction with Big Stonecoal Trail and Forest Road 80. There's a designated backcountry campsite at this junction.

513 — Big Stonecoal Trail — 4 miles, starts at the headwaters (near highway 80) and follows the streamcourse of Big Stonecoal Run south 3½ miles to a junction with Red Creek Trail. Much of the northern part of the trail is on an old railroad bed; the southern part follows a logging road. Some of the area is forested, but there are also treeless areas. You will pass a number of waterfalls and rapids.

There are four designated camping areas along the way. The first campsite is at the north end of the trail, just off highway 80. The second is just past the mouth of a small intermittent stream in an open area. The third is past a second small stream; and the fourth is at a junction with Dunkenbarger Trail.

Shortly after this junction and about a mile north of Red Creek, you will see Rocky Point Trail coming in from the east.

554 — Rocky Point Trail — 2 miles, connects Red Creek Trail north of Fisher Springs with Big Stonecoal Trail. It heads uphill from Red Creek, then south around the southern end of Breathed Mountain (elevation 3820) and north again to meet Big Stonecoal Trail.

510 — Fisher Springs Trail — 2 miles, runs northeast from the mouth of Fisher Springs Run at Red Creek along an embankment above the creek for a mile, then northeast across a high plateau another mile east to Forest Road 75. Elevation ranges from 3500 feet at the creek to 3900 feet at Forest Road 75.

552 — Little Stonecoal Trail — 1¾ miles, runs north and west from the mouth of Little Stonecoal Run to a junction with Cabin Mountain and Dunkenbarger Trails. It follows the creek for the first mile in a climb of 800 feet from 2800 feet to 3600 feet. Waterfalls are plentiful. We are told that parts of this trail may become overgrown from time to time by fast-growing rhododendron.

Cabin Mountain Trail — 2½ miles, continues northwest from the north end of Little Stonecoal Trail through wooded land and a couple of tree-less areas 2½ miles to Forest Road 80. Then it proceeds along the road to a junction with Stonecoal and Breathed Mountain Trails and on north outside the Scenic Area along the slopes of Cabin Mountain.

552 — Dunkenbarger Run Trail — 1¼ miles, connects Little Stone-coal and Cabin Mountain Trails with Big Stonecoal Trail. It passes through mature forest on a railroad grade.

Rohrbaugh Plains Trail — 3 miles. This trail, opened by the Forest Service and the Potomac Appalachian Trail Club in the fall of 1973, is one of very few in the scenic area that gives you a look at the open plains of the Sods away from a creek bank. It runs north from the Dolly Sods ·Picnic Area to Fisher Springs Run just west of Red Creek. The trail is blazed with blue paint.

Trails in the Otter Creek Area
Location: Take U.S. Route 33 and West Virginia Highway 4 east 12 miles from Elkins to the Alpena Gap Recreation Area. Turn north on a gravel road, past several strip mines, to the road's end at the headwa-ters of Otter Creek. (Forest Road 91, the Stuart Memorial Drive, heads west from this road just before its end to nearby Bear Heaven Camp-ground and on into Elkins.)
Length: There are 56 miles of interconnecting trails in the Otter Creek drainage.
USGS Quads: Parsons, Mozark Mountain, Bowden, and Harman, W. Va.
Description: Otter Creek basin is a high, wild plateau of some 18,000 acres that towers over the hills and valleys that surround it in north-eastern West Virginia. It is completely uninhabited and seems much more remote than its size would indicate because it incorporates an en-tire watershed system. The mountains that rise to the east and west of Otter Creek cut off even the sounds of civilization.

Timber in the area was last cut over 60 years ago; and since there are many fast-growing species of trees in the region, the forest is so well-grown today that ferns and grasses, rhododendron and laurel are the main understory. Most of the terrain is wooded, but there are three notable bogs with Canadian-zone vegetation. Trails that we describe touch two of those bogs.

This area shelters a stable breeding population of black bear. There are also wild turkey, deer and grouse, and trout fishing is allowed on Otter Creek between its mouth at Dry Fork and Big Springs Gap.

Otter Creek and the trail which runs alongside it form the heart of this wilderness. The stream flows north from a swampy area just north of Dry Fork mountain (at the end of the Alpena Gap road) some 11 miles to empty into Dry Fork Creek. A hike along this trail will give you the best look at the entire area. There's an Adirondack shelter located near the trail's midpoint at the mouth of Devil's Gulch Creek at the junction with the Moore Run Trail. Here's a detailed description:

Otter Creek Trail — 11 miles. The entire route follows an old railroad bed and offers fairly easy walking. The trail crosses the creek five times and in wet weather may require some knee deep wading.

After the first mile, Yellow Creek Trail branches off to the left (west).

At mile three, you reach a junction with Mylius Trail, which runs east about half a mile to connect with the area's other major trail running along the top of Shavers Mountain (Shavers Mountain Trail, 11 miles).

At mile four, just past Devil's Gulch, you pass Moore Run Trail heading left (west) up to and along Moore Run Creek. Elevation on the creek at this point is 2750 feet. The shelter here has accommodations for six people, and the area around it is flat and ideal for setting up tents. There is also a picnic table.

Possession Camp Run is the small stream coming down a draw from the east just south of Moore Run.

At mile 5.5 you cross from Randolph into Tucker County. The creek elevation is a little lower now — about 2300 feet. Hills slope up on both sides to more than 330 feet. The creek and trail curve east just past mile 8 at Big Springs Gap. Big Springs Gap Trail runs west from this point to connect with a road that leads north four miles to the town of Parsons.

From Big Springs Gap to the trail's end at Dry Fork Creek is a distance of just over 2¾ miles. There is a steep drop down to Dry Fork and a bridge across it to connect with West Virginia Route 72 some 2½ miles south of the town of Hendricks.

Spur trails east and west from Otter Creek Trail:

Yellow Creek Trail — 3 miles, leads west from an elevation of 2990 feet at Otter Creek along the banks of Yellow Creek for 1¼ miles to a swampy area and a junction with McGowan Mountain Road and the Little Black Fork Trail. Little Black Fork Trail heads west on Little Black Fork Creek one mile, then cuts south across a peak of Dry Fork Mountain — elevation 3850 feet — and down to Stuart Memorial Drive (just east of Stuart Knob).

The Yellow Creek Trail follows McGowan Mountain Road west and north for half a mile before branching left and north to parallel the road for 1¼ miles. This part is within sight and sound of traffic on the road and for that reason is not highly recommended. Yellow Creek Trail deadends at a back country designated campsite and becomes McGowan Mountain Trail just south of the road crossing.

McGowan Mountain Trail — 2⅔ miles, continues north parallel to and on the east side of McGowan Mountain Road. It follows bluffs above the road downhills from 3870 feet to 3350 feet at another designated campsite and a junction with Moore Run Trail.

Moore Run Trail — 4 miles, heads west from Otter Creek (at elevation 2750) at the shelter just north of Devils Gulch. It runs north to join Moore Run, then west to a swampy area (elevation 3200 feet) and junction with Turkey Run Trail at mile 2.5. This spot is one of the three bogs we mentioned earlier. The trail continues west another 1½ miles to the designated campsite (elevation 3350 feet) at a junction with McGowan Mountain Trail just east of McGowan Mountain Road. This trail is uphill all the way, a climb of some 600 feet through mature forest. There are occasional good views of Otter Creek.

Turkey Run Trail — 2 miles, runs north to connect Moore Run Trail with Turkey Run Road (which connects with McGowan Mountain Road and leads north four miles to the town of Parsons). Most of it follows gentle slopes up to, along and down from the wide flat top of a spur of McGowan Mountain. Elevation on top is about 3600 feet. The trail ends at the road near the headwaters of Turkey Run Creek. Much of the timber is spruce and hemlock.

Green Mountain Trail — 5 miles, runs east from Otter Creek at a designated campsite (elevation 2250 feet) just south of Turkey Run Creek. It connects with Shavers Mountain Trail at an elevation of 3700 feet. Most of the climbing is in the first mile, a very steep grade up from 2250 to 3400 feet. The trail on top of Green Mountain after the first mile curves south and then west to reach Shavers Lick Run at mile four. At the headwaters of this creek is another of the Canadian-zone bogs.

Go north downstream half a mile to a fork, then turn south to reach the ridgetop of Shavers Mountain and the junction with Shavers Mountain Trail in another half mile.

Big Spring Gap Trail — one mile, goes west from the Otter Creek Trail at the big bend three miles from the junction with Route 72 at Dry Fork. There's a designated campsite at the junction of Otter Creek and Big Spring Gap Trails. You will climb in the mile's walk from 2050 feet at Otter Creek to 2550 feet at the wilderness boundary and road that leads north to Parsons.

Shavers Mountain Trail — 13 miles. This trail follows the ridge top of the mountain that forms the eastern boundary of the Otter Creek Wilderness. Portions of this trail can be found farther south in the Greenbrier District of the forest, but there are gaps between that part of the trail and this.

Shavers Mountain Trail actually begins at the Alpena Gap Recreation Area on U.S. 33, but some maps label the first two miles as Middle Mountain Trail. You can also reach it from the headwaters of Otter Creek and beginning of the Otter Creek Trail by taking the Hedrick Camp Cutoff Trail one mile east to the top of Shavers Mountain.

About 3¾ miles north of the Hedrick Camp Cutoff, you will come to another link with the Otter Creek Trail. The Mylius Trail runs downhill and west about a mile to Otter Creek Trail. It also runs downhill off the east slopes of Shavers Mountain to connect with West Virginia Route 12 at its junction with state route 162 on Glady Creek.

Elevation on the Shavers Mountain Trail varies between 3600 and 3815 feet. The last 2½ miles follow a dirt road that leads east across Dry Fork to West Virginia Route 72 five miles south of Hendricks.

Loop trips can be made using a variety of the side trails connecting the long Shavers Mountain and Otter Creek Trails.

Tennessee

This state is unique among those in the Southern Mountains in that its officials have made a concerted effort to coordinate their outdoor recreation facilities into an interrelated system. Now being developed is a series of seven long scenic trails that will incorporate many existing trails, campgrounds and scenic areas in state and city parks, the Cherokee National Forest and the Great Smoky Mountains National Park. From a total of 21 state parks existing in 1965, there are now more than 115 existing and proposed outdoor recreation areas.

The need for a wide distribution of trails of all types was recognized by the Tennessee Trails System Act of 1971. The Act provides the authority and guidelines for development of hiking, equestrian and bicycle trails in and near urban areas and in the remote wilderness areas in the state.

Two trail systems were authorized by this Act. The Tennessee Recreation Trail System will be composed of relatively short, urban-oriented trails while the Tennessee Scenic Trail System will be made up of long distance trails located in the remote natural areas of the state.

A trails coordinator was hired by the state to plan routes and acquire land, and an umbrella Tennessee Trails Association was formed in 1968 to represent the various groups, both public and private, with an interest in trails.

More Information: Trails Administrator, Tennessee Department of Conservation, 2611 West End Avenue, Nashville, Tenn. 37203.

Cherokee National Forest

The Cherokee National Forest forms a long, narrow strip along the eastern border of Tennessee from Virginia to Georgia with its eastern boundary following the state line. The forest's 600,000 acres are split into two sections by the Great Smoky Mountains National Park.

North of the park, the mountains are long, narrow ridges running from northeast to southwest. Between the ridges are valleys wide enough to support some settlement. South of the park, the forest tends to be more rugged and sparsely inhabited. The Tellico Ranger District immediately south of the Smokies is particularly wild. Government owned land there is of considerable size. Together with the adjoining areas of the Nantahala National Forest in North Carolina, the Tellico forms one of the largest blocks of wild land in the Appalachians.

The Cherokee offers splended opportunites for hikers. Numerous trails follow its creeks and ridges, and some of these are seldom travelled. Many trails are suitable for day hikes, and trips of a week or more also can be arranged.

Trails in the Tellico Ranger District

The Tellico Ranger District runs from the Little Tennessee River in the north to a point about five miles south of the town of Tellico Plains. It has few roads and fewer settlements, but many trails.

This area also has the European wild boar, a distinction whose value is rather dubious. It seems that in the first decade of this century, an English company called Whiting Manufacturing bought some large tracts of timber in North Carolina, just across the state line from the Tellico. The company's hired manager decided to start a hunting lodge on Hooper Bald, one of the peaks of the Snowbird range, brought in several wild animals, including wild boar. When the project was disbanded, the boar took to the woods.

Today the animals are firmly established in the Tellico and adjoining areas in North Carolina as well as in substantial areas of the Smokies. They can weigh anywhere from 200 to 400 pounds, and they are armed with razor-like tusks and very sharp hoofs.

These animals are also hunted for about two months of the year, and as a result they are likely to be extremely cautious about getting near people. They are generally nocturnal and tend to spend the day holed up out of sight in a rhododendron thicket or some similarly out-of-the-way spot.

Certainly, however, if you see a wild boar, give it a wide berth. Your chances of actually seeing one are fairly slim, although you may well see the rooted up earth that boars leave behind when they feed. However, boar hunters are a different matter. During the October and November boar season, stick to established trails and avoid trying any cross country exploring. While on the trails, wear something bright red or international orange. You should also do this during the November and December deer season.

Road access to this district is via the town of Tellico Plains, TN, on Tennessee Route 68. From there, proceed on Forest Roads.

95 — Fodderstack Trail — The south end of this trail is actually on Bob Bald, a peak on the North Carolina side of the border. It connects there with trails in the Nantahala National Forest's Cheoah district. The north end of the hiking trail is at the junction with the Pinestand Ridge motorcycle trail at big Fodderstack. Road access from the north is through the jeep trail which ends at the junction of Forest Roads 26 and 59 about five miles north of the Double Camp Recreation Area.

Length: Total length from Bob Bald to Farr Gap is 11 miles. The hiking trail from Bob Bald to Big Fodderstack is about five miles.

USGS *USGS Quads:* Big Junction, Tennessee, and Whiteoak Flats, Tennessee.

Description: The Trail heads north from Bob Bald (5100 feet), heading downslope along the ridge line to Cherry Log Gap which is 4400 feet above sea level. The trail from the north Fork of Citico Creek comes in at the gap.

In this area, the trail often follows the state line. The trail itself is marked with white paint blazes shaped like large block "i's". The state boundary is marked with orange paint blazes on trees. Do not confuse the two marks, since the trail splits from the state line north of Cherry Log Gap.

Between Cherry Log Gap and Big Fodderstack, the trail changes little in elevation. It generally skirts the peaks — Chestnut Knob and Rockstack — on their western slopes, returning to the ridge line at the gaps. Lowest point along this section is 3800 feet in Harrison Gap, just south of Big Fodderstack.

A few extremely large hemlocks and oaks are found along the trail here, and there are numerous excellent views to both east and west.

There is no water along the trail from Cherry Log Gap to Fodderstack. In a few spots, there are damp rocks that might produce enough flow to provide drinking water in wetter times, but don't count on it.

The slopes above and below the trail where it circles around the peaks are too steep to allow for camping, but in the gaps there are flat areas large enough to put up a tent.

In the gap immediately north of Big Fodderstack, another trail crosses the path. This is the Pinestand Ridge motorcycle trail. Take it to the left, and it leads down Pinestand Ridge to Citico Creek. Take it to the right, and it leads to the jeep road that heads north to Farr Gap.

Three hiking trails branch off from the jeep road north of Fodderstack. In order, south to north, they are the Mill Branch Trail (which goes west), the Crowder Branch Trail (which crosses), and the Stiff Knee Trail (which goes east). It is less than a mile from the Pinestand — Fodderstack Trail junction to the intersection with the Mill Branch Trail.

96 — Mill Branch Trail — Between the motorcycle trail north of Fodderstack to Forest Road 59 about 2 1/2 miles north of Double Camp Recreation Area.

Length: 3.2 miles Whiteoak Flats
Description: This trail is not shown on the USGS Quad. Mills Branch is a creek running west from just below Big Stack Gap, which is 3400 feet high. Heading east the trail drops to 3250 in a few hundred yards, reaching the head of the stream at that altitude. About 1/2 mile downstream a tributary enters from the south, and another ¾ mile along, another stream enters from the same direction. Between these two streams, the trail drops about 700 feet, from 3000 feet to 2300. One mile beyond the second tributary, the trail meets Forest Road 59. Mill Branch flows into Doublecamp Creek just west of the road.

About one mile north of Mill Branch, a trail heads east from the jeep road down to Slickrock Creek. Just north of this, the Crowder Creek Trail goes west from an open area that was once a homestead site.

84 — Crowder Creek Trail — From jeep trail 59 west to Forest Road 59 about three miles north of Double Camp Recreation Area.

Length: 2.5 miles

USGS Quad: Whiteoak Flats, TN

Description: From the jeep road, the trail drops 200 feet in about 1/2 mile, hitting the head of Crowder Branch at 3100 feet. It follows the north bank of the stream for the next mile, and in the last mile, crosses the stream several times. Three tributary streams come in from the south along the trail.

The ground flattens out somewhat as Crowder Branch nears Doublecamp Creek. The west end of the trail strikes the road just south of the bridge over Double Camp. Elevation, 1900 feet.

106 — Stiff Knee — This trail heads east from Farr Gap where the Fodderstack Jeep Trail meets Forest Roads 59 and 26. It follows Slickrock Creek as far as the Little Tennessee River. See North Carolina, Cheoh District of the Nantahala National Forest for details on the eastern end of the trail.

Length: 4 miles

USGS Quad: Whiteoak Flats, TN; and Tapoco, N.C. *Description:* The trail goes east along the slope of the ridge from Farr Gap, dropping gradually from 2800 feet to 2400. It then drops into the hollow and Slickrock Creek which it follows eastward.

Six separate trails fan out from Citico Creek and Forest Road 35 between Boundary Lake and Double Camp Recreation Areas. From north to south, they are:

100 — Rocky Flats — The north end of this trail is at Forest Road 59 about 2 miles north of the Double Camp Recreation Area. The south end is at Forest Road 35, 1/2 mile east of Double Camp.

Length: 3.4 miles

USGS Quad: Whiteoak Flats TN.

Description: The trail heads east from 59 between Mill Branch and Rocky Flats Branch at about 1850 feet. It goes southeast uphill to 2300 feet and then back down to cross Rocky Flats Branch at 2100 feet about 1/2 mile from the trail head. Shortly, it crosses a prong of Rocky Flats Branch and then goes southwest back up the slope of Pine Ridge. It follows the 2300 foot contour along the ridge before dropping down a draw to Citico Creek and the road at 1500 feet.

Going north from Boundary Lake, Forest Road 35 winds downhill into the valley of Citico Creek. Where it strikes the creek, a road branches off to the east, crossing the creek. This is Forest Road 29 which dead ends less than half a mile from its beginning. The remaining trails in this area branch off from 29. From north to south they are the Pinestand Ridge Trail, the North Fork Citico Trail, the Brush Mountain Trail, the South Fork Citico Trail, and the Grassy Branch Trail.

99 — Pinestand Ridge Trail — Between Forest Road 29 and the Fodderstack Trail.

Length: 5.1 miles *USGS Quad:* Whiteoak Flats, TN *Description:* This is the motorcycle trail mentioned in the description of the Fodderstack Trail. Since it is a motorcycle trail, it is likely to be an undesirable spot on summer weekends. However, during the week and off season there is little traffic. It is the most direct route between Forest Road 29 and the Fodderstack Trail.

From the dead end of 29, the trail crosses the creek heading northeast at about 1660 feet. Once across, it climbs rather quickly with several switchbacks up to over 2000 feet. It crosses a small creek just as it starts up the hill. This is the last water on the trail.

Once up on the ridge, the trail climbs steadily but gradually up to about 4000 feet at its junction with the Fodderstack Trail.

98 — North Fork of Citico Creek Trail — From Forest Road 29 to Fodderstack Trail.

Length: 3.5 miles *USGS Quad:* Whiteoak Flats, TN. *Description:* Glenda Daniel and Jerry Sullivan hiked his trail and found it extremely beautiful and also extremely strenuous. It had been three years since a trail maintenance crew had been through here, and a lot can happen in the southern mountains in that amount of time. Rhododendron and laurel along with herbaceous growth of various kinds had obscured the trail in many areas. Apparently a wind storm had been through at least once, because downed timber on the upper creek was very common. In places the combination of fallen logs and rhododendron reduced the trail to a tunnel, and they had to crawl through on their bellies.

You should be prepared for eventualities like this, however, when you depart from the more commonly used trails. Altogether, it took them nine hours to negotiate the length of this trail. Fortunately, they had allowed ample time to complete the loop hike they had laid out for themselves, so the long struggle up the creek didn't throw them off schedule. Since they had to follow the creek bed to get to their destination, they couldn't get seriously lost even if they could not follow the exact route of the trail.

Water was no problem, since they were walking along the bank of a stream and even a serious delay would not have left them short of food. They had planned a three-day hike, but had taken along an extra day's food as an emergency ration.

The lower portion of the creek, about two miles long, gave no warning of what was to be. Starting from 29, they crossed Citico Creek on a low water bridge. Just across the creek, the trail forked and they took the northern fork to the left. Following along the creek for a few hundred yards, they came to the confluence of the North and South Forks of Citico Creek. Here the trail forks again, and they again took the northern fork. It led across an old bridge that may have been built to support a narrow gauge logging railroad. The bridge had a concrete and steel structure, but it was covered with old planking that was beginning to rot out.

Beyond the bridge, the trail follows what is apparently an old road. bed or railroad bed. It is broad and level and easy to follow. Block "i" blazes in white on tree trunks are frequent and easily visible. After about a mile and a quarter, a tributary stream comes in from the north, and a half mile farther along, there is another one. Between these two, two streams come in from the south.

A few hundred yards beyond the last tributary, two streams, the Indian Valley Branch and another unnamed creek, flow into the Citico from the North. Up to this point, good campsites have been common, but beyond here, the creek banks get steeper and the hollow gets narrower, and campsites are scarce.

Glenda and Jerry camped just beyond Indian Valley Branch.

They started out the next morning, things changed quickly. The slopes of the hollow got steeper and closer together. There were a lot of hemlock trees and ferns, and the air was a bit damp. The white blazes disappeared, to be replaced by red plastic ribbons tied around tree trunks.

The guy who had tied these streamers up had been very frugal. He wasn't going to waste any plastic, so he tied them about 200 yards apart. Also, they had been tied on a long time ago, and long exposure to the weather had bleached them out to a powdery gray that almost matched the trunks of the yellow poplars they were often wrapped around.

The only way to operate in these situations is slowly. Rushing ahead if you are going wrong will only make you wronger faster. If you still can't see anything, take your pack off and lean it against a tree. Backtrack a little ways; investigate in a couple of directions.

If you still can't find anything that looks like a trail, but you know you are supposed to keep following the stream bank, then it is time to treat the whole excursion like a cross country hike. Just pick out the easiest looking route in the direction you want to go.

Taking it slow in a sense is armchair advice. When you are picking your way over slippery, moss covered rocks, struggling through the rhododendron patches, and scrambling up steep slopes, there ain't no way to go but slow.

Alertness is a quality that should be cultivated by hikers. It is very easy when you are strolling along a smooth path to start day dreaming, to amble along with your head miles away. But when the trail ahead is obscure and the terrain demands that you watch where you put your feet, you will find yourself noticing a lot of other things too: the tiny wildflower on the forest floor or the wren flitting about in the underbrush. It's a great way to clean out your senses.

In the two miles beyond Indian Valley Branch, a tributary comes into Citico from the north, then three come in from the south, another from the north, and a fourth from the south. You are climbing all this time, from 2200 feet at Indian Branch to over 3000 at the last tributary. The creek tumbles over two rather spectacular waterfalls along this stretch, the highest having a single drop of perhaps 40 feet.

A few hundred yards beyond that fourth southern tributary, the creek forks, and the trail follows the north fork to the left. The rhododendron virtually enclosed the narrow stream at this point, and the trail simply follows the rocks of the creek bed uphill. If you are going on to hike along the Fodderstack Trail, you should fill your canteens before you leave the creek behind.

The trail ends at Cherry Log Gap, where Glenda and Jerry actually saw a downed cherry log. They also saw the Fodderstack Trail running north-south as well as signs identifying the land to the east as a North Carolina bear sanctuary. They had arrived.

97 — Brush Mountain Trail — From Forest Road 29 to Forest Road 217-H. 217-H is basically not navigable by ordinary automobiles. However, one can drive a short distance north from Forest Road 217 at Beech Gap along this route. The condition of the road will depend a lot on the weather, but since the weather can change rather rapidly, it is best to err on the side of caution and do less driving and more walking.

Length: 6 miles *USGS Quads:* Big Junction, TN, and Whiteoak Flats, TN. *Description:* At the dead end of Forest Road 29, cross Citico Creek on the low water bridge. Follow the trail along the creek to the left until you reach the bridge where the two forks of Citico Creek flow together. Turn right there and follow the south fork of the creek. Less than 1/2 mile south of this point, Ike Camp Branch flows into Citico Creek from the southeast. The trail forks here, and you will follow the left fork up Ike Camp Branch. The elevation here is about 1900 feet, and the trail climbs steadily along the creek. Two tributaries come in from the north, then about 1 1/2 miles from the creek mouth, the stream forks. The trail follows the left fork uphill, passing the head of the creek at 3300 feet and climbing steeply up onto Brush Mountain at 3600 feet.

Turning southeast, the trail climbs slowly along the ridge top, reaching 4000 feet in about 1/2 mile. Where the trail ends at the road, it is possible to turn north, follow 217-H to its end, and then head east·to hit the Fodderstack Trail at the state line near Cherry Log Gap.

105 — South Fork of Citico Creek Trail — From Forest Road 29 to Forest Road 2l7-G and Forest Road 217-H. 217-G is another short dead end road that heads north from 217-I. It is also reasonably passable in good weather, but not really recommended for travel in an ordinary passenger car. According to rangers at the Tellico district station, the first mile of the road north of 217-I is all right, but it is pushing your luck to try to drive beyond that point unless you have a four-wheel drive vehicle.

Length: 7.8 miles

USGS Quads: Whiteoak Flats, TN; and Big Junction, TN. *Description:* From the dead end of Forest Road 29, cross Citico Creek on the low water bridge and follow it around to the left for a few hundred yards. Where the north and south forks of Citico Creek come together, turn south along the west bank of the south fork. After 1/2 mile, the Brush Mountain trail branches off to the left.

The Citico Creek Trail continues south just over a mile to where Eagle Branch flows in from the south and the South Fork of Citico turns east. In that mile, three tributaries flow in from the west. About ¾ mile east of this turn, the trail climbs up on the ridge along the north bank, rising about 400 feet in l/2 mile. It follows the 2800 foot contour southeast, continuing on the slope for about ¾ mile, and climbing up to 3000 feet at the top of a narrow, steepsided gorge.

The trail crosses a tributary that comes in from the northeast and then turns southeast for a mile, crossing another tributary from the southwest and one from the northeast. Where a second tributary comes in from the southwest, a branch of the trail leads up it for l/2 mile to the end of Forest Road 2l7-G.

A few yards beyond the branch, another stream comes in from the northeast. The trail then goes through a narrow gorge and then out onto a wider, flatter area where the trail stays south of the creek. The creek then divides and the trail follows the south (right) fork.

The trail follows the stream uphill to about 3600 feet, and then beyond the head of the creek goes steeply up the draw, climbing about 650 feet in just over l/2 mile, crossing 2l7-H and ending at the state line.

9l — Grassy Branch Trail — From Forest Road 29 to Forest Road 217-I. *Length:* 4.5 miles *USGS Quads:* Whiteoak Flats, TN; and Big Junction, TN. *Description:* While Forest Road 29 provides road access from the north, this trail actually begins where Eagle Branch flows into the South Fork of Citico Creek. From there at an altitude of 2200 feet, the trail goes south climbing slowly along the creek to 2400 feet where Eagle Branch and Grassy Branch fork. Grassy Branch is the fork to the east (left). The trail follows it for about a mile and a half, goes through a narrow draw and past a tributary at 3l50 feet. The creek then forks again, with the trail following the western fork about 1/3 mile north to the head of the creek. From there it is an easy climb for about 200 yards to 217-I.

102 — Flats Mountain Trail — From Forest Road 217-I just west of the Hemlock Knob Fire Tower north to Forest Road 35 about one mile north of the turnoff to the Indian Boundary Recreation Area.

Length: 6.5 miles USGS Quads: Whiteoak Flats, TN; and Big Junction, TN. Description: The trail begins with a short climb from 217-I up to the ridge of Flats Mountain, a narrow north-south ridge that forms the trail route for most of its length. Reaching the crest of the ridge at 3800 feet, the trail heads north, reaching the high point of Flats Mountain (3853 feet) in about 1/2 mile. The trail continues north past the head of Footes Creek to Forest Road 35.

The area between Forest Road 217-I and Forest Road 210 which parallels the Tellico River, contains six hiking trails. All of them follow creeks over most of their length. **103 — The Long Branch Trail —** From Forest Road 217-2 about 1/2 mile north of Forest Road 210. The trail dead ends at the right of way of the proposed Forest Road 217, a highway that was laid out to travel along Sassafras Ridge into North Carolina. Complaints by environmental groups have been successful in stopping the construction of the road, and the Forest Service is currently looking for an alternate route which will have less impact on the semi-wilderness character of the Tellico area.

Length: 2.7 miles USGS Quad: Big Junction, TN. Description: The trail heads north from the North River Road at about 1700 feet, following the banks of Long Branch Creek. It climbs to 1800 feet and continues along the west bank of the creek. After 1 to 1 1/2 miles, the trail leaves the creek to head uphill toward Sassafras Ridge, climbing from 2000 feet at the head of the creek to 3200 at the ridge.

101 — Hemlock Trail — From 217-2 about 1 1/2 miles north of Forest Road 210 to the Hemlock Knob tower. The tower is just south of Forest Road 217-1.

Length: 3.5 miles USGS Quads: Big Junction, TN, and Bald River Falls, TN. Description: The trail follows Hemlock Creek north from the road, beginning at an altitude of 1800 feet. Tributaries come into Hemlock from the northwest at 1/3 mile, the northeast at one mile, and from the northwest again in another 1/2 mile. About 1/4 mile beyond this last tributary, the creek forks, and the trail follows the right or east fork. From there, at 2100 feet, the trail climbs steeply for about 2 miles up to Hemlock tower at 4019 feet. The road lies just to the north about 150 feet below the tower.

92 — McNabb Creek Trail — From Grassy Gap on Forest Road 217-1 south to 217-2 about 1 mile west of the North River Recreation Area. The Grassy Branch Trail ends just across from this trail at 217-1.

Length: 3.7 miles USGS Quads: Big Junction, TN, and Bald River Falls, TN. Description: Heading south from Grassy Gap, the trail heads downhill quickly to the head of McNabb Creek which it follows for the remainder of its length.

In the first mile, you will descend 600 feet from 3400 to 2800. At 2800 feet, major tributaries come into the creek from east and west. In the next mile, the trail descends another 600 feet as the banks gradually widen out.

For the next 1 1/4 miles, the altitude drops gradually from 2200 to 2000 feet. Hampton Lead is the long mountain to the west, and Brushy Ridge parallels the creek to the east. The last 1/4 mile of the trail is a gradual downslope to 1900 feet.

93 — Laurel Branch Trail — From Forest Road 217-2 about three miles north of the North River Recreation Area. The trail ends at Forest Road 217-1.

Length: 3.1 miles *USGS Quad:* Big Junction , TN *Description:* The trail leaves the road headed north at about 2000 feet following Laurel Branch upstream. A tributary comes in from the west at about 1/4 mile, another at one mile, and a third at 1 1/2 miles. Two more streams come in from the west with the next mile. Beyond this last, a tributary comes in from the east, and the trail takes the left fork. The altitude here is about 2700 feet. The trail follows the creek up to about 3000 feet and then leaves it to climb rather steeply up to 3800 feet to Sassafras Ridge.

137 — Big Cove Branch Trail — Follow Forest Road 217-2 about five miles beyond the point where it spiits off from Forest Road 210. The trail ends at jeep trail 86 about two miles north of Forest Road 210.

Length: 3.2 miles *USGS Quad:* Big Junction, TN *Description:* The trail crosses the North River, heading southeast from Forest Road 217-2 and 2000 feet. The trail skirts the hillside for a short distance and then follows Big Cove Branch. It follows the creek for about two miles and then, at 3000 feet, climbs Whigg Ridge to Deep Gap at 3500 feet and then goes quickly downslope to the Sycamore jeep trail at 3000 feet.

89 — Sugar Cove Trail — North from Forest Road 217-2 about six miles beyond its junction with Forest Road 210. Ends at the state line.

Length: 2.4 miles *USGS Quad:* Big Junction, TN. *Description:* The trail follows the hillside above Sugar Cove, climbing from 2700 feet at the trailhead up to 4320 at Beech Gap along the state line ridge.

There are five trails on the Tellico south of Forest Road 210:

88 — Bald River Trail — The north end of the trail is at Forest Road 210 just west of the Bald River Falls Recreation Area. The south end is at Forest Road 126 immediately west of Holly Flats Recreation Area at the bridge over Little Cove Branch.

88-A — Cow Camp Trail — This one-mile trail connects the Bald River Falls Recreation Area with Forest Road 210 over a low hill.

Length: The Bald River Trail is 5.6 miles. Cow Camp Trail is one mile. *USGS Quad:* Bald River Falls, TN *Description:* The trail follows the river for its entire length. The elevation is 1400 feet where the Bald River

flows into the Tellico and 1840 where the Little Cove Branch crosses
Forest Road 126.

107 — Henderson Mountain Trail — The trail begins at Forest Road
210 about five miles east of the Bald River Falls campground. It ends
at the Sugar Mountain motorcycle trail (Trail 90) on Sugar Mountain.
Length: 5.7 miles *USGS Quads:* Bald River Falls, TN; and Big Junction,
TN. *Description:* This trail actually begins on the south bank of the Tellico River across from Forest Road 210, so there is no direct road access from this end. The trail crosses a low hill, climbing from 1600 to
1920 feet, and then drops back to 1760 where it hits Panther Branch
which it follows for about two miles.

Leaving the creek, the trail climbs to Henderson Top, 2800 feet and
then goes southeast along Camp Lead, crossing Forest Road 126 at
2600 feet and then going up Maple Lead to the summit of Sugar
Mountain, 3600 feet.

Virginia

The southern Appalachians begin in Virginia. To the north, the peaks of
the Appalachian chain are comparatively low in elevation. The mountain
country is somewhat less rugged and more open to settlement.

Virginia is a great place for exploration, especially for hikers without
long experience in wilderness travel. Roads flank the ridges and cross
the mountains at frequent enough intervals to make most areas accessible even to weekend travellers. If you do get lost, civilization is generally nearer at hand than in the less settled areas to the south.

More information: The Appalachian Trail in this state is maintained
by nine separate organizations which are each responsible for a section of the path. If you are interested in meeting other hikers, get in
touch with these clubs. The Appalachian Trail Conference, Inc., P. O.
Box 236, Harpers Ferry, West Virginia 25425 can give you information
on the local clubs.

George Washington
National Forest

The George Washington comprises well over 1,000,000 acres of land.
It extends from the northern edge of the Jefferson Forest in the south
to Strasburg, Virginia., only 100 miles from Washington, D.C., in the
north. It is divided into sections that follow the ridges northeast, extending into West Virginia in many areas.

Maps and information: Forest Supervisor, George Washington National
Forest, 210 Federal Blvd., Harrisonburg, Virginia 22801; telephone
703-433-2491.

Trails in the Dry River District
The district offers a number of trails scattered over its length.
Current information: District Ranger, 510 N. Main, Bridgewater, Virginia
22812; telephone 703-828-2591.

1020 — Shenandoah Mountain
Location: Take U.S. 33 to the Virginia-West Virginia border and turn
south on Forest Road 85. A short distance from the highway, the road
forks. The left fork climbs to the High Knob Fire Tower while the right
fork continues south briefly before deadending at the trail head. South
end of the trail is at Bother Knob.
USGS Quad: Brandywine, Virginia.
Description: The trail follows the ridge line south from High Knob, with
elevations varying from about 3600 to 3800 feet. On the southern half
of the trail, two side trails come in, almost together, from the west. One
leads to a dirt road that parallels the trail. The other crosses that road
and heads down Miller Run to end on private property.
To the south, the trail climbs to 4344 on Bother Knob, then goes
briefly downhill to a dirt road (Forest Road 85). You can take this road
south about two miles to Virginia 924. Or you can take it east to Flagpole Knob and the Slate Springs Mountain Trail about two miles away.

428 — Slate Springs Mountain Trail
Location: From Flagpole Knob about five miles north out a dirt road
(Forest Road 85) from Virginia 924 to U.S. 33 at Rawley Springs, Vir-
ginia.
Length: Eight miles
USGD Quads: Brandywine, Virginia, Rawley Springs, Virginia
Description: Forest Road 85 continues east from Flagpole Knob for a
few hundred yards. Trail 428AA branches off to the south, and 428
continues east where the road turns sharply north.
The trail follows the ridge east, dropping from over 4000 feet to
3900 feet about one mile out. There, the trail forks with 428 heading
north and 428A heading south.
Trail 428 heads north along a narrow ridge that flattens out at the
hamlet of Maple Springs about two miles away. The trail follows the
dirt road north through the community. Where the road ends on Chestnut Ridge, the trail turns east, beginning a slow descent along the
ridge. It continues to drop until it reaches Bum Run, which it parallels
on a dirt road into Rawley Springs.

428A — Slate Springs Trail
Location: From Trail 428 east of Flagpole Knob to Virginia 257 near
the forest boundary about 11 miles west of Dayton.
Length: Four miles
USGS Quad: Brandywine, Virginia, Reddish Knob, Virginia, and Briery
Branch, Virginia
Description: From the fork where it splits from Trail 428, this trail
heads southeast down a ridge. At Pond Knob, trail divides in three;

take the middle tine. It crosses Oak Knob at 3500 feet and goes east from there to a fork. Take the south fork, continuing out the ridge. At another fork about ½ mile farther, take the left — east — tine. The trail ends at the road near Rocky Run.

428AA — Slate Springs Trail
Location: From Forest Road 85 at Flagpole Knob to Hone Quarry Run. Trail down Hone Quarry Run continues as far as Hone Quarry Dam. Dirt Road leads to Hone Quarry Recreation Area.
Length: Four miles
USGS Quads: Brandywine, Virginia, and Reddish Knob, Virginia
Description: The trail heads south from the road, dropping from 4200 feet to 3400 feet in the first mile. Altitude is 2300 feet where the trail meets Hone Quarry Run. From there, follow the jeep trail southeast to the campground.

435 — Hone Quarry Mountain
Location: Take Virginia 257 west from Dayton. Inside the forest boundary, road turns south, becomes Virginia 924. Trailhead is ½ mile south of Forest Road 62 on 924. To get to the other end, take 924 west to Forest Road 85 and north one mile to Forest Road 539, which heads back east.
Length: Eight miles
USGS Quads: Reddish Knob, Virginia, and Briery Branch, Virginia
Description: Forest Road 259 is a gated road, open only during hunting season. The trail follows it east for two miles, dropping steadily from 3900 feet to 3400. One mile beyond the end of the road, the trail forks, with the south fork being a side trail down the side of Hone Quarry Ridge to Mines Run and the Mines Run Trail.

One mile beyond this fork is another. The Big Hollow Trail goes off to the left. In another mile, a trail branches to the right — south — to Virginia 924 just below Briery Branch Dam. The main trail continues on down the ridge to the road, elevation 1700 feet.

430 — Big Hollow Trail
Location: From the Hone Quarry Mountain Trail to the Hone Quarry Recreation Area.
Length: Two miles
USGS Quad: Reddish Knob, Virginia
Description: Heading east from the Hone Quarry Mountain trail at 3220, the trail drops steadily to 1950 where it hits Hone Quarry Run just above the campground.

Mines Run Trail
Location: From Virginia 924 just above Briery Branch Dam to a dead end up Mines Run.
Length: 3 miles
USGS Quad: Reddish Knob, Virginia
Description: The trail follows the creek from the road at 2050, feet,

climbing to 2600 feet at the dead end. About halfway along, a trail to the north climbs up the ridge to the Hone Quarry Mountain Trail.

431 — Timber Ridge Trail
Location: Begins at the Reddish Knob fire tower. Take Virginia 924 10 miles from the forest boundary to Forest Road 85. Turn left — south — and go two miles to the Reddish Knob tower. At the eastern end, take Forest Road 101 four miles south from 924. The trail head is just north of Hearthstone Lake.
Length: Eight miles
USGS Quad: Reddish Knob, Virginia
Description: The Reddish Knob tower is at 4397. The trail heads east from there, dropping downhill for about ½ mile to a fork at 4100 feet. Take the south (right) fork down Timber Ridge.

Four miles from the trailhead, the Sand Spring Mountain Trail branches off to the left at 3700 feet. The Timber Ridge Trail goes southeast down Hearthstone Ridge, dropping steadily to 1781 feet at the road.

Sand Spring Mountain Trail
Location: From the Timber Ridge Trail to Forest Road 101 two miles north of Hearthstone Lake.
Length: Three miles
USGD Quad: Reddish Knob, Virginia
Description: Leaving the Timber Ridge trail at 3700 feet, the trail heads east down to 2000 feet at the road.

425 — Chestnut Ridge
Location: From Bridgewater, Virginia, take Virginia Route 42 east to Virginia 727, just outside of town, and follow the latter road southeast to Virginia 730. Take 730 into the forest to the Stokesville community. Take Virginia 718 west past Stokesville. Just past the bridge over the Little River, turn north on Forest Road 101 for about 500 feet. Then go west on Forest Road 95. After another 500 feet a short, deadend road turns north to the trail head. Western end of the trail is at Little Bald Knob.
Length: Seven miles
USGS Quads: Stokesville, Va., Reddish Knob, Virginia, Palo Alto, Virginia.
Description: From the eastern end, the trail begins at 1600 feet and goes north briefly upslope to 1800. It then turns west along the ridge, climbing steadily to 2700 feet and 1½ to two miles. A half mile farther west, the Little Skidmore gated jeep road comes in from the south.

The trail continues up Chestnut Ridge, climbing to 3000 feet. It turns north briefly to meet the Grooms Ridge Trail, doubles back to the south, and then turns west again; from 3200 feet at the junction, it climbs to 4300 on Little Bald Knob.

A trail goes north from Little Bald Knob, following a ridge line for about five miles, angling east to meet Forest Road 85 about a mile north of the Shenandoah Recreation Area.

To the south, a trail goes from Little Bald Knob down to Forest Road 95 at Camp Todd.

424 — Grooms Ridge Trail
Location: From the Chestnut Ridge Trail to Forest Road 101 about 1½ miles south of Hearthstone Lake.
Length: Four miles
USGS Quad: Reddish Knob, Virginia
Description: The trail follows Big Ridge, dropping steadily but never steeply, eastward, from 3200 feet at the junction to 1700 feet at the road.

North River Trail
Location: Follows the river upstream (north) from Forest Road 95 to the Shenandoah Recreation Area.
Length: Four miles
USGS Quad: Palo Alto, Virginia
Description: Starting about 2½ miles north of Camp Todd at 2700 feet, the trail heads up river to 3000 feet before making a sharp climb to the west up to the campground at 3600 feet.

422 — Dull Hunt Trail
Location: Take Virginia 763 from Harrisonburg. About a mile past the forest boundary Forest Road 72 goes off to the left. This very curvy road goes six to seven miles to White Oak Flats and the gated jeep road of Dull Hunt Trail. A branch of the trail meets Forest Road 72 about five miles beyond this point. The trail ends at Forest Road 240 which winds 2½ miles over Leading Ridge down to the Little Dry River and Forest Road 87.
Length: Eight miles
USGS Quads: Cow Knob, Va., and Rawley Springs, Virginia.
Description: From the gated road at about 3300 feet, the trail heads northeast down Trail Ridge, turning north and then dropping with a series of switchbacks down to 1800 feet at Slate Lick Run, two miles from the trail head. Crossing the creek, it climbs up on Gauley Ridge to 2200 feet, turns northeast for ½ mile and then doubles back west going steeply downhill into Dull Hunt Hollow, meeting Bible Creek and following it northeast at 1930 feet.

A branch of the trail continues across the creek, rather than turning down it, and turns northwest up Middle Mountain, climbing to 2800 feet quickly and then more slowly to 3200 feet where it meets Forest Road 72.

The main trail continues down to the confluence of Bible Run and Spruce Lick Run, which comes in from the west. Here the trail forks. Follow the fork up Spruce Lick Run less than ½ mile to Forest Road 240. The other branch continues down Bible Run onto private property.

447 — Shenandoah Mountain
Location: This trail has the same name as trail number 1020, but it is actually the northern end of a long trail in the Deerfield Ranger District. From Forest Road 95 just west of Forest Road 85 to Tearjacket Knob and the sections of this trail in the Deerfield District.
Length: 3.5 miles
USGS Quad: Palo Alto, Virginia
Description: This trail was described to us as "good but steep." From 3000 feet at the road, it climbs quickly up the ridge to 4000 in about one mile. It follows the ridge south to Tearjacket Knob — 4200 feet — and connects with the trails coming north past Hardscrabble Knob.

Trails in the Lee District
More information: Stop at the Visitor Center on U.S. Route 211 between Luray and New Market, open seven days a week from April to November. Telephone 703-740-8310. Or contact the District Ranger, Professional Building, Edinburg, Va. 22824; telephone 703-984-4101.

Massanutten Mountain Trail

Location: There are two ways to reach it from the north. To hike the entire 23 miles, one would locate the intersection of the trail (orange-blazed) at its junction with State Route 613 approximately one mile east of the intersections of State Route 613 and 678. The trail head (not visible from the road) is across the road from the fish hatchery near the home of the superintendent. The second, and easier, way to locate the trail is to start at the bridge over Passage Creek at the north end of the picnic grounds in Elizabeth Furnace Recreation Area. (Cars left in the picnic grounds overnight should have a note displayed that car owners are hiking.)
Distance: 23 miles
USGS Quads: Strasburg, Bentonville, Rileyville, Luray, all in Virginia. PATC Map G
Description: The trail follows the ridge line of Massanutten Mountain, a geologic oddity, in that it rises abruptly out of the floor of the Shenandoah Valley of Virginia, near Strasburg, extends southwest for 60 miles, then disappears just as abruptly, near Harrisonburg, Virginia.

At the bridge over Passage Creek, pick up the blue-blazes of the Big Blue trail and follow that trail east and southeast for 1.5 miles to its junction with the Massanutten Mountain Trail in Shawl Gap. The elevation at Elizabeth Furnace is about 700 feet, whereas on top of the ridge it is 1500 feet.

At Shawl Gap the Big Blue and the Massanutten Mountain trail follow the same route south for approximately 6 miles to Veach Gap. The hiker follows both blue blazes and orange blazes. Those who are backpacking are urged to stay overnight at the excellent Little Crease shelter in Veach Gap. It is big, well lighted, and has plenty of sleeping space in its four bunks and ample floor space. The traffic areas in front of many shelters become muddy holes in even moderately wet weather. Not at Little Crease! The area in front of the shelter is paved with heavy field stone. It has table space, a toilet and a good source of water in the little stream in front of the shelter.

From the shelter the trail goes generally east to regain the ridge elevation. One mile from the shelter the two trails split, the Big Blue going east toward the South Fork of the Shenandoah River, while the orange-blazed Massanutten Mountain trail goes south. In 4 miles the white-blazed Milford Gap trail goes east to the Hazard Mill Canoe Camp. The main trail continues southwest, crossing another side trail 4.5 miles farther on. About 4 miles beyond that junction, a side trail heads to Kennedy Peak and the observation tower, at elevation 2560. Continuing on south on the main trail for 2 more miles leads the hiker to State Route 675. Bear right on Route 675 for 1.7 miles to the Camp Roosevelt campground.

Signal Knob Circuit Hike
Distance: 10 miles
USGS Quad: Strasburg, Virginia; PATC Map G (see in particular the enlarged inset map of the Elizabeth Furnace area on reverse of Map G.)
Description: Signal Knob is a historic spot where both Confederate and Union troops maintained a signal station during the Civil War. The stone breastworks built to protect the site from attack are still evident. There are several ways that one may reach Signal Knob, but since circuit hikes are always more interesting than straight "up and back," hikes we will describe a circuit taken by Edward Garvey in mid-July, 1975, with his son Kevin and three other members of Explorer Post 681 of Falls Church, Virginia.

They had camped overnight at the family campground in the Elizabeth Furnace Recreation Area. Early next morning they walked to the campground entrance and across the hard surface Route 678. The trail sign at that point read:

Bear Wallow Trail	0.6 miles
Signal Knob	5.1 miles
Signal Knob Parking Lot	1.7 miles

A ten-minute walk took them to the Bear Wallow Trail, which they followed until it cut across the Big Blue Trail. Turning left on the blue-blazed "Big Blue", they followed both trails until their intersection with Little Passage Creek. The Bear Wallow Trail ends at that point.

To reach Signal Knob, turn right (northeast) on an unblazed but clearly defined trail. In 0.3 miles, pass Sand Spring on right, the sole source of water for Confederate troops stationed on the Knob. Follow the trail for approximately 2 miles to the top of Signal Knob at 2105-foot elevation. From the Knob one has an unobstructed 180 degree

view of the Shenandoah Valley. The spot is still used for communications, but today the communications take the form of an educational
television transmitting equipment tower.

For your return trip take the *unblazed* trail past the television tower.
PATC Map G shows this as a red-blazed trail but the map is incorrect.
The trail goes generally south and east. Plan enough time for the return trip so that you can enjoy the outstanding views from the Shenandoah Valley Overlook at 1900 feet, the Fort Valley Overlook at
1800 feet, and the Buzzard Rock Overlook at 1500 feet. In July and
August allow additional time for picking and eating blueberries at many
spots along the trail. About .2 miles before reaching the Signal Knob
parking area, the trail crosses a gushing stream which emanates from
a walled-in enclosure some 50 feet off the trail. Upon reaching the
parking area, one can return to the starting point via Route 678 or one
can postpone the road walking a bit by taking the yellow-blazed trail
from the parking lot which intersects the road near the picnic area.

Allow approximately 5 hours for the hike. Water is available at several points along the circuit.

The
Jefferson National Forest

Over 1,500,000 acres of land are within the boundaries of the Jefferson National Forest; 546,000 acres are actually owned by the United
States. The land extends in long strips from the Tennessee and Ken-
tucky lines in the southwest to beyond Roanoke to the north.

The elk that used to roam the mountains are long gone, but these
magnificent animals have been reintroduced here.

Mount Rogers, at 5729 feet, is the highest point in Virginia. The
peak and some 150,000 acres around it have been set aside as a National Recreation Area.

Other than the Appalachian Trail, the major trail in the Mount Rogers
area is the Iron Mountain Trail, which follows an old route of the A.T.

If you are looking for a long trip, the A.T. and the western section of
the Iron Mountain Trail can be combined into a loop over 50 miles
long. If you want a good hike on a slightly less heavily traveled path,
head for the eastern section of the Iron Mountain Trail.

More information and maps: Forest Supervisor, 3517 Brandon Ave.,
Roanoke, Virginia. 24018; telephone 703-343-1581.

Trails in the Marion District
Current information: U.S. Forest Service, District Ranger Office, 1102
N. Main St., Marion, Virginia 24354; telephone 703-783-5196.

301 — Iron Mountain Trail
Location: From the intersection of Virginia Route 16 and Virginia Route
650 west to the Appalachian Trail 2½ miles east of Damascus, Virginia.

Length: 24 miles
USGS Quads: Trout Dale, Virginia, (east to west) Whitetop Mountain, Virginia, Knooarock, Virginia, and Damascus, Virginia.
Description: When the A.T. was rerouted in 1972, this trail was re-marked with yellow blazes. Watch for these, since a number of other trails and logging roads intersect the Iron Mountain Trail. Three trail shelters, all near water, lie along the route, remains of the time when this was the A.T.

From the road at 3400 feet, the trail heads west, descending to cross Comers Creek at about 1½ miles. The trail follows the creek briefly to Comers Creek Falls and then starts uphill, rising about 4000 feet as it heads west. Just under seven miles from the start, the Iron Mountain Trail crosses the new A.T. From here, you could take the A.T. south to Mount Rogers or north to loop back around to where the A.T. crosses Virginia 16 near your starting point.

The trail climbs to the top of Flat Top at 4451 feet, and about one mile beyond, it reached the Cherry Tree shelter. To the west, the trail stays on the ridge, reaching the trail down Little Laurel Creek at about 10 miles.

Thirteen miles from your beginning, the trail hits Virginia Route 600 which it follows briefly to the north before heading west again. The Forest Service Skulls Gap Picnic Area is located off Virginia 600 on the trail route.

About two miles west of Virginia 600 is the Straight Branch Shelter. West of here, the trail follows the ridge top of Iron Mountain. Parts of this area are open fields.

The trail crosses Forest Road 90 19 miles from the beginning, and a half mile farther along it reaches the Sandy Flats Shelter. The junction with the A.T. is about four miles west of the shelter.

Several streams pass through the area, providing fishing as well as cooking water. Hunters use the trail during deer season. One portion is open to motorbikes from May to November. Horses can be used also.

166 — Mount Rogers Trail

Location: From Va. Route 603 at the Grindstone Recreation Area to the Appalachian Trail at Deep Gap.
Length: 6.9 miles
USGS Quad: Whitetop Mountain, Virginia (quad does not show trail)
Description: From the campground, the trail climbs along Grindstone Branch and then up onto ridge at 3600 feet. It continues up rather quickly to 4400 feet and heads southwest along the west slope of Mount Rogers reaching 5000 feet before descending slightly to meet the A.T. at Deep Gap (4800 feet).

The Deep Gap shelter is just to the west of the trail junction. You can follow the A.T. west a short distance to get a look at the high meadows on the slopes of Whitetop, the second highest mountain in Virginia.

To the east it leads 1½ miles to the top of Mount Rogers. Unlike Whitetop, Mount Rogers is heavily wooded with Fraser fir and red spruce. This is Canadian zone forest like the crests of the higher Smokies and Black Mountains farther south. Mount Rogers is the northernmost station for Fraser fir. North of here, the equivalent species is balsam fir.

301 — Iron Mountain Trail
Location: The eastern section of the trail begins at U.S. 21 at the intersection with Forest Road 57 east of the Comers Rock campground. It ends at the beginning of the Bournes Branch Trail.
Length: 10.5 miles
USGS Quads: Speedwell, Virginia, Cripple Creek, Virginia, Austinville, Virginia.
Description: Another ridge top trail. About four miles along, the Horse Heaven Trail comes in from the north. The trail ends at Jones Knob, where the Bournes Branch Trail continues east.

An Outward Bound group maintained this trail in 1973, so it should be easy to follow. They cleared out brush and painted yellow blazes along the route.

306 — Henley Hollow Trail
Location: From U.S. Route 21 two miles south of Speedwell, Va., to the Horse Heaven Trail.
Length: 1.4 miles
USGS Quad: Speedwell, Virginia.
Description: Heads southeast from the road, up Henley Hollow, climbing from 2485 at the road to 3100 feet where it meets the Horse Heaven Trail.

307 — Horse Heaven Trail
Location: From the Henley Hollow Trail to the Iron Mountain Trail.
Length: 3.1 miles
USGS Quad: Speedwell, Virginia
Description: The trail follows Horse Heaven ridge east from the Henley Hollow Trail at 3500 to 3800 feet. It turns south on a dirt road that carries it downhill to Forest Road 14 along the East Fork of Dry Creek. It then climbs up to the south and the Iron Mountain Trail at 3744 feet.

308 — Rocky Hollow
Location: From Virginia Route 619 east of Speedwell to the Horse Heaven Trail. Take 619 from Speedwell to the bridge over Cripple Creek. A dirt road goes off to the south here, follows the creek from a short distance, and then crosses it at a ford. The trail begins south of the ford.
Length: 2.5 miles
USGS Quad: Speedwell, Virginia.
Description: The trail heads up Laurel Hollow from the ford and then

climbs up onto a ridge at 3400 feet. It passes a spring just before joining the Horse Heaven Trail.

317 — Bournes Branch Trail — From Iron Mountain Trail at Jones
Knob to Virginia Route 602 just north of the Sheperds Corner camp-
ground. Jones Knob is just east of the intersection of the Iron Mountain
Trail and Virginia Route 653.

Length: 6 miles

USGS Quads: Cripple Creek, Virginia, Austinville, Virginia

Description: Heads east from the Iron Mountain Trail, dropping off
Jones Knob at 3400 feet down to Bournes Branch. Bournes Branch
runs into Brush Creek which the trail follows to Virginia 602.

310 — Yellow Branch Trail

Location: From the Bournes Branch Trail to Va. 602

Length: 3.5 miles

USGS Quad: Cripple Creek, Virginia

Description: This trail branches off to the north from the Bournes
Branch Trail two miles from the Iron Mountain Trail. It quickly hits Yellow Branch which it follows north. The trail hits a dirt road along the
way. When that road forks, follow the left fork to Virginia 602.

The Appalachian Trail

"The story of the Appalachian Trail has been many times told; it cannot be told too often."

The above quotation is from the book, *The Appalachians*, by Maurice Brooks. And indeed the story of the Trail does need to be told often. Each year a new body of young hikers — and thousands who are not so young — arrive on the scene eager for a place to test or acquire their hiking skills. And what better place than on this granddaddy of all long distance marked hiking trails. Secondly, the Appalachian Trail is in trouble. Approximately 800 miles of the Trail is still in private ownership and there is a continuing encroachment of mountain top ski developments, mountain top summer home developements; and roads, radio and television towers threaten to squeeze the Trail right off the map.

"If enough good people don't know about a beautiful place, chances are it won't be a beautiful place very long."
Ansel Adams

Today there are 36 hiking club organizations that maintain assigned sections of the 2000-mile trail. In many cases the maintenance work is shared with the national forest or national park through which the trail passes. Today, as in 1925, the Appalachian Trail Conference is the coordinating organization for the entire trail.

More information: Write to the Conference or obtain one of the other books dealing with the Trail: Appalachian Trail Conference, P.O. Box 236, Harpers Ferry, West Virginia 25425; telephone: 304/535-6331. Please enclose 25 cents to cover the cost of the information packet that will be sent to you.

Length: 2000 miles

Description: Almost 500 miles, or one-fourth, of the entire Appalachian Trail follows the crest of the Blue Ridge mountains of Virginia. Part of the time the Trail straddles the Virginia-West Virginia line and at times it actually leaves the Old Dominion and wanders over into Wild Wonderful West Virginia. Unfortunately, some of the Appalachian Trail Conference maps (in ATC Publications 5 and 17) slow the Trail coming close to, but not entering, West Virginia.

The Appalachian Trail crosses over from Tennessee into southwestern Virginia near the friendly little town of Damascus. From here the Trail promptly proceeds to Virginia's two highest mountains — Whitetop (5530 feet) and Mt. Rogers (5729 feet), continues northward through the Jefferson National Forest, goes through another friendly hikers' town, Pearisburg, reclimbs the mountain outside of Pearisburg and makes its first brief trip into West Virginia. From there it swings back east into Virginia, goes to the north of Roanoake, climbs the mountain and plays hide and seek with the Blue Ridge Parkway as the Trail wends its way north to the James River. At the James the trail leaves Jefferson National Forest, within whose friendly boundaries it has meandered for 250 miles. The 28 trailside shelters, well equipped and well maintained, plus the beauty of the mountains through which the Trail passes, make this 250 miles an especially pleasant segment. There are tremendous rhododendron displays throughout the Jefferson during late May and early June.

At the James River, the Trail drops to its lowest elevation (750 feet) since it began down in Georgia. It now enters the George Washington National Forest and continues in that Forest for 78 miles until reaching the Shenandoah National Park. This is a rugged and beautiful 78 mile stretch marked by a series of mountains in the 3500-4100 foot elevation range that are divided by river gorges. The hiker begins at the James River (elevation 750) and climbs within a few miles to 3550 feet. Further north, the hiker descends into the Tye River Gap (elevation 900 feet) and begins a strenuous 3000 foot climb to the summit of Three Ridges. Seven trailside shelters dot this 78 mile stretch.

At U.S. Route 250 (I-64), the Trail leaves the George Washington National Forest, enters the Shenandoah National Park and intersects the Skyline Drive some 25 times on its 94-mile course through the Park. The 17 shelters along the Appalachian Trail within the Park have been declared out-of-bounds for overnight use by Park regulation, but the footway itself is, by consensus, considered to be the best designed and best maintained of any similar length of footway in the 2000 mile long trail. Backpackers must obtain permits on entering the Park.

Leaving the Shenandoah National Park in northern Virginia, the Appalachian Trail comes on hard times. North of State Route 55 at Linden, Virginia, the Trail becomes largely a matter of road walking until it leaves the Virginia-West Virginia line near Harpers Ferry, West Virginia, and crosses the Potomac River into Maryland. The last three miles of the Trail provide tremendous views of the Shenandoah and Potomac River Gorges and of the village of Harpers Ferry. It is safe to say that the 51 mile stretch of Trail between the Park and the Potomac is the one in the most critical danger and provides the lowest quality hiking experience of any comparable 51 miles throughout the 2000 mile Trail.

Throughout its almost 500 mile traverse of Virginia, the A.T. is never very far from the West Virginia state line. In two places it actually crosses over into West Virginia for short distances.

The first of these is near the town of Pearisburg. From the outskirts of Pearisburg, the Trail proceeds west and north and crosses into West Virginia on Peters Mountain. It proceeds along the West Virginia side for some miles before turning east in Virginia and on to the Blue Ridge Parkway area north of Roanoke.

In northern Virginia as the Trail approaches Harpers Ferry, West Virginia, it again swings over into West Virginia for several miles before descending onto U.S. Route 340 and crossing the Potomac into Maryland.

The Trail enters Maryland on the east end of the Sandy Hook bridge (U.S. Route 340). It then drops down to the Chesapeake and Ohio Canal towpath, which it follows for 1.5 miles. Leaving the canal, it crosses underneath U.S. Route 340 and then climbs Weverton Heights to the top of the ridge. There are excellent views of the Potomac River Gorge and of Harpers Ferry from lookout spots along the Trail.

From atop Weverton Heights, the Trail proceeds north along South Mountain for the remainder of its traverse through the state. It leaves Maryland at Pen-Mar on the state line after first skirting Camp David, the brief vacation spot for U.S. Presidents. In all, some 37 miles of the Trail goes through Maryland, and there are five shelters on this stretch. The State of Maryland has been making steady progress in acquiring land throughout the length of the South Mountain area.

Midwestern Trails

7

The Midwest does not have the riches of the east or the west—there are probably more miles of trail just around the Finger Lakes of Upper New York State than in the whole Midwest. But it does have trails. And some of them cross country that is both beautiful and, in its own way, quite wild.

There is still some empty country in this crowded Midwest, and some trails that very few people use. Jerry Sullivan and Glenda Daniel once hiked for four days on the North Country Trails, 60 miles, without encountering another human being.

Illinois

Illinois ranks well down on the list of states in the amount of recreational land per citizen. This status, unfortunately, is reflected in the shortage of hiking trails. Most of the state parks have hiking trails or "nature" trails, but since the parks generally are small, the trails usually are short.

People are unlikely to come from afar just to hike in Illinois. But if you live in the state, there are some pleasant places for a day's outing.

Illinois and Michigan Canal Towpath
Location: The canal was the first shipping route between Lake Michigan and the Illinois River, which flows into the Mississippi. It is still possible to hike along the towpath south of Joliet. The town of Channahon off U.S. 6 is a good place to start. You can continue down the path as far as Morris.
Length: About 15 miles.
Description: Along this stretch of the bank the Du Page, Des Plaines, and Kankakee Rivers combine to form the Illinois River. The canal parallels the Des Plaines and then the Illinois, and the towpath follows the narrow raised strip of land that divides the canal from the river. There are bluffs where the Kankakee flows into the Des Plaines, and the McKinley Woods Forest Preserve is at this spot. A bridge here allows hikers to cross the canal to the preserve, and you can return to Channahon via country roads.

If you continue on to Morris, you pass through the deepening valley of the Illinois, with a mixture of farms, industry, and a few strip mines along the way.

139

Illinois Prairie Path

Location: West of Chicago along the old right-of-way of the Chicago, Aurora & Elgin Railroad. Its eastern end is in Elmhurst, west of the Tri-State Tollway and south of St. Charles Road. You can get on it from York Road, Spring Road, or Illinois 83. The trail is marked at all road intersections with easily visible Illinois Prairie Path emblems. Heading west, it passes through the suburbs of Villa Park, Lombard, Glen Ellyn and Wheaton. It then splits, with one branch going northwest toward Elgin and the other southwest toward Aurora. This latter branch splits again, with a northern branch going to Batavia.

Length: 40 miles.

Description: Years ago, the "Roarin' Elgin" ran Toonerville Trolley-style electric trains across the corn fields from Chicago to Aurora and Elgin on the Fox River. The railroad has been defunct for some time, but thanks in large part to the efforts of Mrs. May Theilgaard Watts, a retired naturalist from nearby Morton Arboretum, the old right-of-way has been turned into a foot and bicycle path.

This is not exactly wild country. The eastern segment of the trail, since it follows an old railroad, takes you directly through the business districts of small towns along the way. Major access points by car are at York Road and Illinois 83 in Elmhurst, Villa Street and Grace Street in Villa Park, Illinois 53 in Lombard, Main Street in Glen Ellyn and West Street in Wheaton.

Most of the path is surfaced with very fine gravel for the bikes and it is as easy to walk as a sidewalk, although softer.

The segment of the path running northwest from Wheaton passes mainly through flat farm country with some marshy ground. The trail crosses Jewell Road just at the edge of Wheaton, Geneva Road at Country Farm Road, Illinois 64 just east of Illinois 59, Illinois 59 itself, Army Trail Road and Dunham Road just south of Stearns Road. You can pick it up at any of these points.

There is a picnic table near a mobile home park where the DuPage River crosses the trail, and there is a roadside park with water and toilets just north of the trail on Route 59. There are few other places where one can stop without trespassing on private property. Even the Forest Preserve has "No Trespassing" signs posted next to the path.

Immediately east of Dunham Road the trail passes by a tiny forest preserve called Pratt's Wayne Woods. Group camping is permitted there, but since the facilities frequently are used by Boy Scouts, it is wise to make reservations. Write: Cook County Forest Preserve District, 536 N. Harlem Avenue, River Forest, Ill. 60305.

The section north of Dunham Road passes a scenic gravel pit on its way into South Elgin.

The southern branch of the trail, which splits southwest from Wheaton, crosses Roosevelt Road and parallels Wiesbrook Road to Illinois 55 which it follows into Warrenville. There are some attractive horse farms along this section, with what may be the only stile in the state of

Illinois, taking the trail over a farm fence. A good part of this section of the trail is surfaced with very large, loose rocks which make for rather tiring walking.

About 4½ miles southwest of Warrenville, a quarter of a mile west of the trail crossing at Eola Road, the Prairie Path branches again. The northern branch runs to Batavia in Kane County, the southern branch goes to Aurora.

The westernmost part of the Batavia section, nearest the Fox River, may be the loveliest part of the entire trail. If you are walking west from Warrenville and want to take this northern route rather than continuing on to Aurora, you will have to detour briefly along the frontage road of the East-West tollway.

After crossing Illinois Route 55, the trail passes alongside the tree-bordered grounds of a National Accelerator Laboratory for little more than a mile. It crosses Farnsworth Road, Hart Road, and then dips down into a box canyon. The old railroad bed here in the Fox River Valley cuts through bedrock of Niagara limestone that was originally worn down by melt-water during the glacial age. The footpath becomes narrow and somewhat hazardous; be prepared to ford a stream several times. Where the path goes under a railroad and state highway 25, you will see rock walls.

On the west side of the highway bridge, the path goes over the scoured surface of the bedrock and then, leaving the stream, swings north. Within the next 1000 feet, there are a dozen or more glacial boulders. As you examine them, particularly where they lie almost on the base of the limestone outcrop, you can understand why they were called "erratics" and why they were such a source of puzzlement to people 150 years ago who knew nothing of the continental glacier. Many are granite, brought from the far north and shaped by ice-scour. One even shows glacial scratches, striae.

The southern trail branch to Aurora passes by fields and farms and at two points crosses a tiny Fox River tributary called Indian Creek.

More information: The Prairie Path is maintained by volunteer labor. Scout troops, the local Sierra Club chapter, and other conservation groups all participate, coordinated by an association called the Illinois Prairie Path (address: P.O. Box 1086, Wheaton, Illinois 60187). You can get an individual membership in this group for $3.00 a year, or you can become a "patron" by giving $100 or more. Family memberships are $5.00. Maps are available free.

This land has not been taken over by the state and turned into a park. A whole host of private and public bodies have rights of various kinds to the land, and the path exists at their sufferance.

Michigan

Michigan undoubtedly offers more than 500 miles of trails in all, and they range in character from the rather domesticated Shore to Shore Trail to the wilderness of Isle Royale.

There is something here for the experienced hiker and for the novice, for someone with a weekend free or a month's vacation.

Isle Royale National Park

Location: Isle Royale is in Lake Superior about 50 miles from the Upper Peninsula of Michigan and 15 miles from the Minnesota shore.

Access: If you have a boat more than 20 feet long or a plane outfitted with pontoons, you can make your own way to Isle Royale. Otherwise, you can take a ferry from Houghton or Copper Harbor, Michigan , or from Grand Portage, Minnesota. There is also air service from Houghton.

There is bus service via Greyhound and local carriers to Houghton and to Grand Portage.

*Length of trails:*There are 26 named trails on the island with a total length of about 160 miles. Some of these trails are only a mile or less and do not connect with other trails, and therefore are in the descriptions that follow.

Description: Isle Royale is a beautiful example of North Woods wilderness. The island is made up of a series of parallel basaltic ridges running from northeast to southwest. Between the ridges are low lying areas of marshes, lakes, and streams. The shoreline is irregular, with many coves and harbors, and a number of small islands lie offshore.

For hikers, Isle Royale offers considerable variety: short easy loop trails near the lodges for day hikes; and long, rugged trails through the wilderness that should be undertaken only by experienced hikers with the proper equipment. Trail heads along the shore away from the lodges are served by water taxis which will deliver hikers to the trail and pick them up later at the same spot or at any other trail head along the shore.

There are 24 campgrounds on the islands, all but four along the shore. The camps are supplied with fireplaces, tables and tent sites. You may not reserve a campsite; but if you cannot get space in a campground, wilderness camping is allowed, with certain restrictions.

A few additional points for hikers: Groceries and freeze dried foods may be purchased on the island. No pets, other than seeing eye dogs, are allowed anywhere on the island. Disposable food or beverage containers cannot be taken into the backcountry. Wheeled vehicles are prohibited, and no outboard motors are allowed on inland lakes.

Water should be boiled for at least five minutes before drinking. Don't try to swim in Lake Superior. The water temperature seldom gets much above 40 degrees. If an inland lake seems warm enough to swim in, it is also warm enough to support leeches.

The trails of Isle Royale range in length from less than a mile to 40 miles. All the trails described here interconnect with each other, making trips of almost any length possible. Although visitors to the islands are not allowed to stay more than 14 days, you can cover a lot of ground in that time.

You will need good boots for these trails. There is not much topsoil on the island, but there are many sharp rocks. The northwest faces of the ridges are frequently quite steep, and boots that give good traction will provide a bit more security.

The island's trails can be divided into four broad categories. First there is a group of trails — mainly short loops — near the Rock Harbor lodge and campground. A similar, but smaller, group is located near the Windigo lodge. Two long trails run on the ridge lines from southwest to northeast. Finally, there are trails branching off from these longer trails and connecting them to campsites.

The trails around Rock Harbor are:

The Albert Stoll, Jr., Memorial Trail — 2.3 miles. The trail generally follows the shores of Rock Harbor and Tobin Harbor. The Indians used to mine copper on Isle Royle, and some remains of their activities still are visible.

Rock Harbor Trail — 10.5 miles. Another shore line trail. This one passes the remains of copper mining done by whites in the 19th century. The Daisy Farm campsite is seven miles from the lodge, and the Moskey Basin campground is at the end of the trail.

The Mount Franklin Trail — branches off from the Rock Harbor Trail, making possible a loop trip of six miles from the lodge. At Suzy's Cave, a stone arch left behind by the retreating shoreline of Lake Superior, it is possible to cross from the Rock Harbor Trail to the Tobin Harbor Trail for a loop hike of four miles.

Tobin Harbor Trail — three miles. The trail is mainly inland through woods, but the water often is visible. The trail joins the Mt. Franklin Trail at one end.

Mount Franklin Trail — 2.2 miles. The trail head is on Rock Harbor about three miles from the lodge. It is reachable by boat or by the Rock Harbor Trail. Three-Mile campsite is near the trail head. The trail crosses the narrow peninsula dividing Rock and Tobin Harbors and then climbs up again to the summit of Mount Franklin, 1074 feet above sea level. Mount Franklin is a part of Greenstone Ridge, and the Greenstone Trail can be picked up here.

Lookout Louise Trail — one mile. The trail head is on the northwest shore of Tobin Harbor, accessible by boat from the lodge. The trail passes a beaver pond called Hidden Lake as it climbs from the shore up to the Lookout. Monument Rock is along the trail, a large, isolated stone that, like Suzy's Cave, is a remnant of a time when the lake waters were higher than they are now. This trail joins the northernmost section of the Greenstone Trail. This section is five miles long and carries its own name (Mt. Franklin — Lookout Louise Trail), but here it is treated as an extension of the Greenstone Trail.

Daisy Farm Trail — two miles and the Mount Ojibway Trail, 1.7 miles.

Both begin at the Daisy Farm campsite and head inland to Greenstone Ridge. The Daisy Farm Trail starts up Benson Creek, a brook trout stream. The creek flows out of Lake Benson, and near its headwaters is a swamp which the trail crosses on a foot bridge. There are carnivorous pitcher plants here as well as the common bog trees, black spruce and tamarack.

The Mount Ojibway Trail ends at the mountain's summit, more than 1100 feet up, where there is a lookout tower.

These two trails combine with a short section of the Greenstone to form a triangle about five miles long with the campground at one angle. The trails traverse both ridge and valley, offering views of bogs, stands of birch, white pine, and the northernmost examples of maples on the island.

Lake Richie Trail — 2.3 miles. This begins at Moskey Basin at the head of Rock Harbor and travels through spruce and fir forests to Lake Richie, which is supposed to be a good spot to catch sight of a moose. The trail joins the Indian Portage Trail at the lake.

There are three main trails in the Windigo area at the southwestern tip of the island.

The Huginnin Cove Loop Trail — seven miles. It is four miles from Windigo to the campground at Huginnin Cove. The remainder of the loop is about three miles. Traces of mining once done alone the first part of this trail include open shafts concealed by vegetation. Watch where you walk.

Two beaver ponds on the way to the cove, and two more on the way back, offer excellent spots to see other wildlife, including moose. There are bald eagle nests in the area, too. The Superior shore around Huginnin Cove is made up of steep bluffs backed by aspens.

Feldtmann Ridge Trail — 14.3 miles. This trail was opened less than 10 years ago. It provides access to some of the most rugged terrain on the island. Feldtmann Ridge itself rises to 1173 feet, and its northwest face is a precipitous cliff nearly 400 feet high. The Big Siskiwit Swamp in this area is the largest on the island. It is virtually impossible to navigate on foot, and hikers are advised to stay on the trail and content themselves with gazing on the swamp from on top of the ridge. However, the trail crosses a bog near Feldtmann Lake that requires a boardwalk 1200 feet long, and that stretch should satisfy most swamp enthusiasts.

The trail starts at the Windigo Ranger station and hugs the south shore of Washington Harbor for about 1½ miles. It then turns inland over a low stretch of Greenstone Ridge to Grace Creek (brook trout). Beyond the creek, the boardwalks alternate with low ridges. Hardwoods predominate in the uplands, with black spruce and alder on the wet ground. A side trail leads to Feldtmann Lake (northern pike).

On the ridge, the woods give way to scattered white pine. There is a lookout tower and splendid views over much of the southern end of the island. The cliffs are undercut, so stay away from the edges.

From the ridge top it is downhill to Siskiwit Bay campground about five miles away. About halfway along is a side trail to Lake Halloran. The Isle Royale Natural History Association recommends a visit to Lake Halloran in early summer when the rare ladyslipper orchid blooms along the southwest shore. The trail ends at Siskiwit Bay campground where it joins the Island Mine Trail.

Feldtmann Lake Trail — 2.5 miles. This connects the Feldtmann Ridge Trail with Lake Superior at Rainbow Cove on Isle Royale's southwest shore. It is about one mile along a stream bank from the cove to Feldtmann Lake. The remainder of the trail skirts the lake to the Feldtmann Ridge Trail junction.

The two longest and most difficult, trails on the island are the Greenstone Ridge and the Minong Ridge trails, and should be attempted only by experienced hikers.

Greenstone Ridge Trail — 45 miles, including the piece from Mount Franklin to Lookout Louise. This ridge is the backbone of the island. The highest peaks are along its length. The northwest face of the ridge tends to be quite steep, while to the southeast the slopes are gentler.

Water is available only at the inland lakes that occupy the lowlands on either side of the ridge, and it must be boiled before drinking. There are three campsites on lakes along the way.

If you wish to start at Lookout Louise and hike the five miles to Mount Franklin, you will get a chance to see some of the sites of prehistoric mining on the island. A few of these sites have been excavated to show their original form. Copper mined in the upper Great Lakes was traded by the Indians as far south as Alabama.

Starting from Rock Harbor, there are a number of ways to reach the trail. The most direct is via Rock Harbor Trail and the Mount Franklin Trail. From Mount Franklin, the trail crosses Mount Ojibway and then reaches a short trail leading to the campsites at Chickenbone Lake.

A dip in the ridge beyond Chickenbone Lake precedes the climb to Mount Siskiwit, 1205 feet high. Here it still is possible to see remnants of trees nearly destroyed in the fire of 1936.

Hatchet Lake campground is on a spur trail seven miles beyond Chickenbone. Then there is a climb to Ishpeming Point, 1377 feet high, where there is a lookout tower. About two miles farther along the trail drops down to Lake Desor and the third campsite. From there it is a long climb to Mount Desor, at 1394 feet the highest point on the island.

From Mount Desor, it is four miles to the junction with the Island Mine Trail. Six miles farther on through a forest of sugar maples and yellow birch is the Windigo Lodge.

Minong Ridge Trail — 26 miles. This was originally constructed to provide access to the northwestern area of the island for fire fighting crews. It still is identified as a Fire Manway on the Geological Survey map. It is rugged hiking that will involve getting your feet wet at some stream crossings and low spots. Water generally is available only at a few points along the way, and it should be boiled before drinking.

The northern end of the trail is near McCargoe Cove and connects to the cove via the Minong Mine Trail, less than a mile in length. The Minong was the largest copper mine on the island 100 years ago, and there was a considerable settlement near it. Nothing remains now but a clearing, some pits and rock piles, and the remnants of the railway used to transport the ore from pit to dock.

Six miles along the trail, there is a campground at Todd Harbor, site of the old Haytown mine, and beyond it is a side trail leading to Hatchet Lake and Greenstone Ridge. A half mile beyond this junction is a short side trail to Pickett Bay where water can be obtained from Lake Superior. After six miles of hiking along the ridge through birches and aspens, another spur trail leads down to the shore of Little Todd Harbor.

There are steep grades between this junction and the Lake Desor spur trail about six miles farther on. This is the last good place to get water before the trail's end. There are swamps, streams and beaver ponds to be waded in the final section of the trail. The last obstacle is Washington Creek. Once you have splashed through that, the Washington Creek Trail takes you into Windigo.

There are five trails more than one mile long running southeast-northwest along the island's short axis.

Indian Portage Trail — 10.6 miles. This is the longest of these branch trails, its name stemming from the belief that Indians used to portage canoes across the island on this route. It should be a good trail for fishermen, since it skirts the shores of four inland lakes, while a short side trail leads to a fifth. Northern pike inhabit all these lakes.

The southern end of the trail is at Chippewa Harbor campground. The spur trail to Lake Mason is a short distance inland, and beyond that the trail stays close to a stream that drains Lake Richie. The trail detours around the lake, meeting the Lake Richie Trail four miles from Chippewa Harbor.

There are no severe slopes on this trail, but the up and down pattern of the island is evident as the trail climbs to Greenstone Ridge past Lakes LeSage and Livermore. Beyond the ridge, it is downhill to Chickenbone Lake campground. The trail follows first the shore of the lake and then Chickenbone Creek to McCargoe Cove.

Siskiwit Falls Trail and Ishpeming Trail — 7.4 miles. These two trails can be treated together conveniently. The Siskiwit Falls Trail begins at Malone Bay at a campground and follows the stream that provides an outlet for Siskiwit Lake, passing Siskiwit Falls along the way. The Ishpeming Trail begins at the lake and climbs to Ishpeming Point on Greenstone Ridge, where it joins the Greenstone Trail.

The trail skirts the lake shore in a southerly direction, crossing a small swamp at the southern tip. Footbridges keep hikers dry during the crossing. Just beyond this swamp is a small stream that is the last reliable source of water for several miles. However, the water must be boiled.

Beyond the stream, the climbing begins. You will enter part of the burned over area from the 1936 fire, and as you go up the slopes, maples, oaks, and white pine will become more common. About ¾ mile from the top if Ishpeming Point, you cross a stream on a footbridge. Beyond this, it really gets steep. At 1377 feet, Ishpeming Point is the second highest spot on the island.

The Island Mine Trail — 5 miles. The trail heads north from the Siskiwit Bay campground, crossing the Big Siskiwit River, Senter Point and Carnelian Beach before turning inland to climb to Sugar Mountain, where it meets the Greenstone Trail. There are a number of interesting points along the way. For example, there is the Siskiwit River, which reverses its flow about every 20 minutes. Lake Superior, like the other Great Lakes, is subject to a phenomenon known as a seiche (pronounced "saysh"). The water in the lake basin sloshes from side to side like beer in a bucket, creating periodic reversals of flow in low-lying rivers such as the Siskiwit.

On Senter Point are the remains of a powder house used to store explosives in the 1870s when the Island Mine was in operation. The mine itself is located about two miles from the shore. Again, be cautious in exploring this area, since some open shafts are covered with vegetation.

It is possible to combine the Feldtmann Ridge, Island Mine, and Greenstone Trails into a loop trip starting and returning to Windigo. Total distance would be about 25 miles.

Lane Cove Trail — 2.8 miles. This trail starts at Lane Cove on the island's north shore and ends at Mount Franklin. Beavers have been active here, and you may see many trees that have been gnawed. Beavers are particularly fond of the stands of quaking aspen along the way.

McCargoe Cove Trail — 2.2 miles. The trail provides a short route from the McCargoe Cove campground to Greenstone Ridge. Along the way it passes the remains of a stamp mill. A spur trail about 100 yards long leads to a dam that used to provide power for the mill. The trail crosses directly over a beaver pond near Greenstone Ridge.

More information: Additional information on Isle Royale is available from Isle Royale National Park, 87 N. Ripley St., Houghton, Mich. 49931. Ask specifically for the list of publications of the Isle Royale Natural History Association. They sell a long list of low priced books on flora, fauna, history, and geology of the island. They also offer guides to hiking trails, topographical maps, and lake survey charts.

The Shore To Shore Trail

Location: This trail crosses the entire Lower Peninsula from Lake Huron

to Lake Michigan. The eastern end is at Tawas City. The western end
of the trail forks, terminating at two small towns, Elberta and Empire.
Length of Trail: This seems to vary according to source. The side trail
toward Mackinaw City is about 70 miles long. The south trail to Cadillac is about 32 miles long. As to the main trail, one source shows 211
miles and the other 271. (A significant disparity which we cannot really
resolve.)
Description: The Shore to Shore Trail is largely the creation of a private group called the Michigan Trail Riders Association. These folks
are primarily equestrians whose principal interest was in a horse trail.
However, the trail is just as good for hikers as for riders.

Since the trail is so long, it has been divided into nine sections for
sake of convenience. Descriptions begin at the eastern end and head
west, saving the north and south branches for last.

Note: The Shore to Shore Trail is marked with blue paint blazes on
trees, fence posts, rocks, or other objects. It also is marked with 4x4
posts at junctions with other trails or roads, especially where there is a
change in direction. The posts are marked with a horseshoe with a foot
print superimposed on it. Under this insignia is an arrowhead that
points the direction. There is also a letter indicating where the trail is
headed. For example, between Mio and Grayling, westbound arrows
are marked with a G and eastbound arrows with an M, and should
keep hikers from getting turned around.

Watch for these posts whenever you arrive at a cross roads or trail
fork. It is sometimes a long way between blazes, especially when the
trail is routed along a road, so if you do take a wrong turn it may take
a while to discover.

Also, the trail is subject to rerouting. Property owners may withdraw
permission for the trail to cross their land, or a better route may be
found through public land. When this happens, the blazes or posts may
disagree with the Michigan Trail Riders Association trail maps. When
there is a disagreement, follow the posts, not the map.

Also, blue blazes are used to mark timber for cutting. Since the trail
is accustomed to the boots of hikers and hooves of horses, it is quite
easy to follow. If you see a blaze that seems to lead off into the
bushes, don't follow it; it is a timber mark.

Tawas City to South Branch Trail Camp — approximately 42 miles.
The trail heads north out of town on Willow Road and continues on
Monument Road into the Huron National Forest. The forest covers
much of the eastern part of the state at this latitude, and the trail will
be in it until just east of Grayling. Once inside the forest boundary, the
trail leaves the highway and goes cross country and on forest roads to
Loud Basin on the Au Sable River.

The Au Sable was Hemingway's Big Two-hearted River, and it is
world famous as a trout stream. The water is amazingly clear. Loud Basin is an artificial lake created by damming the Au Sable, and there are

smallmouth bass, northerns, and walleyes in its waters.

The countryside near the river is rather hilly, with extremely sandy soil covered with jack pine, cedar, red pine and white pine. Most of the trees are small, but there are magnificent red and white pines that were apparently left as seed trees the last time the place was cut over. They tower over the rest of the trees.

This sandy, wooded country continues all the way to Lake Michigan, with moderate hills alternating with flat to rolling areas. There are islands of hardwoods, but it's mainly conifers.

The trail crosses Michigan 65 just south of the river and then heads west between the river and the road. Just past Bass Lake Road, it turns north, following the river. There is a developed campsite at Gordon Creek, with water and toilets. The camp is about eight miles inside the Huron National Forest, one of many trail camps maintained by the Michigan Trail Riders.

There are Forest Service campgrounds at Corsair Bridge and at Rollways Road. The Corsair site can be reached by staying on Monument Drive after the trail leaves it and going north about one mile. You can get back to the trail by going west one mile on Pond Rd., a short distance north of the camp. The Rollways camp is along the Au Sable where Rollways Road intersects Michigan 65.

The South Branch camp is also on Rollways Road. Follow this north from where the trail branches off. Markers will lead you into camp.

South Branch Camp to Michigan 33 — 48 miles, more or less. The trail continues to follow the river, skirting Bamfield Pond, another impoundment where there are said to be fish. About 30 miles from the beginning of this section, there is a ford to the north bank of the Au Sable for horsepersons. Hikers should stay on the south bank. Four miles beyond the ford, there is a bridge across the river to McKinley on County 602. Still south of the river, there is a marker pointing the way off 602 to the McKinley trail camp. This is undeveloped.

The Forest Service has a nice campground on Mack Lake about 1½ miles south of the trail. There is a forest road leading to it from the trail about three miles east of Michigan 33.

If you want to make a detour from the trail, you can head north on Michigan 33 into Mio to see a statue of the Kirtland's in front of City Hall.

Michigan 33 to Grayling — approximately 48 miles. This section of the trail is a microcosm, containing samples of most of the sights to be seen on the entire trail. There are large tracts of woodland, a few farms, a look at the Au Sable, and some sections where the trail follows paved roads bordered by houses.

About 12 miles from the start is a trail camp with water and toilets. Just beyond it is the Lost Creek Sky Ranch, one of several dude ranches serving riders along the trail. It is rather disconcerting to walk for miles through quiet woods and then suddenly come upon Xanadu.

The ranch is made of neo-rustic, natural finish wood, with lots of rough finished logs for pillars and beams. It has a bar, a restaurant, and rooms to rent ($8 per night if you share a bath). There is entertainment on Saturday nights.

Heading west from the ranch, the trail parallels a paved road for about a mile. It is off the road with a thin screen of trees between hiker and pavement. For another mile, however, you walk right on the shoulder of the road. On both sides are summer homes.

Where the trail reaches County 489, it heads back into the woods. Luzerne is about 2½ miles south of this point. The path stays in the woods until it crosses Michigan 72 at the south branch of the Au Sable. Canoe Harbor Camp Ground is on the Au Sable a mile south of the trail. This is about 20 miles from the Lost Creek Sky Ranch.

The trail heads straight west from Canoe Harbor to Four Mile Trail Camp, where there are water and toilets. It then turns north to Grayling, entering along Michigan 72. It is about nine miles from Canoe Harbor to Four Mile Camp, and another eight to Grayling.

Grayling to Kalkaska — 50 miles. The trail follows Robert Road north out of Grayling and then goes overland, turning west about 1½ miles south of Frederic. The trail to the north branches off here. The eastern portion of this section is in the Au Sable State Forest, and the western in the Kalkaska State Forest.

There is a trail camp at Goose Creek about 22 miles from Grayling, and there are two state forest campgrounds along Manistee Road about ½ mile south of the trail.

The Kalkaska State Forest is well supplied with lakes, and there are a number of them within one mile of the trail. The trail leaves the forest at Drake Road and crosses a few miles of private property before reentering Kalkaska Forest on State Road. The Sky Valley Ranch is on the trail five miles east of Kalkaska. It has a motel, camping and a heated pool.

Just east of Kalkaska is a trail camp with water and toilets.

Kalkaska to the Junction of the Elberta and Empire branches — 51 miles. The trail goes almost straight west out of Kalkaska and then turns south to cross Island Lake Road five miles from town. A mile south, it joins North River Road, and just past the junction with South River Road is the Guernsey Lake trail camp which has toilets but no water. Go north a little more than half a mile from the junction of North and South River Road and you reach Guernsey Lake Forest Campground, a state run campground.

It is another eight to nine miles to Forks Campground in the Fife Lake State Forest. To reach it, take Supply Road south ½ mile from the trail. Four miles farther west is the Schnecks Place Trail Camp where the trail south to Cadillac branches off.

Mayfield is about five miles west of Schecks Place, and a mile north of it is the Brown's Dam campground. This is at the south end of a collection of lakes.

There are more lakes near the western end of this section, perhaps a dozen within a few miles of the trail, some quite large. The Mud Lake Trail camp is north of the trail one mile on Gonder Road, then west a half mile, north again a quarter mile across the dam, then east into the camp. Mud Lake is a large area that has been flooded to attract waterfowl, and it's a good spot for birders.

The Junction to Elberta — 32 miles. The trail goes south on Gonder Road past U.S. 31 for one mile. It then turns east on St. Johns Road for two miles and south again on Reynolds Rd. The Gass Lake Forest campground is about six miles from the beginning of the section. Take a dirt road east through Clary Crossing about two miles to the camp. This is on another waterfowl flooding.

The Wallin Trail Camp is at Wallin Road and Long Road, about 12 miles beyond Mud Lake. It has water and toilets. From here the trail heads almost staright west to Elberta, initially through the Fife Lake State Forest and then through private property. The last eight miles or so are straight down Grace Road. The trail enters town on Michigan 22. It is about 20 miles from Wallin to Elberta.

There is camping north of Elberta. Take Michigan 168 to Beach Road. Go west to the beach and then south a half mile on a jeep track.

The Junction to Empire — 32 miles. The trail goes west for two miles on Fewins road and then angles northwestward another two to the Platte River trail camp. This is undeveloped but very nicely situated near the Platte River and Bronson Lake. The trail heads north on Mill Road for a mile and then west again on Hooker Road. If you stay on Mill Road and go two miles north, then east on Almira Road a half mile and then south a half mile, you will reach Lake Ann Forest Camp on Lake Ann, the largest of the dozen or so lakes in the area.

The trail follows Hooker Road for 3½ miles and then turns north about six miles to the Gerry Lake Trail Camp which has water, toilets, and swimming in Gerry Lake. You cross into Leelanau County north of Gerry Lake and then turn west going cross country to Kitlinger Frederickson Road. Turn north about 1½ miles and walk the last few miles along Michigan 72. Follow 72 to a dead end and turn north one block past a hardware store to the Empire trail camp.

Grayling to Hardwood State Forest — 70 miles. This is the least developed section of the trail. It has fewer trail camps, but there are campgrounds near the trail. Eventually, this will go all the way to Mackinaw City.

The trail heads northeast from the fork, and after about six miles a side trail leads east to Babbitt's Riding Stable where campsites are available. A mile north of the Otsego County line, you can turn west on Marlette Road for two miles, then go south for one mile to the Lake Marjory Forest campground. This is in the Pigeon River State Forest, as is much of this section of the trail.

Marjory Lake is one of several near the trail in this area. Near Horseshoe Lake, the trail turns east for about eight miles and then north along Gingell Road, crossing an area of private land about five miles long before reentering the Pigeon River Forest.

It is 17 miles from the Forest boundary to Elk Hill trail camp, which has toilets but no water. About one mile south of this camp is the Pigeon River Forest campground, which you can reach by taking Hardwood Road a mile west from the trail.

In Cheboygan County, much of the trail is in Hardwood State Forest. About four miles north of the county line, turn northwest on Osmun Road for ¾ mile, then west on the first cross road for another mile to Campsite Road. This angles southwest for about another mile to Pine Grove Forest campground.

Two miles north of the Osmun Road, the trail passes the Dog Lake flooding, and 11 miles further on, the Stoney Creek flooding. Both of these are good waterfowl areas. The trail ends at the intersection of Merchant Road and Michigan 33.

Cadillac to the Main Trail — 32 miles. The south end of this branch trail is about 1½ miles east of U.S. 131 on Airport Road. This road at the north end of Cadillac is shown as "No. 36 Road" on the map, but the road sign on the ground says Airport. The Gateway camp at the end of the trail has water and toilets.

The trail goes almost straight north through a hilly area with many lakes in the Fife Lake State Forest. Twelve miles north it passes Manton and crosses Michigan 42. It follows back roads north into the forest again, and eight miles north of Manton enters Missaukee County. The undeveloped Hopkins Creek trail camp is in Missaukee County.

The trail quickly heads northwest into Grand Traverse County, passing through another area rich in lakes. Spring Lake campground is just off U.S. 131 about two miles north of where the trail crosses that road. About 10 miles north of 131, this branch meets the main trail. The branch actually splits, with one fork going straight north and the other west. Take the west fork if you are heading for Lake Michigan. Take the north if you want to east.

More information: Write to the Michigan Trail Riders Association, Rt. 5, Box 312-A, Traverse City, Mich. 49684, which offers a year's membership and a guide to the trail for $5.

Porcupine Mountains Wilderness State Park

Location: The park is on Lake Superior about 17 miles west of Ontonagon. It comprises more than 58,000 acres of some of the wildest country in the Midwest.

The shoreline of Lake Superior forms the northern border of the park. The eastern edge is a few miles west of — and parallel to — Michigan Route 64. The southern border is irregular, running more or less west from the village of White Pine to the mouth of the Presque Isle River in Gogebic County.

There are only two paved roads. One is Michigan 107, which enters

the park from the east, and ends a few miles into the park at a parking
area which also is a trail head. The other road is South Boundary
Road, which heads straight south from 107 just inside the eastern end
of the park. It turns west at the southern edge to Presque Isle Campground. There are four other campgrounds scattered along the South
Boundary Road, as well as one on Union Bay just off 107. Everything
else in the park is accessible only on foot.

Length of Trail: There are 17 named trails in the park with a total
length of 85 miles. They range in length from one mile to 16 miles, and
interconnect in various ways, making it possible to put together a hike
of almost any length.

Keep in mind the nature of the terrain if you are planning a trip. Vertical miles take longer than horizontal ones.

Description: The mountains are formed of a series of long ridges with
valleys running roughly parallel to the Lake Superior shoreline. The ap-
proximate mean elevation of the lake is 602 feet, while the highest
point in the "Porkies" is 1958 feet. Elevations more than 1500 feet are
fairly common, and this makes the park demanding country to hike in.
Trails may go up and down hundreds of feet within a few miles.

There are streams to cross on many trails. The rivers are one of the
glories of this park, and the trails frequently follow them. To get an
idea why, consider this: A trail parallels the Little Carp River for 5½
miles. In that distance, the river drops nearly 700 feet. Only the most
spectacular drops get named "falls," but rapids are more or less common. There are lakes, too, in the valleys.

There are some rather plush facilities, principally nine cabins, eight
with four bunks each and one with eight bunks. Four of the cabins are
along the Superior shore at Speakers Creek, the Little Carp River, the
Big Carp River and Buckshot Point. Four are on the high lakes in the
valleys of the Porcupine Mountains. They are at Lake of the Clouds,
the Lily Pond and Mirror Lake. Mirror Lake has two cabins, one with
eight bunks. The last cabin — called the Section 17 cabin — is on the
Little Carp River at Greenstone Falls, about 1200 feet up. None of the
cabins can be reached by road.

You can reserve a cabin by writing to the Park Supervisor, Porcupine Mountains State Park, Route #2, Ontonagon, Mich. 49953. Reservations are accepted for any date after January 1 of that year. The
cost is $4 a night for the four-bunk cabins, and $6 a night for the eight
bunk cabin. There are also special rates of $40 and $70 to rent a cabin during deer season.

There are three Adirondack shelters available on a first-come, first-
serve basis for $1.50 a night. These are three-sided structures with
bunks. Finally, you can camp beside the trail — for $1.50 a night —
anywhere except within ¼ mile of a cabin or shelter.

Backpackers are required to register at the park office before setting
out. Fires are allowed in the park.

Lake Superior — 16 miles. The trail follows the lake shore northwest from Presque Isle campground to Buckshot point. There it turns inland to end at Michigan 107. It starts atop high bluffs, but for most of its length the shore line is somewhat less steep, and the trail usually is within 20 feet (elevation) of the water. There are four cabins and a shelter along this trail. Their locations — and distance from the Presque Isle River — are: Speakers Creek — two miles, Little Carp River — six miles, Big Carp River — seven miles, Buckshot Point — 14 miles. The shelter is near Lone Rock about 12 miles from Presque Isle. Lone Rock is in the lake about 200 yards offshore. The trail from Buckshot point to 107 climbs about 550 feet in two miles. For fishermen, this trail offers lake trout, rainbows, and salmon, especially around the mouths of the streams.

Pinkerton Trail — three miles. This is near the western end of the park. It runs north from the South Boundary Road to the mouth of the Little Carp, passing through virgin hemlock along the way. It meets the Lake Superior Trail and the Little Carp Trail at its northern end.

Little Carp River Trail — 11 miles. It begins at the river's mouth where there is a cabin as well as the junction with the Pinkerton and Lake Superior trails. It follows the river upstream for 5½ miles, and there are four falls big enough to have names in that span. In between are innumerable rapids. The Section 17 cabin is six miles from the trail's beginning, altitude about 1200 feet. The Lily Pond cabin is three miles farther on — altitude 1500 feet. The trail ends at Mirror Lake, altitude 1531, 2½ miles from the Lily Pond. There is brook trout fishing in the Little Carp, and other trout in the Lily Pond and Mirror Lake. The Lily Pond has a soft bottom and fishermen should not try to wade it.

You can get to the Little Carp River Trail from the South Boundary Road via an access road called Little Carp River Road. The road is quite short and gives way to a trail that joins the Little Carp River Trail between the Section 17 cabin and the Lily Pond.

Cross Trail — five miles. This joins the Little Carp River Trail to the Big Carp River Trail and the Lake Superior Trail. The Section 17 cabin is at the south end and the Big Carp River cabin at the north.

Lost Lake Trail — 4½ miles. It connects the South Boundary Road with the Government Peak Trail. It is two miles from the road to Lost Lake, and another 2½ miles to the junction. Lost Lake Trail joins Government Peak Trail between Union Spring Trail and North Mirror Lake Trail.

Correction Line Trail — three miles. This runs between the Big and Little Carp River trails, crossing some extremely rugged terrain. It climbs about 500 feet in one mile and crosses Landlookers Creek and a small tributary of the Big Carp. The Mirror Lake cabins are at its west end, and there is an Adirondack shelter at its east end.

Lily Pond Trail — three miles. This heads south briefly from the Little Carp River Trail at the Lily Pond and then turns east to end at Summit Peak Road, an unimproved road running north from the South Bounda-

ry Road. Highest point on the trail is more than 1700 feet. The Lily
Pond cabin is at one end, and parking is available on Summit Peak
Road north of where this trail meets it.

South Mirror Lake Trail — 2½ miles. This follows Summit Peak Road
north from the South Boundary Road. You can leave your car in the
parking area and continue on foot to Mirror Lake with its two cabins. A
side trail one mile long leads west to Summit Peak (the mountain, not
the road), the highest point in the park at 1958 feet. You can see Lake
Superior from there and get a magnificent view of the mountains as
well.

Big Carp River Trail — nine miles. The trail begins at a parking area
at the end of Michigan 107. For the first two miles, it follows a steep
escarpment southwestward, providing excellent views of Lake Superior
from a height of over 1400 feet. It thens turns south down into the fairly broad valley that divides the escarpment from the next ridge line
south. The Big Carp River runs through this valley parallel to the lake
shore and then it — and the trail — turn toward the lake, tumbling
through a narrow gorge. Shining Cloud Falls, the second highest in the
park, is about one mile from the mouth of the river. It is five miles from
the beginning of the trail to the shelter at the junction with the Correction Line Trail. At the end of the trail is the Big Carp River cabin. The
trail crosses the river and a number of smaller streams as well.

North Mirror Lake Trail — four miles. The trail begins at the end of
107, climbs over the escarpment to the valley of the Big Carp and then
up again to the lake. Mirror Lake is at 1431 feet, the highest lake in
the state. This is probably the most physically demanding trail. In one
stretch it climbs more than 300 feet in about half a mile.

Government Peak Trail — eight miles. This trail branches south from
107, following the Big Carp River as far as Trap Falls — about two
miles. There is a shelter here. The trail then turns west to Government
Peak, which is 1850 feet high and the second highest point in the
park. This trail joins the North Mirror Lake Trail less than a mile from
the Mirror Lake Cabins.

Overlook Trail — three miles. This is a side trail that forms a loop east
off the Government Peak Trail. It begins one-half mile south of 107,
and returns to the main trail one mile south of the road. There are
some good views from the high places as well as stands of virgin timber along the way.

Escarpment Trail — four miles. This is a spectacular trail along the
escarpment east from the end of 107. Lake of the Clouds is in a valley
visible from the trail. Cloud Peak and Cuyahoga Peak are crossed
along the way, and the trail ends at 107 where the Government Peak
trail joins it.

Union Springs Trail and Impoundment Trail — 5½ miles. These are
separate trails, but it is convenient to treat them together. The Union
Springs Trail heads east from the Government Peak Trail to Union
Springs, which produces 700 gallons of water a minute. The spring is

two miles from the trail's beginning. From the spring, the Impoundment Trail goes east 3½ miles to South Boundary Road. The impoundment is an artificial lake in Union River where there are supposed to be brook trout.

Presque Isle — One mile. From the Presque Isle campground to the Lake Superior Trail. The Presque Isle is the largest and most spectacular of the park's many rivers.

Minnesota

All but a few of the trails of any length in this state are within the Superior National Forest adjacent to the Canadian border and Ontario's Quetico Provincial Park. Most of them are in the northern third of that forest, within the million-acre roadless domain of the Boundary Waters Canoe Area.

There are hiking trail networks of more than five miles each in 36 Minnesota State Parks, too. However, the 1971 state legislature authorized funds for several more long trails. Some of them may be finished by the time you read this book.

More information: Trail Coordinator, Division of Parks and Recreation, 320 Centennial Building, St. Paul, Minnesota 55155.

Superior National Forest Trails

Seven separate trails from this forest are described on the following pages. Items of general information and some regulations that apply to the entire area are detailed here.

The geology of the region includes numerous outcroppings of granite, and some of the most spectacular shorelines are formed by the unyielding vertical rock faces formed by this rock.

The terrain along most of the trails is flat to gently rolling, although those in the east, along the Laurentian Divide, have more elevation fluctuations than those in the west. The land is almost completely forested.

Anyone entering the Boundary Waters Canoe Area must obtain a free travel permit in person from a Superior National Forest office or from an outfitter or resort owner in the area. Forest Service ranger stations are located in Ely, Cook, Tofte, Two Harbors, Aurora, Isabella, Virginia and Grand Marais.

More information: Contact the Forest Supervisor, U.S. Forest Service, P.O. Box 338, Duluth, Minnesota 55801; or the ranger station nearest to the trail or trails you wish to hike.

Crab Lake Trail
Location: The Crab Lake Trail begins at Cook County Highway 12 (the

Gunflint Trail) at the east end on Long Loon Lake and proceeds northeast to a Laurentian Divide line at the west end of South Lake on the
International Boundary.
Length of Trail: Five miles
Description: The trail follows the east boundary of Loon Lake, then
skims along a patch of open country before reaching the lake for
which the trail was named. It then proceeds through a fir and aspen
woods to a watershed along the Laurentian Divide, then downhill slightly to South Lake.

Cummings Lake Trail

Location: The trail begins at Forest Road 644. This forest road turns
west off highway 116 just north of Fenske Lake Campground. The trail
runs west cross country and along abandoned logging roads to Cum-
mings Lake.
Length of Trail: Five miles
Description: This path stays just inside the Boundary Waters Canoe
area for most of its length, so no snowmobiles or motorcycles will mol-
est you. It crosses a narrow strip of water between Coxey Pond and
Silaca Lake about halfway along; but since the trail at this point is on a
logging road in fairly good condition, you are unlikely to get your feet
·wet. Part of the trail is in woods and part is through open country.

Eagle Mountain Trail

Location: The trail begins at Forest Road 153 about five miles west of
Two Island Lake Campground. It proceeds north cross country to Brule
Lake at the north end of Forest Road 326.
Length of Trail: Nine miles
Description: This trail provides some scenic vistas and the most climb-
ing you will encounter on trails anywhere within the Superior National
Forest. About halfway along, you will reach Eagle Mountain, highest
point in Minnesota at 2301 feet.

The trail is in good condition (in the Boundary Waters Canoe Area
— that means no swamps to cross). It runs almost directly north
through woods to Eagle Mountain, then proceeds northwest to Brule
Lake by way of the Brule Lookout Tower.

La Croix Trail

Location: It begins at Forest Road 116 about five miles east of the
Meander Lake Recreation Area and continues north to Stuart Lake.
Length of Trail: Eight miles. Actually, the trail is supposed to be 12
miles long, reaching to Lac La Croix on the International Border, but
that portion of the trail beyond Stuart Lake is in poor condition.
Description: The trail enters the Boundary Waters Canoe Area about
1¼ miles north of the highway. It continues through a forest of birches
and conifers and along the western shores of Mule Creek to Stuart
Lake. Between the fourth and fifth miles, you will cross a half mile
patch or so of relatively open country. If you hike the trail in mosquito

season, this will provide welcome relief.

The path is wet and muddy in several spots. It is used both for hiking and horseback riding in the summer.

Kekekabic Trail

Location: The Kekekabic Trail extends from the Gunflint Trail (County Highway 12), 50 miles northwest of Grand Marais, to Fernberg Road (County Highway 18), 20 miles east of Ely.

Length of Trail: 38 miles. Parking space is available at both ends.

Description: This trail was constructed during the 1930s for firefighting and for servicing the Kekekabic Lookout Tower, which is no longer in existence. The eastern half of the trail is in good shape, but the western half is not. Some rough scrambling and deep wading occasionally is necessary. The Gunflint Tower near the eastern terminus is used as a radio tower. Visitors are requested not to climb it. There are remnants of the old Paulson iron ore mine, which was active during the 1890's, also near the east end. Be careful of the pits, especially in winter when the snow may obscure the openings. A log bridge over the gorge between Ogishkemuncie and Agamok Lakes, constructed in 1968, provides a striking scenic attraction.

The trail covers terrain that is level to gently rolling with only a few steep grades. It is well marked and easy to follow. In summer, swamps and water crossings along the trail might require getting your feet wet. Some of these places will be rerouted and others bridged sometime in the future.

Lakes scattered along the trail provide for drinking water (boil it before drinking), but hikers should carry a canteen for the long stretches between lakes.

Detailed area maps showing the trail are available from local outfitters or from the W. A. Fisher Company, Virginia, Minn. 55792. Map numbers 113 and 114 cover the entire trail. U.S. Geological Survey maps of the area are available, but they don't show location of the trail.

Superior Forest rangers suggest a minimum of three days for a leisurely trip over the 38 miles in the summer. In winter, plan from five to eight days. Your speed will depend on whether you are breaking snow all the way, your physical condition, and how strongly you feel like stopping and building a warm fire. Most people using the trail don't cover ground as quickly as they thought they would.

Norway Trail

Location: The trail begins one mile east of the Lake Jeanette Campground on Forest Road 116. This highway, known locally as Echo Trail, proceeds northwestward through the forest from the town of Ely, where a majority of the region's private outfitters are located.

Length of Trail: Eight miles.

Description: The path travel almost directly south from the forest road across gently rolling land to Trout Lake, one of the larger bodies of water in the forest. Norway Creek crosses the trail about 4½ miles south of the Lake Jeanette Camp, and small lakes are visible at several points along the way.

There are no established campsites at trail's end on Trout Lake, but you may set up your own, keeping forest regulations in mind.

The last half mile of the trail is within the Boundary Waters Canoe Area. The path is useable in winter for snowshoeing and cross-country skiing and that portion outside the BWCA is available for snowmobiling.

Sioux-Hustler Trail

Location: This trail begins on Forest Road 116 about three miles east of Camp Jeanette and winds north of the road in a loop that eventually will bring you back to the Forest Road via the recreation area at Meander Lake and Forest Road 467.

Length of Trail: 27 miles.

Description: This trail is not recommended for amateurs. The hiker will encounter brushy spots and windfalls at many locations along the way. Some parts of the trail are difficult to follow and all streams must be waded. The terrain varies from flat to gently rolling. Wilderness campsites are provided on Emerald Lake, Devils Cascade, and Pageant Lake.

Proceeding north from the western terminus of the trail you will cross a snowmobile trail after walking about two miles. You will follow it northwest for half a mile or so, then split off to the right to head directly north for Lower Pauness Lake. Skirting its east side, you will reach the first campground at Devils Cascade (about five miles from the trail's beginning).

The path north from this campground passes through heavy forest, and you will encounter no major streams for about four miles.

Shortly after crossing the first major stream, the trail begins to turn east and then south around the upper side of Range Line Lake.

The second trailside campground is north of the footpath, just across from Range Line Lake on Pageant Lake.

Heading south you will pass Hustler Lake and Emerald Lake (another campsite) and a short stretch (about ¼ mile) of open country.

The trail leaves the Boundary Waters Canoe area about four miles south of Emerald Lake, so snowmobiles are permitted along this last segment.

It ends at Meander Lake Recreation Area, where there are picnic tables but no camping facilities. To get back to your car, take Forest Road 467 south to Forest Road 116 and head west for about five miles.

Missouri

This is a favorite Midwestern state for spring hiking. The season comes early to the Ozarks, for one reason; the mosquitoes are not as vicious as they are farther north, for another.

Most of the long hiking trails are found within one of the state's two national forests, the Clark and the Mark Twain. State parks and forests limit trail lengths to two miles.

The Boy Scouts have developed several trails not detailed here. The Moses Austin Trail is 14 miles long, most of it on federal land. It begins about 11 miles west of Potosi on State Route 8. The John J. Audubon Trail makes a 12-mile loop that runs north of Womack, southwest of Clearwater, and southeast of Farmington. For further information on these footpaths, write the Boy Scouts of America, 4568 W. Pine Blvd., St. Louis, Missouri 63108.

More information: State highway maps and general tourist information are available from the Missouri Tourism Commission, Box 1055, Jefferson City, Mo. 65101; and the Missouri Department of Conservation, 2901 N. Ten Mile Drive, Jefferson City, Mo. 65101.

Clark National Forest

Berryman Trail

Location: The Berryman Trail is a riding and hiking trail making a loop through a sparsely settled part of the Potosi Ranger District of the Clark National Forest. It may later link up with a proposed state-wide system of horse riding trails.

The starting point is an old Civilian Conservation Corps (CCC) campsite known as the Berryman Camp, located 17 miles west of Potosi on State Highway 8 and one mile north on Forest Road 2266.

Length of Trail: 24 miles

Description: The trail is designed for single file traffic through a variety of Ozark topography, scenery, and timber types.

There is a five-acre national forest campground with eight tent spaces on the site of the old CCC camp. Picnic tables, fireplaces and flush toilets are provided.

From the Berryman Camp the trail winds more or less directly west for a mile and a half, then turns sharply north and east. You will cross three fire trails before coming to the Edward Beecher Campground. This camp boasts an artesian well in addition to fireplaces and picnic tables.

Two miles north of this campsite, the trail crosses Forest Road 2265, and half a mile farther on it curves again to the west. At mile 10½ you will reach another campsite with an artesian well, Harmon Spring Camp.

From Harmon Spring, the trail turns east and meanders up and down hill to the Brazil Creek Camp, adjacent to County Highway W at mile 14½ of the loop trail. Local legend has it that the Jesse James gang frequently camped here when journeying through the country. There are eight tent spaces in this tiny park, plus picnic tables, fireplaces and flush toilets.

From Brazil Creek Camp, the trail drops south and you will cross three more fire trails before crossing Forest Road 2265 at mile 18½. You will pass through Elm Lick Hollow and begin to edge west again in Kemlin Hollow (around mile 20). Another four miles will bring you back to the Berryman Camp and your car.

Big Piney Trail

Location: The easternmost point of this loop trail begins 10 miles west of Licking and is accessible by state highway 32 and county routes N and AF. You also may begin your hike from the westernmost point at the Roby Lookout Tower, six miles south of Fort Leonard Wood on Highway 17.

Length of Trail: The Big Piney Trail winds through 17 miles of the Paddy Creek area of the Clark National Forest (Houston district). All motorized traffic is prohibited.

Description: The forest here is lush in the summer, mature hardwoods laced with grapevines and wildflowers of every description. The trail crosses Little Paddy and Big Paddy Creeks, both offshoots of the Big Piney River. They are clear and fast-moving little streams but may or may not be safe for drinking without boiling the water. This part of Missouri is favored by canoeists as well as hikers, and nearly every resort rents canoes and fishing tackle.

Paddy Creek Campground is the only designated campsite on the entire route. If you plan to do the entire 17 miles, you will probably want to leave your car at the Roby Lookout Tower, hike to Paddy Creek Camp, spend the night, then walk back along the other half of the loop the next day.

The trail proceeds east from the fire tower about a mile before branching. The northern route is longer (about 9½ miles to Paddy Creek Campground) because it is more winding. You will walk east along this northern part about three miles before encountering a fire lane which parallels the trail for a mile or so. Just before you cross the lane, there is a scenic overlook with nothing but undulating forest to see in all directions.

Between the fourth and fifth miles you will pass through a Box Canyon, and somewhere around the sixth mile the trail crosses Forest Road 220. You can take a shortcut south on this road to the campground if you are getting tired of the deep woods or mosquitoes are getting too pesky.

If you prefer to continue, the trail loops gently around to the south after passing the forest road. About Mile 8, there is another lookout point on a bluff from which you may catch a glimpse of the Big Piney River to the east.

You will be heading west again before you come to the camp. Fires are permitted but there may not be any cut or split wood on hand. Use only dead or down wood if you have to scrounge for your own camp-fire fuel.

Starting off again the next morning you will come to a small lime-stone cave just after crossing Big Paddy Creek, and you will cross a fire lane and the first of three watering ponds somewhere around Mile 4.

Little Paddy Creek crosses the trail about a mile and a half from the junction with the trail's northern half. Another mile and you are back at the lookout tower. Climb up and see where you have been.

More information: To find out more about this section of the Clark National Forest contact the District Ranger at Houston, Mo. 65483.

Rock Pile Mountain Trail

Location: In the Madison County section of the Clark National Forest south of Fredericktown. The path begins at Faro Lookout Tower and travels south over undeveloped logging trails to Rock Pile Mountain.

To get to Faro Tower from Fredericktown, take State Highway 67 south to County Road C. Go west on C to Cedar Mountain. Continue west there on a forest road and follow it until signs direct you along the first road to the left. This road will lead you up to the tower.

Length of Trail: Five miles

Description: This trail is recommended only to experienced hikers armed with plenty of stamina and a good compass. It has come to the attention of hiking enthusiasts only by word of mouth and wasn't devel-oped for recreational purposes at all. The compass is necessary be-cause there are no blazes to keep you to the path and the fire lanes that crisscross all forest roads may confuse you. Rock Pile Mountain is almost due south from Faro Tower. Get specific directions from a local ranger before you start out.

Taum Sauk Trail

Location: The Taum Sauk Trail lies between two sections of the Clark National Forest. It begins at the Elephant Rocks State Park near Gran-iteville and runs south and west to end at tiny Johnson Shut-Ins State Park. On the way it climbs up and over Taum Sauk Mountain, highest elevation point in the state. From St. Louis to the trail's beginning is a drive of about 100 miles.

Length of Trail: 28 miles

Description: This path was established in 1958 by the Boy Scouts and is still managed and heavily used by them. If you wish to hike it, you should contact the Boy Scouts of America, 4568 W. Pine, St. Louis, for reservations.

Trace Creek Trail

Location: In that section of the Clark National Forest immediately west of Potosi and Ironton. To reach Keith Spring, the forest recreation area that is the starting point for this trail, take state highway 21 north from

Ironton to the junction with state highway 32 north of Belleview. Take 32 west about 11 miles to Keith Spring.
Length of Trail: Five miles.
Description: This little trail runs entirely through deciduous forests and involves little climbing. There are three creeks to cross within the five miles, all ideal picnic sites. There are no campground facilities at Keith Spring, nor are there any along the trail with the exception of a primitive hunter's cabin just before the junction of the trail with County Road DD.

The footpath ends at a secondary road about half a mile west of another intersection with Highway DD. To avoid retracing your steps back to Keith Spring, you can walk west and south along the road instead. When the county road intersects Forest Road 2391, take the forest road south to state highway 32 and the state highway east for a mile to Keith Spring.

The campground within easiest driving distance of the Trace Creek Trail is about 20 miles west at Davisville, still within the Clark National Forest. To get there from Keith Spring, drive west on highway 32 to county road Z at East End. Drive north on Z to the Czar lookout tower, then go north and west on county road V to Davisville.

Mark Twain
National Forest

Whites Creek Trail
Location: In the Winona-Doniphan-Van Buren Ranger Districts of the Mark Twain National Forest, east of Poplar Bluff and not far from the state's boot-heel. To reach the trail's easternmost end at Camp Five Pond, take state highway 160 west of Doniphan to county highway J. Take J north about six miles to the camp. There is ample space for car parking there and picnic tables with fireplaces, but no overnight camping is permitted. There is a campground, however, about halfway between Doniphan and the trail head, at Buffalo Creek on Forest Road 3145.
Length of Trail: 20 miles
Description: The steep hills and deep hollows in this region were formed by tributaries of the Eleven Point River cutting into the impressionable limestone. This kind of rock, also known for its susceptibility to fossil imprints is predominant throughout the Ozark mountains.

The Whites Creek Trail makes a good two day hike if you get an early start. Bliss Spring Campground is located about halfway along the loop trail.

West of Camp Five Pond the trail winds along on more or less level ground through heavy hardwood forest for a couple of miles before beginning a gentle ascent to Whites Creek.

At the creek about 3½ miles from the trail's beginning, the trail branches to begin the loop. If you take the northern route, you will begin climbing almost immediately, ascending 300 feet to the top of a mountain in less than two miles. From this peak you will have a good view of Bliss Hollow to the south and the impressive Eleven Point River itself. The Corps of Engineers waged a campaign several years ago to dam the Eleven Point, but conservationists prevailed and it was made a National Scenic River.

The west slope of the mountain is gentle, and the trail follows a ridge line for about two miles between Bliss and Brawley Hollows.

It begins a sharp descent and a gentle curve to the south around mile 7. The Eleven Point River is almost immediately below you now at its spectacular Horseshoe Bend. The trail continues along a ridge, but at a lower elevation than before, between the river on the west and Barn Hollow on the east.

Bliss Creek Campground, about 8½ miles by trail from Camp Five Pond, is situated on the riverbank at the southern end of Bliss Hollow. Because this camp is so far from main roads, it is used almost exclusively by hikers from the trail and by fishermen floating the Eleven Point. There are no picnic tables, but there is a well.

Heading back east from Bliss Spring, the trail stays between steep hillsides in Bliss Hollow for most of a mile, then climbs sharply to a ridge overlooking Orchard Hollow. It follows the brow of the ridge around to the south for a mile, then descends again to Whites Creek and a mile-long side trail that leads to Whites Creek Cave.

The main trail from this point heads north and then quickly south in another horseshoe bend for about a mile and a half along Whites Creek to Fiddler Spring.

It heads north then, still along the stream bed for about 1½ miles, to the point where the trail first branched. Retrace your steps of the previous day back east to Camp Five Pond.

Ohio

The big story in Ohio is the Buckeye Trail. This will eventually form a great loop from Toledo to Cincinnati to Cleveland. Most of it is complete now.

The Buckeye Trail

Location: The Buckeye Trail begins at the Ohio River in Cincinnati. One branch extends northward through Dayton as far as a small town called Lockington. This branch will eventually reach all the way to Toledo. The other branch heads east, passing south of Chillicothe, Lancaster, and Zanesville. It then turns north, passing east of Cambridge and through Massillon. Just north of Massillon, it splits into two parts. One part skirts the western edge of Akron and the eastern edge of Cleve-

land. The other branch goes around Akron to the east and then heads north toward Lake Erie. The two branches meet just south of the lake, and the trail ends on the lakefront near a spot called Fairport Harbor.
Length of Trail: About 760 miles.
Description: Before getting into a detailed description of the entire trail, it might be a good idea to take a look at how this rather amazing footpath was put together. The Buckeye Trail is largely the creation of a group of hiking enthusiasts who call themselves the Buckeye Trail Association. They conceived the idea, planned the routes, and actually laid out and marked the path.

Ohio is a densely populated state without any large tracts of publicly owned land. Consequently, the trail is mainly confined to roads. Where it leaves the roads, it frequently crosses privately owned land. Permission for hikers to use this land is, of course, dependent on the continued goodwill of the land owners, which means hikers should be extra careful not to disturb anything.

The trail is atop a levee along the Mad River and on a similar structure on the Miami. At Taylorville, it crosses a dam and then follows the bed of the Miami-Erie Canal. Levees and canal towpaths, with brief detours onto riverside roads, make up the entire remainder of the trail.

Some points of interest along the way include the Johnson Farm, a project of the Ohio Historical Society. The society is restoring an old farm and a section of the Miami-Erie Canal. Rides in a canal boat will be offered when the project is completed. The farm is between Piqua and Lockington. Restored buildings include a house of the 1810-15 period, a log barn dating from 1808, and a brick spring house. At the end of the trail in Lockington is a museum offering exhibits from the earliest days of settlement in Ohio.

For campers, Mr. Shelton Prudhomme, 2535 E. Ross Road, Tipp City, Ohio 45371, offers use of his land by advance arrangement. The campsite is about half way between Taylorsville and Tipp City 1½ miles east of the trail on Ross Road. The site is near a 50-foot waterfall, and only hikers are allowed to use it.

Hikers will have to wade Loramie Creek just south of Lockington. During high water season, detour around it by road.

Shawnee State Forest

Shawnee Backpack Trail
Location: In the Shawnee State Forest along the Ohio River west of Portsmouth. The trail is a loop that begins at a parking area on Ohio 125 about ½ mile south of State Forest Road 16.
Length of Trail: About 20 miles
Descriptions: The countryside here is hilly and covered with hardwood forest. Elevations along the trail range from above 1200 feet on the hilltops down to less than 700 feet in the hollows. The trail crosses a

number of hollows, so there is a good deal of up and down walking.

The trail heads east from the start, crossing Forest Road 1 after about three miles and Forest Road 14 after another three. Along the way, it crosses six separate hollows. These are dry most of the time, but they may have running water in wet seasons. Just beyond Forest Road 14 there is drinking water and a primitive campsite on the hillside above Zarne Hollow.

The trail heads northwest from here, roughly parallel to 14. It crosses Forest Road 1, and then goes straight west for about five miles. There is another campsite at the head of Rock Lick Hollow, and drinking water is available where the trail touches Forest Road 6 near Copperhead Lookout Tower. The trail crosses Route 6 twice along this stretch before heading south for about three miles back to the starting point.

The main trail is marked with orange blazes, and side trails to campsites are marked with white. Camping is permitted only in the prepared campsites, and fires are allowed only in fire rings at these sites. There are rattlesnakes and copperheads in this area, and a snake bite kit should be carried.

Registration forms are provided at the starting point, and all hikers are required to fill them out before starting on a hike.

Planometric maps of the Shawnee State Forest and topographic maps of the trail itself are available from the Ohio Department of Natural Resources, Division of Forests and Preserves, Fountain Square, Columbus, Ohio 43224.

Wayne National Forest

Vesuvius Trail
Location: In the Wayne National Forest, one mile east of Ohio Route 93 eight miles north of Ironton.
Length of Trail: 15 miles
Description: The U.S. Forest Service has created the Lake Vesuvius Recreation Area around an artificial lake created by damming Storms Creek. The trail is a loop that winds through the hilly wooded country starting and ending near the Vesuvius Iron Furnace. The furnace was built in 1833 and used to smelt iron until 1906.

The recreation area has two campgrounds with 69 sites, five picnic grounds, a boat dock with 40 rowboats for rent, a space for private rowboat mooring, and a bathing beach. Powerboats are not allowed.

Further information on this area is available from the District Ranger, Wayne National Forest, Ironton, Ohio 45638.

Wisconsin

The Wisconsin Department of Natural Resources only recently became aware of a need for public hiking trails; but once aware, it lost little time creating facilities. You will find all the state-run trails well-maintained, though not all of them have the mileposts hikers cherish as proof they are really making progress.

Wisconsin terrain is ideal for hikers. Seldom is it entirely flat and treeless, but just as seldom are trails so steep you are tempted to throw your backpack off into a distant gorge and crawl the rest of the way on your hands and knees.

More information: Most state parks and state forests contain short hiking trails of a mile to a mile and a half in length not detailed here. You can find out more about them by writing the Wisconsin Department of Natural Resources, Box 450, Madison, Wis. 53701. Snowmobile trails in the Nicolet National Forest can be used by hikers in summer. The forest supervisor can be contacted at the Federal Building in Rhinelander, Wis. 54501.

Chequamegon National Forest

Mt. Valhalla Trail
Location: In far northern Wisconsin roughly straight west of Washburn, a town on the shore of Lake Superior. To reach it from Washburn, take Bayfield County Route C west to the Mt. Valhalla Recreation Area.
Length of Trail: 17 miles. The trail loop begins and ends at Mt. Valhalla.
Description: This marked trail is part of a network of snowmobile trails that the Forest Service has opened up in this area. When there is no snow on the ground, hikers can use the facilities. The countryside is hilly, with the typical northern forest cover of jack pine, aspen and birch.

There is a chalet at Mt. Valhalla (the area has been used for training the U.S. Olympic Ski Team) with drinking water available. Leaving the chalet, the trail climbs to a high hill from which you can see Lake Superior. The Birch Grove Campground is 4.7 miles south of Mt. Valhalla. It offers pit toilets, drinking water and fire rings. There are 16 campsites, and the daily use fee is $2.00.

Beyond Birch Grove, the Long Lake Picnic Ground (6.5 miles from Mt. Valhalla) has drinking water and toilets, a beach with change houses and picnic facilities.

North of Mt. Valhalla is the Sun Bowl, a large valley with few trees.

In addition to the trail markers, each intersection of the trail with other trails or with forest roads is numbered. The number at the intersection corresponds to a number on a sketch map of the area which is available from the Forest Service Office, Park Falls, Wis. 54552, or from the District Ranger, Washburn, Wis. The district office can also supply a planometric map on a scale of ½ inch to the mile.

Flambeau Trails

Location: There are 11 different interconnecting trails in the Flambeau system, all located in the Park Falls Section of the Chequamegon National Forest. There is an access point with a parking lot just off Wisconsin State Route 70, about five miles east of Fifield. Most of the trails in the system begin at this point, branching out to the north, south and east.

The longest of the trails, Number 111, does not begin at the access point. It's western end is at Blockhouse Lake and can be reached by taking Wisconsin 182 east from Park Falls to Forest Road 648. Go north on 648 for about two miles. The trail intersects 648 at Forest Road 153.

Length of trails: The trail numbers and lengths are as follows: 101: 15.4 miles; 102: 10.6 miles; 103: 2.2 miles; 104: 6 miles; 106: 0.6 miles; 107: 01. miles; 108: 0.8 miles; 109: 1.2 miles; 110: 05 miles; 111: 24.8 miles; 119: 0.6 miles.

Description: These trails were originally cut to restrain meandering snowmobilers, but the forest service has added bridges over streams so they can be used all year. A warning note in the words of the Forest Service: "The Flambeau Trails are managed for multiple use: snowmobiling, hiking, hunting, walking, horseback riding, trail bike riding, etc."

This is rolling to flat country covered with a typical northern forest vegetation: birch, aspen, spruce and jack pine. There are numerous lakes, ponds and small streams, and the South Fork of the Flambeau River also flows through the area. There are also extensive areas of marshy land, some of which has been set aside as waterfowl refuges.

In this kind of country, it is a good idea to stay on the trails. There are no landmarks to speak of, and it is easy to get lost.

Trail 101 begins at the access point and winds eastward for 15.4 miles, ending just west of Pike Lake. There are two forest service campgrounds north of the trail. A bit more than halfway along the trail you can turn off north on Forest Road 148 to the Smith Rapids campground which is between one and two miles from the trail. Two miles beyond 148, you can turn north on Trail 111 approximately three miles to Fishtrap camp (Note: there is no water at this camp). Both of these campgrounds are along the Flambeau River.

The land around Pike lake is privately owned, but there is a campground on the north east shore called Stein's Oak Grove. Campsites are $2.50 per night and there is a beach, boat launching facilities and boats for rent.

Trail 102 heads south from the access point past Spur Lake (2-3 miles), Sailor Creek (3 miles), Gates Lake (4-5 miles), Nichols Lake (6 miles) and the Squaw Creek Flowage (8-10 miles), ending at the Forest Boundary. The Squaw Creek Waterfowl Area is near this trail. From the Squaw Creek dam, take Forest Road south two to three miles to a county campground on Solberg Lake. This campground also has a beach, boat dock and boats for rent.

Trail 103 branches off 102 just south of Sailor Creek. It follows the creek westward, ending at the forest boundary. Beyond the boundary, there is a poor road that leads to the Sailor Creek Flowage campground approximately two to three miles away.

Trail 104 begins at the western edge of the access point, meandering northeast and then looping back southeast to join Trail 101 about three to four miles east of the access point. The entire 104-101 loop is about 10 miles long.

Trails 106 through 110 are very short, serving mainly to connect some of the larger trails; 106 runs north from the access to 104. If you want to take the 104-101 loop, starting out on 106 would shorten things slightly. Trail 107 joins 104 and 106 just north of the access. Trail 108 branches north from 101 about a mile east of the access and heads northeast to join 104. This is another alternate that could shorten the 104-101 loop. Trails 109 and 110 are best considered together. They head north from the northernmost point of trail 104 and end at Forest Road 152.

Trail 111, the longest in the system, starts two to three miles from the east end of 101. It meanders north and then east, ending at Blockhouse Lake. Along the way it crosses the Flambeau near Fishtrap campground. While it does not touch any lakes until trail's end at Blockhouse Lake, it passes within a mile or two of more than a dozen.

It is possible to make a complete loop of just under 50 miles by taking trail 101 east from the access point to trail 111. Then take 111 to its end. From there, walk south along Forest Road 648 about 1.5 miles, then east on Wisconsin Route 182 for another mile and a half to Forest Road 152. Take 152 south about 1.5 miles, then east a few hundred yards to where trail 109 hits it. Trail 109 connects to 104 which takes you back to the access point.

Finally, trail 119 is a short north-south walk connecting trails 101 and 108 just east of the access point.

More information: It is rather difficult to describe a trail network like this one in words. With a map, the whole thing becomes immediately clear. The District Ranger, Park Falls ranger District, City Hall Building, Park Falls, Wis. 54552, can supply you with a planometric map of the entire Chequamegon National Forest (scale ¼ inch to the mile). This map shows the three longest trails (101, 102 and 111), as well as information on campsites. The Ranger also will supply a rough sketch map of all the trails, and some information on the trails and their use.

The U.S. Geological Survey quadrangles are Park Falls and Pike

Lake. The Pike Lake quadrangle is a planometric map on a 1:48,000 scale. At this time the only topographical map of the area is the 1:250,000 scale. The City Hall building in Park Falls is right on Route 13, and it might be a good idea to check in there for any last minute information before you start hiking.

Rock Island State Park

Location: Rock Island State Park is a 900 acre, wooded island at the northernmost tip of the Door County peninsula which makes up the eastern shore of Lake Michigan's Green Bay.

The peninsula is accessible by two state highways, #57 from Green Bay and #42 from Manitowoc. The park, which allows no motorized vehicles, is accessible by two pedestrian ferries, operated privately with contracts from the state. One ferry leaves twice daily (at 10 a.m. and 2 p.m.) during the summer from the mainland port of Gills Rock. The other leaves hourly between 9 a.m. and 4 p.m. during July and August from Washington Island's Jackson Harbor. In spring and fall (June 1 to July 1 and September 4 to October 15) the ferry from Washington Island to Rock Island leaves at 10 a.m., noon, 2 p.m. and 4 p.m.

Washington Island lies between the mainland and Rock Island and is definitely worth a visit by itself. If you go that route, however, you must take an extra ferry. A fleet of three car ferries runs frequently in July and August between Gills Rock and Washington Island (every half hour when traffic is heavy). In spring and fall, the gaps in service can sometimes be up to two hours, and from December through March the boats run only twice daily. But, if you want to visit Rock Island in the winter, though, you have to rent a snowmobile or trudge across the ice.

Length of Trail: Approximately eight miles of interconnecting trails.

Description: The trails in this state park are ideal for beginners or for hikers shaking down new equipment. The terrain is varied, but there is no steep climbing. Trail surfaces are well-maintained (no jagged rocks or potholes), and mosquitoes are few, even in the wettest springs and summers. There is only one campground, from which all the trails are easily accessible, so day hikes are in order and there is no need to carry more than a picnic lunch.

The campground is located on the southwest side of the island; there are 40 sites, most of them on the shore but some inland as well. All are far enough apart to insure privacy. Pit toilets, picnic tables, fireplaces and firewood are available. Drinking water is available at a faucet near the dock. There is an electric generator on the island, so there is no need to pump water by hand. Fees for camping are $2.25 a night per site, and checkout time is 3 p.m. A state park ranger lives permanently on the island and is available at all times for information, advice or aid.

The main trail, which takes about three hours to hike at a leisurely pace, skirts the edge of the island all the way around it. Two more trails cut across the interior from east to west. To understand some of the things you will see on these trails, it helps to know a little of the island's history.

Archeologists from Lawrence College in Appleton have developed several excavation sites adjacent to the trail on the southern shore of the island which reveal the location of one Indian village dating from the 16th century. They also have found remains of some storage buildings and defense ramparts thought to have been erected by LaSalle's men.

In 1836 the first lighthouse in the state of Wisconsin was built on Rock Island and named for the original Potawatomi settlers. Its interior is closed today to visitors, but the exterior is still in excellent condition. The beautifully landscaped grounds behind it and the panoramic view make it a perfect resting point on your trek around the island's periphery.

A brother of Daniel Boone, his two sons and David Kennison, the last surviving member of the Boston Tea Party and a veteran of Bunker Hill, were among English residents of the early and mid-19th century.

You are sure to want to stay at least a week once you are there, but if you do you will have to make supply trips back to Washington Island. Owners of the Karfi ferry charge $1.60 round trip for commuters, $2 for folks carrying camping gear.

Any hiking you do on Washington Island will have to be on public roads; there are no trails. A number of people live year-round on this 36 square mile island.

There are grocery stores, bars, a community center, post office and a number of cottages and motels. One public campground is located on the north shore at Schoolhouse Beach. Several festivals are scheduled on the island during the summer. Two fish boils are held annually in July. For up-to-date information, you can contact the Washington Island Tourist Bureau, Washington Island, Wisconsin. 54246.

Park Falls—Tuscobia Trail

Location: The Park Falls-Tuscobia Trail is another of the state-maintained trails that follows an old railroad bed. It runs from Park Falls on State Route 13 in northern Wisconsin (about 50 miles south of Lake Superior) west on a meandering line across country to Tuscobia, a tiny hamlet four miles north of Rice Lake on State Route 53.

Length of Trail; 74 miles. Most of the trail's eastern half, however, runs adjacent to, or very near, county highways E and EE and State Highway 70.

Description: The western part of the trail contains the most spectacular scenery, since you will be passing through the Meteor Hills country. The elevation is more than 1800 feet, almost as high as it gets in Wisconsin, but since the trail does follow an old railroad bed you will not encounter grades steeper than five to six per cent.

About two miles from the western end of the trail you will cross Tus-cobia Creek; if the weather is dry you might miss it. Two miles farther on, however, you may have to detour a few hundred feet to the north and cross the Brill River on a highway bridge of a town road leading into the, village of Brill.

From Brill the trail angles northeastward toward State Highway 48 and the town of Angus. Shortly after passing through Angus you will detour again, this time to a highway bridge on 48, to get across a nar-row stream of water connecting Balsam and Red Cedar Lakes. The next small town is Birchwood; it's approximately 7½ miles between Brill and Birchwood.

After Birchwood, there are no more detours for 17 miles. The few streams that cross your path will be easily fordable — Malviney Creek, 33 Creek, Knuteson Creek just past the town of Yarnell and Swift Creek at Lemington. This segment takes you through some of the wild-est, most remote land in northern Wisconsin.

Just before reaching the town of Couderay, you will have to detour south on town roads to avoid having to swim the Couderay River and Eddy Creek.

The trail parallels state highways 27 and 70 for five miles between Couderay and the town of Radisson (named for the first white man to visit the area — in 1659). Rock Creek crosses the trail just before Ra-disson; but since you are immediately adjacent to the highway, there is no inconvenience.

At Radisson you will have to hike highway 70 east two miles to a town road, then south ½ mile to intersect the trail again.

Six miles east of Radisson is the town of Ojibwa, another — you guessed it — detour across the Chippewa River highway bridge — and the only authorized campground you will encounter along the trail ($2.25 per night). Camping is allowed anywhere beside the trail for your other nights out, but rangers caution hikers to leave each site as they found it when leaving in the morning. Carry out empty all contain-ers you carried in full. Campfires are allowed but small stoves are pre-ferred.

The 6-unit Ojibwa campground is one mile east of the town. Toilets and drinking water are available.

The trail runs adjacent to highway 70 again for the five miles be-tween Ojibwa and Winter. There is a ranger station at Winter, and the ranger there is in charge of maintaining the trail. You might want to consult him about current conditions on the trail ahead of you. At Win-ter you will be hiking right on the highway for about three-quarters of a mile.

About two miles east of Winter you will encounter the Brunet River, an excellent place to fish for walleye, as are many of the streams in this area. To get around the river, take highway 70 north ¼ mile to a town road, then walk ½ mile east to intersect the trail again. After

about seven more miles you will cross Fly Blow Creek (small detour)
and then come upon the twin towns of Loretta and Draper, one mile
apart.

The last stretch of the trail, 19½ miles between Draper and Park
Falls, is occasionally marshy and crisscrossed with creeks — Thornap-
ple, Log, Pine and Butternut. For most of this distance, it is best to
walk along the edge of county highways EE and E.

When you encounter a private property sign about two miles west of
Park Falls, take the town road there north to County Highway B and
follow that on into town.

Hardly anyone but Boy Scouts has hiked the Park Falls-Tuscobia
Trail so far, because theoretically it is not finished. The trail is only for
hikers who do not mind a few hardships — such as wading a creek or
two and making your own campsite along the trail instead of stopping
in one maintained by park or forest rangers. Isolation itself has many
charms. Your chances to see birds, deer and other game are much
greater than if you stick to more civilized walks.

North Country Trail

Location: Eastern end of the trail is just west of Mellin — a town on
Wisconsin Route 13 — and its western end is three miles south of Iron
River, Wisconsin, which is on U.S. Route 2. To reach the western end
of the trail, take Bayfield County A south from Iron River to Lake Ruth.
The trail starts at County A just south of the lake. Its beginning is
marked by a large wooden sign.

The eastern terminus can be reached by taking Hillcrest Ave. west
from Mellin. This street becomes Forest Road 390 about 2½ miles
west of Mellin, and the trail branches off to the left from the road about
three miles from town. This end of the trail is also marked with a large
wooden sign.

Length of Trail: 60 miles.

Description: Someday, there is supposed to be a North Country Trail
connecting the Appalachian Trail in Vermont with the proposed Lewis
and Clark Trail in North Dakota. At present, only two sections of this
proposed trail are completed. One is in the Allegheny National Forest
and the other is this section in the Chequamegon National Forest.

The trail is marked with either orange or yellow diamond-shaped
blazes, and there are frequent signs giving the distance to the next notable landmark along the way. The eastern two-thirds of the trail is
marked with numbered posts every mile.

The landscape ranges from rolling to rather rugged. In the Penokee
Mountains, some upgrades get pretty long and steep, but generally
speaking the walking is not especially difficult.

Fall is incredibly beautiful in this area. The hardwoods of the forest
are mainly maple, the aspen that is known locally as popple, and birch.
Their fall colors are punctuated by the occasional conifer. The bugs
are gone, and for birders; the fall migration is in full swing.

Of course, you do have hunters. September is bear season. In October it is grouse and partridge, and towards the end of November it's deer.

There are several Forest Service campgrounds on or just off of the trail. These have pit toilets, wells, fireplaces and access by road. You can lay out a trip that will allow you to stay at one of these every night, but the Forest Service will not object if backpackers camp anywhere along the trail. Fires can be built along the trail with the usual precautions. Use only dead wood, and be sure the fire is out before you leave it.

What follows is a detailed description of the trail beginning at the eastern end. The trail heads southwest from Forest Road 390, but this is the section that beavers have dammed. If you want to avoid the pond created by these industrious rodents, continue west on 390 to F. R. 604. Turn south on 604 and follow it until you pick up the trail 2½ miles from its beginning. There are plans to put a bridge across the pond, but check with the rangers to find out whether this has been done before you start walking.

The country here is heavily forested, rolling hills. Just over eight miles from the trail's beginning, you will cross the Brunsweiler River. The river widens out into a beaver pond where the trail crosses it, and local residents come here to fish for muskies.

There is a campground at Three Lake, 10 miles from the beginning of the trail, and an Adirondack Shelter just beyond it. There is another campground at Beaver Lake (13 miles). The trail splits here, with the right fork continuing on, while the left fork leads to the campground.

The Marengo River is 18½ miles from the trail's beginning. This beautiful fast rushing stream flows through a gorge in the Penokee Mountains. There is another shelter on the eastern side of the gorge, and on the ridge that forms the western side, there is an outcrop that gives a beautiful view of the mountains.

Tallest summits of the Penokees are only 1600 feet above sea level. But to flatlanders, all mountains are a surprise and a delight.

Moving west from the Marengo, the rugged country gradually gives way to more rolling land. Thirty miles from trail's beginning is Porcupine Lake, where there is another shelter. Two and a half miles farther on, you strike a side trail that leads to Twin Lakes Campground, about half a mile away. The campground is located on a narrow piece of land between two lakes. It has just under 100 sites. Bald eages often soar over the trail here, as this is their nesting area.

Three miles beyond the Two Lakes turnoff is one that goes to the picnic grounds at Lake Owen. The section of the trail between Two Lakes and Lake Owen contains some virgin white pine.

There is more virgin pine — one tree is about 51 inches in diameter — just north of Wisconsin Route 63, which the trail crosses 40 miles from its beginning. About one mile west on 63 is the tiny hamlet of

Drummond (general store, restaurant, motel and three bars).

Beyond 63, you cross the Long Branch River as well as about a dozen small lakes. One of these, Perch Lake, has a campground. To get to it, turn off the trail at Forest Road 223 (45 miles). The camp is about three miles from the trail.

The trail ends at Lake Ruth where there is a privately owned resort with spaces for tent campers, a nice beach and a small bar and store where you can buy a few food items — bread, milk, butter, eggs — as well as soft drinks and beer.

More information: The Chief Ranger, Chequamegon National Forest, Park Falls, Wis., can supply a planometric map of the forest that shows the trail. The scale is ¼ inch to one mile. He also can send you a mimeographed map of the North Country Trail, a detailed list of points of interest along the trail, and some advice for hikers.

U.S. Geological Survey quadrangles are Mellin, Marengo, Grandview, and Drummond. The first two of these are the usual 1:62,500 topographic maps, and they show the trail as far west as the Marengo River. The Grandview and Drummond quadranges are 1:48,000 planometrics that do not show the trail.

If you are interested in shorter walks on the trail, here are a few: Lake Three Campground to Brunsweiler River and return: 3.8 miles; Lake Three Campground to Marengo River and return: 16.8 miles; Beaver Lake Campground to Marengo River and return: 10.8 miles; Two Lakes Campground to Marengo River and return: 28 miles; Two Lakes Campground to Lake Owen Picnicgrounds and return: seven miles; from Forest Road 228 to Forest Road 392 and return: 12.8 miles (there are five lakes along this stretch of trail).

Ahnapee Trail

Location: The Ahnapee Trail follows an abandoned railroad bed from the town of Algoma, 11 miles north of Kewaunee on the shores of Lake Michigan, to Sturgeon Bay at the southern end of the Door County peninsula. The southern terminus is about one mile north of Algoma on County M. Watch for a small sign on the right identifying the trail. The northern end is at County U near the southern city limits of Sturgeon Bay. You can also get on by taking County J east out of Forestville or by driving to Maplewood where State Route 42 crosses Kawaunee County H.

Length of Trail: 15 miles.

Description: The Ahnapee Trail makes a pleasant day hike if you camp at nearby state parks and drive over early in the morning. Potawatomi State Park is only 20 minutes by car from the Sturgeon Bay trail access, and Point Beach State Park at Two Rivers is about a 40 minute drive from Algoma.

The countryside is level to gently rolling with a mixture of farms and small patches of woods, mainly hardwoods. There are small dairy and beef herds as well as swine, and several corn fields and apple and cherry orchards. Apples grow wild along the trailside, too, so in season you can eat your fill.

About five miles of the trail — between Algoma and Forestville — runs along — and at one point across — the Ahnapee River, a scenic meandering stream. There is a reservoir behind a small dam at Forestville, and marshy ground along the trailside for part of the way.

The tiny hamlet of Maplewood is located almost exactly halfway, if you are doing the entire trail, and it makes a good stopping point. There are a couple of bars and a grocery store where food, corn plasters and moleskin are available for hungry and blistered hikers.

North of Maplewood, the route crosses County O a mile or so past country H and meets County S about three miles south of Sturgeon Bay.

Southwestern Trails

When you say "the American Southwest," most people tend to think of a lot of desert, relieved by man-made oases like Phoenix. But experienced hikers know that many of America's best mountain ranges are in the Southwest, and to these high places they make yearly pilgrimages to camp in cool forests and alpine meadows. Every state in the Southwest except Arizona and Texas has peaks over 13,000 feet high, and Arizona is not far behind, with Humphreys Peak at 12,611 feet. You can even climb a 10,000 foot peak just 39 airline miles from the Los Angeles City Hall.

Most of this mountain land is public land, and open to the hiker in summer, the skier in winter. Best of all, the southwestern states have more than 50 federally designated wilderness areas, forever set aside by the government for self-propelled recreation. No roads and virtually no buildings are allowed in these protected enclaves. Those who seek solitude and pristine surroundings will find them in these sanctuaries of the spirit.

Despite this surfeit of mountains, the Southwest has plenty of deserts and near-deserts. And here, too, the hiker who wants to lead a simple yet fulfilling life for a few days will find endless sources of fascination. The attractions of the desert are more subtle than the soaring peaks of the glaciated Colorado mountains, than the waterfalls of Yosemite National Park. But it is this very subtlety that entrances those who have sat quietly watching the mesquite-bush shadows grow longer as the sun sinks, the sand cools and the creatures of the desert stir from their heat-induced torpor. We suggest you not miss this experience.

Arizona

Arizona is blessed with some of the finest backcountry of any state. In variety it spans the spectrum from the stark deserts of drifting sand in the southwest corner to the Grand Canyon and back to the desert areas of the Petrified Forest National Park in the northeast. It also has abundant sub-alpine spruce fir forests throughout much of the northern half of the state and on the isolated Sky Islands in the extreme southeast.

Arizona has seven national forests, two national parks and 14 national monuments. The national forests alone account for over 12 million acres.

The state has something for everyone — anytime of the year. Areas above 6000 feet are best visited in the summer (temperatures of minus 40° and lower have been recorded in some locations). Any area not snowed out will make a fine winter trip.

The Chiricahua Mountains

The Coronado National Forest in southeastern Arizona consists of nearly 1.8 million acres in twelve isolated mountainous units termed "Sky Islands." With peaks rising some 6000 feet above the desert floor, the Chiricahua Mountains are the epitomy of these "Sky Islands".

The visitor can expect the 300 miles of trails to cover the entire spectrum from "hard to find" to "impossible to loose." The range's large variation in elevation results in year round hiking opportunities.

Chiricahua Wilderness Area
Location: Southeast of Wilcox, bordered by Interstate 10 on the north and U.S 80 on the east. There are numerous approaches to the Chiricahua Wilderness — the most popular is from the Rustler Park Campground. This campground can be reached from Wilcox via Arizona Route 186 and Forest Road 42. It can also be reached from U.S. 80 through Portal and Forest Road 42.
U.S.G.S. Quads: The area is covered by the Portal and Chiricahua Peak 15' Quadrangles. Although, a smaller scale, the 5 color map distributed by the U.S. Forest Service is more accurate. Description: This 18,000 acre wilderness takes in most of the high country including 9796 foot high Chiricahua Peak. Due to snow conditions, visiting is best from April through November, although ski touring is becoming more popular and winter use is increasing.
Description: The dense, almost primeval fir and spruce forests are in marked contrast to the Sonoran Desert below. Water, although far from abundant, is available at some springs and in the headwaters of a few of the streams on the east side of the crest.

Chiricahua Crest Trail
Beginning at Rustler Park there are 13½ miles of trails along the crest of the range termed the Crest Trail. For nearly the entire length this trail remains above 9000 feet with peaks rising several hundred feet higher. From Rustler Park the most popular route is to hike up the administrative road — sometimes passable in a car — 1½ miles to 9000 foot high Long Park. This is the Wilderness Area Boundary.

From Long Park the Crest Trail is either level or climbs gradually for the 3¾ miles to Junction Saddle. Side trips to Centella Point, Fly Peak, and Cima Cabine are on many hikers list. Water can usually be found at Tub Springs, Booger Spring, and Cima Cabin.

At Junction Saddle the Crest Trail splits. It is 3¼ miles down the west, or right, branch to its terminus at 9373 foot Monte Vista Peak and its lookout. Taking the east branch it is five miles to the 9000 foot Sentinel Peak. Along this section of the Crest Trail water can usually be found at Eagle Spring. Although there is no view from the heavily forested summit the climb to the summit of Chiricahua Peak is still worth the effort.

Most hikers are content with spending two or more days backpacking along the Crest Trail. For the more aggressive, there are a dozen or more developed trails that leave the crest and descend by either canyons or ridges to the base of the mountain.

Chiricahua National Monument
Location: Southeast of Wilcox. Monument Headquarters is 42 miles southeast of Wilcox on Arizona Route 186.
U.S.G.S. Quads: The Monument is on both the Cochise Head and Chiricahua Peak 15' Quadrangles. Many of the trail locations on these maps are in error.
Description: Approximately 10,000 acres of the Chiricahuas has been established as a unit of the National Park Service to preserve the integrity of this wildly eroded volcanic area. On a smaller scale, though, in many ways the spires, columns, arches and balanced rocks rival those of Bryce Canyon in Utah.

Overnight camping is allowed in the campground just north of the Visitor Center. The rest of the area has been designated for day use only and other than the campground no camping is allowed on or off the Monuments trail system.

There are over 20 miles of trails in the Monument, all of which are in very excellent condition.

Except after rains when the creeks are running there is no dependable source of water along the trails.

Echo Canyon-Heart of Rocks Loop
This 8½ mile loop hike is perhaps the most scenic in the Monument. The beginning can be found at the Echo Parking Area six miles above the Visitor Center. The trail begins by descending through the amazing "Wall Street" down Echo Canyon and after 2½ miles joins the Heart of Rocks Trail at the low point of the trip. Turning left at the junction it is just over a 1000 foot climb back to the plateau above and the junction with the Heart of Rocks Loop. This one mile side trip is a must. From the Heart of Rocks Loop it is 3½ miles back to the Echo Parking Area past three trail junctions, turning right at the first two and left at the last.

Natural Bridge Trail
Some of the more remote country in the monument can be seen along this five mile round trip to the largent bridge in the area. The beginning

of the trail is signed and can be found at the pull-out on the Monument Road 1½ miles above the Visitor Center.

Description: The trail climbs 500 feet in the first mile and then levels off before descending into Pickett Park. This half mile long park is dominated by Arizona Cypress and tall pines. Leaving the park, the trail climbs a ridge to the viewpoint. The bridge, 26 feet high and 37 feet across, is just east of the viewpoint.

Apache National Forest

Straddling the Arizona-New Mexico border — with 670,000 acres in Arizona — the Apache National Forest is a forest of contrasts.

The north half is high forested plateau country and one of the south-west's favorite playgrounds. In the winter the Sunrise Ski Resort is busy with some of the finest ski touring to be found in Arizona. In the summer it comes alive with vacationers seeking the cool high climate and its many fishing streams and lakes. The second largest mountain in Arizona, 11,590 foot Mt. Baldy, is located here surrounded by the Mount Blady Wilderness Area.

In contrast, the south half is an area of deep rugged canyons and isolated peaks. Much of this section is in the Blue Range Primitive Area.

Mount Baldy Wilderness Area

Location: Twenty miles southwest of Springerville, Arizona. Bordered by Arizona Route 260 on the north and Arizona Route 273 on the east. Trailheads are at Sheep Crossing Campground on State Route 273 and at Phelps Cabin on the same road two miles to the south.

U.S.G.S. Quads: The area is covered by the Mt. Ord 7½' and the Big Lake 15' Quadrangles.

Description: Although there are only 13 miles of developed trails within this 6975 acre Wilderness Area, they comprise a loop trip through one of Arizona's finest sub-alpine areas. Five of the 13 miles are along trout streams. The forest service requires permits for overnight camping in the area and they allow only five persons per permit.

Mount Baldy Loop Trail

This trail begins at the Sheep Crossing Campground, elevation 9000 feet, on the West Fork of the Little Colorado River. The beginning is signed and is adjacent to the Wilderness Area Boundary.

The first 3½ miles up the West Fork is through a series of beautiful open meadows bordered by dense spruce and fir forests. The Arizona Game and Fish Commission keeps this section of the stream stocked with trout — an Arizona fishing license is required.

After 3½ miles, in an exceptionally beautiful meadow the stream divides with the trail following the left branch. At this point the meadows are left behind and the trail ascends much more stteply for the next 2½ miles to a trail junction on the crest of the range.

Taking the trail to the right it is another mile and 500 feet of climbing to the summit of 11,590 foot Mt. Baldy. To the left it is 5 miles down the East Fort of the Little Colorado River to Phelps Cabin just two miles by road from the Sheep Crossing Campground.

The last two miles down the East Fork is through a series of meadows that rivals those on the West Fork.

Blue Range Primitive Area

Location: Fifty miles south of Springerville, Arizona. Bordered by U.S. 666 on the west and New Mexico Route 180 on the east. There are numerous trailheads in the area. The popular Bonanza Bill trailhead can be found where Forest Road 232 connecting New Mexico Route 180 with the community of Blue crosses the state line.

U.S.G.S. Quads: The Primitive Area is covered by the Blue and Hannagan Meadow 15' Quadrangles along with the Dutch Blue and Alma Mesa 7½' Quadrangles.

Description: 210,000 acres are included in the present Blue Range Primitive Area, which is divided for much of its length by the Blue River. West of the Blue River the country climbs very steeply to the fir and spruce covered plateau some 4000 feet above while to the east is more broken pine country. It is this eastern side that offers the best choices for backpackers but water is scarce. The best time to visit the area would be in July and August after the summer rains when the creeks are running and water is assured.

Banjo Bill Trail

This popular trail begins on the Arizona side of the state line and heads south. Except for several short climbs and descents it remains fairly level for the nine miles to Campbell Flat. Bear Valley 1½ miles further south is one of the jewels of the range and makes fine camping if water is available.

From Bear Valley it is 4 miles and 1500 feet of climbing to 8550 foot Bear Mountain with its lookout tower. The view from here gives an excellent panorama of the Primitive Area. It is another 6 miles down Largo Creek to the Blue River and an additional 6 miles by road back to the trailhead.

Superstition Mountains

The 2.9 million acres of the Tonto National Forest makes it the largest in Arizona. Within its boundaries are four Wilderness Areas containing over 1500 miles of trails. The condition of these trails are as varied as the country they traverse.

In the southern part of the forest is the Superstition Wilderness Area. This has long been a favorite of treasure hunters and hikers alike. The legend of the "Lost Dutchman Mine" along with numerous books and

movies have probably made this the most publicized Wilderness Area
in the country.

Superstition Wilderness Area

Location: Approximately 35 miles east of Phoenix. Bordered by Arizona
Route 88 on the north and U.S. 60 on the south. The Peralta Canyon
approach can be reached by taking U.S. 60, eight miles southeast from
Apache Junction to a well signed turn-off. It is seven miles north on
Forest Road 77 to the trailhead.

U.S.G.S. Quads: The most popular section is covered by the Goldfield
and Weavers Needle 7½' Quadrangles. It takes several more quads to
take in the entire Wilderness Area.

Description: Forgetting all the tales and legends the Superstition Mountains are one of the finest examples of Arizona's rugged, sometimes
harsh, semi-arid mountainous areas. The elevation range between 2000
and 5000 feet makes it perhaps too hot for summer hiking but an ideal
location for those winter trips. Many springs are dependable but others
are not and if the creeks are not running water should be carried.

Peralta Canyon-Needle Canyon Loop

The Peralta Canyon Trail begins at the turn-around at the end of Forest
Road 77 and is well signed. For the first two miles up Peralta Canyon
the trails climbs between massive cliffs but still the first time visitor will
be unprepared for the view when he readhes the crest at Fremont
Pass. The almost tortured country beyond is dominated by the rock
spire of Weavers Needle—the object of so many stories.

Descending the north side of the pass the trail passes Piper's Spring
at the base of the Needle and continues on through Granite Saddle to
Blacktop Pass. From this pass the trail drops into Needle Canyon approximately 7½ miles from the beginning. It is an interesting five miles
back to the cars on the Needle Canyon Trail. Once on the Needle Canyon Trail an excellent alternate is to go downstream to Marsh Valley
and back to the cars via La Barge Canyon and the Dutchman Trail.
This route is nine miles and goes by Charlabois, Music, La Barge, and
Bluff Springs all of which usually have water.

Grand Canyon National Park

Arizona's premier attraction is the Grand Canyon. From the pine forests
on the rim to the Colorado River 5000 feet below it is a scenic wonder,
a geological textbook and an ecological and biological museum.

Location: Northwestern Arizona, bordered by Interstate 40 on the south
and U.S. 89 on the east. The south rim can be reached by going 82
miles northwest from Flagstaff, Arizona on U.S. 180. The north rim is
45 miles south of Jacobs Lake, Arizona on State Route 67. State
Route 67 is closed during the winter.

U.S.G.S. Quads: It requires several 15' Quadrangles to cover the entire
park. The Bright Angel 15' Quadrangles covers the Bright Angel and

Kaibab Trails.

Description: Numerous trails descent into the Canyon and many others connect with them forming an extensive trail system. The Park Service does not maintain these backcountry trails and travel is by permit only. The Park Service does maintain the excellent Bright Angel and Kaibab Trails which are the normal routes used by most people hiking into the Canyon.

Day use on these well-maintained trails does not require a permit. However those planning on staying overnight will need a camping permit. These are obtainable at the Visitors Center.

The Canyon can be hiked anytime of the year, however almost unbearable temperatures at the bottom during the summer makes Fall and Spring preferable. Water is available at specific locations on the Bright Angel and North Kaibab Trails.

Bright Angel Trail

This trail begins just west of the El Tovar Hotel on the west side of Grand Canyon Village. Water is available at rest stops 1½ and 3 miles below the rim as the trail drops 3100 feet in the 4½ miles to Indian Gardens. Water is also available here and camping is allowed by permit. From Indian Gardens it is another 1300 foot descent and three miles to the suspension bridge leading to the Bright Angel Campground just north of the river. Because the South Kaibab Trail is steeper and without water most hikers find it preferable to descend the Kaibab and climb out the Bright Angel.

South Kaibab Trail

The trailhead can be found on Yaki Point four miles east of Grand Canyon Village on the south rim. There is no water on this trail as it descends 4700 feet in seven miles to the river. A suspension bridge carries the trail over the river, and the Bright Angel Campground is just a short distance beyond.

North Kaibab Trail

A continuation of its namesake south of the river, this trail continues on to the north rim. Going north from the Bright Angel Campground it is only a half mile to Phantom Ranch. This spectacular canyon resort is run by the concessionaire and has rustic accommodations if prior arrangements have been made.

From Phantom Ranch the trail climbs gradually up the creek bottom, past scenic Ribbon Falls, to Cottonwood Camp. This is the only location on the trail where camping is allowed. A camping permit is required. It is another two miles to Roaring Springs. These springs are the source of the water in Bright Angel Creek and through an engineering marvel they are also one of the water supplies for the south rim and power supplies for the north rim. In the last 3½ miles to the rim the trail becomes quite steep as it gains the remaining 3400 feet.

Colorado

For many Americans, "Rocky Mountains" and "Colorado" are almost synonymous. Yet the fact is that the Rockies extend from central New Mexico far into Canada. The Rockies consist of many mountain ranges, most of which most Americans have never heard of like the Absaroka Range, the Beaverhead Mountains and the Cabinet Mountains.

Nevertheless, all the highest peaks in the Rockies are in Colorado, and it is peaks that give mountains their mountain-ness. Colorado has about 50 peaks over 14,000 feet in elevation, depending on what you count as peaks. According to *Good's Atlas of the United States,* all land over 10,000 feet is colored red, and Colorado is the bloodiest state of all. Once the terrain sweeps up from the High Plains to the fabulous Front Range west of Denver, it never comes down again, not in Colorado.

You could spend lifetimes hiking the high trails of Colorado and barely begin to leave your mark. The problem for the Colorado backpacker is an embarrassment of riches. Having to make a choice, this book describes trails in Rocky Mountain National Park and in Maroon Bells-Snowmass Wilderness, near Aspen in the western part of the state.

Black Lake Trail
Length: 10 miles (round trip)
Highest Elevation: 10,600 feet
Elevation Gain: 1400 feet
USGS Quad: McHenrys Peak, Colorado (7½ minute)
Highlights: Though Black Lake is near one of the most popular and most visited areas of Rocky Mountain National Park, it offers the backpacker solitude in a splendid setting at the head of Glacier Gorge. Located at the end of a scenic trail that traverses varied terrain, this camping spot will satisfy fisherman, photographer and naturalist, and even the person who simply wants a little peace and quiet.
Location: From the Beaver Meadows entrance station to Rocky Mountain National Park, drive west ¼ mile to the Bear Lake road. Turn south onto it and go 8 miles to the parking area at Glacier Gorge Junction. The trail head is across the road from the parking area.
Note: Back-country camping in the Park is permitted only at designated sites, and backpackers must carry a permit. These may be obtained at a ranger station a day or less in advance of hitting the trail.
Description: A large sign with directions to everywhere marks the beginning of the trail. Cross the wooden bridge over Chaos Creek to the trail-use register and sign it. Another large sign near the register marks a trail fork, where the route goes to the right on a wide trail well-used by day-hikers and horsemen. Climb gently through an aspen-evergreen forest, passing some beaver dams and shallow ponds. Many aspen

trees near the trail have obviously been cut by beaver's teeth. Past the dams, you leave the trees and meet Glacier Creek, in a gorge on our left. This creek will be your intermittent companion until you reach Black Lake.

The trail becomes rocky as it begins to rise more steeply, and soon you come to Alberta Falls, where the water is cool and sweet. The trail turns sharply right, up and away from the creek, then swings back around high above it. The many chipmunks and golden-mantled ground squirrels on the early part of this trail are used to the heavy human traffic, and derive much of their sustenance from it, as people stop to offer the little animals handouts of nuts and bread.

The trail swings away from Glacier Creek again, switchbacking up the slope, then loops around to the left and comes to a fork. The left branch is the start of the North Longs Peak Trail; you go right, toward Mills Lake. It is easy going for the next half mile as you contour around the steep, rocky side of one of the Glacier Knobs, obtaining a good view of lofty McHenrys Peak ahead. In a thin forest of lodgepole pine and Engelmann spruce, you come to two trails within a few feet of each other. The first goes right, to Lake Haiyaha and Bear Lake. The second also goes right, to Loch Vale, Andrews Glacier, and Lake of Glass. Beyond this junction the trail steepens somewhat, and in a few minutes you come to a bridge crossing of Icy Brook. In the next ½ mile, the trail makes a series of short, steep switchbacks as it enters Glacier Gorge, crosses Glacier Creek on a wooden bridge, and then levels out nearing Mills Lake.

Up the canyon to the south, you can see the morainal ridge that forms the lip of the cirque in which Black Lake lies. Towering above it are Chiefs Head Peak, the jagged, dramatically named Keyboard of the Winds, and famous Longs Peak. On both sides of Mills Lake and Glacier Gorge, talus slopes rise sharply to high cliffs so steep that timber is limited to a narrow band at the bottom of the gorge, between Mills Lake and Black Lake.

Now you amble along the nearly level trail past the east side of Mills Lake and shallow Jewel Lake. From here on the trail is narrower and not as well maintained—it is a backpacker's trail, and one is not likely to meet many other people. Short, steep climbs alternate with meadows and marshy areas where logs or corduroy bridges assist the hiker across wet spots. Wildflowers grow in profusion in the meadows — ragwort, cow parsnip, harebell, larkspur, columbine, mountain bluebells, monkshood. and many more. At Black Lake, look for the little red-topped succulent plant called kings crown.

After a stiff climb up from Ribbon Falls, you reach the lake, almost surrounded by cliffs, with Chiefs Head Peak and the Spearhead looming high above. There are nice campsites here, on the east side where a little stream comes down. Fishing for brook trout is excellent if you hit at the right time.

Odessa Lake Trail

Location: See directions for the Black Lake trip. Continue one more mile to road's end at the Bear Lake parking area.

Length: 9 miles (shuttle trip)

Highest Elevation: 10,600 feet

Elevation Gain: 1100 feet

USGS Quad: McHenrys Peak, Colorado (7½ minute)

Highlights: This scenic trip is an ideal conditioner for more strenuous hiking. It presents mountain scenery ranging from broad forest expanses to soaring cliffs rising to the Continental Divide. The traveler will encounter jewel-like mountain lakes and tumbling creeks, where fishermen will be eager to try their luck. This is an excellent family trip.

Description: From the Ranger Station Information Booth near the west end of the parking area, take the right-hand trail, which leads around the north side of Bear Lake. Within 200 yards, you come to an unsigned trail branching right, up the hill. This is the real start of your route, and the start of a wildflower show from here to Odessa Lake that includes many gardens of yarrow, groundsel, paintbrush, aster, pearly everlasting, golden banner, columbine and mountain bluebells.

Ascend the moderately steep trail through lodgepole pine for ⅓ mile to a fork, and turn left. As the trail rises gently, the forest changes to a cool, hushed mixture of subalpine fir, Colorado blue spruce and Engelmann spruce. Ahead you can see the peaks of Knobtop and Notchtop mountains, and to the right is Mt. Wuh. After a short ½ mile, at another trail junction, we turn right. The trees thin and the trail becomes steeper as you traverse an open slope. On your right, across Mill Creek, Basin Trail Ridge rises high in the distance. The trail takes you back into the forest, where you cross a small, treeless boulder field and soon come to a sign marking Mill Creek. Shortly thereafter, between signs announcing Two River Lake and Lake Helene, you are at the elevational high point of your trip. The trail bends sharply right and begins a moderate descent to Odessa Lake, visible in the gorge below. In the gorge, turn left onto the short side trail to the lake. To reach the campsites, go across the bridge over Fern Creek to the lake, go right for a few yards, then right again up the hill and away from the lake a short distance.

Leaving Odessa Lake, you walk back to the main trail, then descend steeply one mile to Fern Lake. At the lower end of Fern Lake, a bridge crosses Fern Creek. From here, fishermen may want to make a one-mile side trip to Spruce Lake to try the excellent fishing there. Spruce Lake is reached via a seldom-used trail, marked by red paint spots on trees, that is often difficult to follow. It leaves the main trail on the left, opposite the hitching post. You continue dropping, parallel to Fern Creek but away from it until you reach the short side trail to Fern Falls, 1½ miles below. A half mile past the falls, you recross the creek, shortly before the junction of the Cub Lake Trail. Just past this junction is a bridge over the Big Thompson River. A large pool in the river at the bridge is ideal for swimming on a hot day. From the bridge you walk along the north side of the river, through thick groves of aspen, over a gently undulating trail for two miles to trail's end at the Fern Lake parking area.

The shuttle is completed by driving 2½ miles east on the dirt road from the parking area, turning right on the paved road you meet, and going 6½ miles to the Bear Lake parking area.

Snowmass Lake - East Snowmass Creek Trail

Location: From Colorado State Highway 82, between Glenwood Springs (37 miles north) and Aspen (5 miles south), turn west at the signed road to the Snowmass-at-Aspen ski area. Follow this road 5 miles to where a signed dirt road to the ski lifts goes right, off the pavement. Take this dirt road 2 miles up and then down to its end ½ mile past the improved Snowmass Creek Forest Service Campground.

Length: 26½ miles (loop trip)

Highest Elevation: 12,700 feet

Elevation Gain: 4300 feet

USGS Quad: Capitol Peak, Snowmass Mountain and Maroon Bells, Colorado (7½ minute)

Description: The first few hundred yards of this trip follow a dirt road through a flat, open area of private property. Soon you come to the signed trail to Snowmass Lake, branching left up the hill through trees. After a short, steep beginning, the trail rises gently-to-moderately, gradually draws away from Snowmass Creek, and bends south. A mixed forest of aspen with Douglas fir and Engelmann spruce provides shade. Below on your right, wide green meadows line both sides of the creek. Wildflowers are happily abundant: in dry places are fireweed, yarrow, aster, harebell, daisies, paintbrush, and squaw currant; in moister spots grow twinberry, Parry gentian, monkshood and mountain bluebells. Where you near Snowmass Creek again are some old, shallow, silted-up beaver ponds. Just past them is a junction with a trail to Capitol Creek. About 1½ miles from the trail head, pass through a wooden stock gate and come to the boundary of the Maroon Bells-Snowmass Wilderness, with a trail-use register. A log crossing of Snowmass Creek here leads to a campsite on the other bank.

The trail continues south on the east side of the creek, past large outcroppings of red sandstone, a common sedimentary rock in this region. The canyon begins to close in on both sides, the forest thins, and ahead the tilted sedimentary beds of point 10293 rise high above. On the left, red and gray cliffs push up into the sky. A small tree sign marks the junction of the Pierre Lakes Trail, 1¾ miles from the Wilderness boundary.

Uptrail we are treated to a view up Bear Creek Canyon on the right, to a little waterfall in the canyon, and to towering, rocky Clark Peak far on the horizon. Wild roses and raspberries grow by the trail, which makes a moderate-to-steep rise through aspen woods and then through open, shrubby areas until it levels out just before the Snowmass Ponds. A home for beavers, these ponds lie in a wide, flat, marshy part of the canyon. You walk through masses of mountain bluebells to the bridge crossing Snowmass Creek, then along the west side past several small ponds, and ascend a few feet to a campsite that overlooks the pond. Here you begin to climb steeply, in a thick Douglas fir forest, the last 2 miles to Snowmass Lake.

At the lake, designated campsites are among trees along the eastern shore. Sheer cliffs around three sides of the lake seem doubly high as they are reflected in the sparkling water. Snowmass Peak, jutting up at the end of a ridge from even higher Snowmass Mountain, dominates the background.

At Snowmass Lake, cross to the south side of the outlet stream and walk a few yards to a trail junction. One sign points out your route to Buckskin Pass; the second marks the Geneva Lake Trail. Turn left and stroll on a nearly level trail through a thick Douglas fir forest. Soon the trail begins to descend moderately, and 1½ miles from the lake you encounter a wet, marshy opening in the forest. The trail skirts wet spots to the north edge of the marsh, crossing Snowmass Creek on the way. You pass a faint trail to Lost Remuda basin, then surge back into forest and begin the 2½-mile ascent to Buckskin Pass. The climb quickly becomes very steep, proceeding via long and short switchbacks to timberline, then via a moderate grade into tundra. This treeless, rocky region has only a thin layer of soil, but it supports a large variety of plants. Low grasses and grasslike sedges are everywhere. Wildflowers here include aster, Indian paintbrush of the red, yellow and pink varieties, and nodding senecio with drooping yellow heads.

In this tundra you climb steeply again, via more switchbacks, to the final stretch that brings you to the pass, and a welcome rest. Crystal-clear views west to Snowmass Mountain and south along red cliffs to the Maroon Bells Peaks divert your attention from the short, steep descent that lies at your feet. Downhill walking is always hard on ankles and knees, and calls for going slow; the first mile here requires extra caution because of the many loose pebbles and stones. The erosion on this stretch demonstrates what can happen when fragile alpine meadows are disturbed, and one hopes that all hikers will stay strictly on the trail. The trail switchbacks down from the pass one mile to meet the signed Maroon-Snowmass Trail, which goes north and south from this junction. Turn north and ascend moderately between two bluffs into a wide gully, at the far end of which is a very steep slope of red sandstone talus. Switching back and forth up the talus brings you to Willow Pass, from where you get a new view back to the Maroon Bells Peaks. Ahead and down to the right is the little basin in which Willow Lake lies. On the left, the slopes of Buckskin Mountain rise to a gentle peak, not 800 feet higher than you are. Going down, there are more switchbacks, but not as steep as those coming up the south side, and more alpine meadows. After a few yards, Willow Lake becomes visible, and in ¾ mile you come to another junction, this one with the East Snowmass Trail. Turning right, continue for another mile, dropping gently to the lake.

There are several adequate campsites around this little lake, and meaty trout in its waters. Willow Creek drains the lake to the northeast, down a long canyon that contains a trail to Maroon Creek road.

Northwest from the lake you can see the gap that is East Snowmass Pass, lying on your route. Except for the climb to the pass, the hiking is all downhill and relatively easy after the short, steep descent from the pass. An early start is advisable. It is a good 1000 foot ascent to the pass, exposed to the morning sun, and even at this altitude the climb can be very hot. You reach the pass by retracing your steps for one mile to the trail junction signed "East Snowmass Pass," then following this new trail for one mile as it drops into a little hollow, veers right, and makes a steep ascent up and around a shoulder of Buckskin Mountain. The rocky trail on the shoulder enters a steep gully, leaving meadows behind, and switchbacks steeply up to the pass (12,700 feet). Great views of mountains rolling away to the north and east, and down the canyon ahead, make this an enjoyable rest stop.

Begin your descent by switchbacking carefully down the rocky slope from the pass and crossing to the west side of the creek drainage. The trail stays high on the west side of East Snowmass Creek canyon, following it down to its mouth. In the upper part of the canyon, the trail is nearly level; then it drops moderately the rest of the way, with only a few short, steep spots. Just below the pass, flower-dotted little meadows appear again. About one third of the way down, you pass through isolated groves of spruce and fir, then thread more open, flowery meadows until the last 1½ miles, which are in a mixed Douglas fir and aspen forest. You come out on the dirt road on which you drove to the parking area, turn left, and walk 200 yards to the car.

One could choose, back at the Pine Lakes Trail junction, to turn west and cross the creek. From here you follow the narrow trail that leads upstream. The trail climbs steadily through open aspen woods for half a mile, then meets Bear Creek near a campsite. You veer west as you ascend along the north side of the creek, where tall grasses, cow parsnip, corn lily, and wild rose decorate the entrance into Bear Creek canyon. On the left, Bear Creek flows sturdily at the foot of a cliff-topped talus slope. To the right, a meadow rises gently to some rocky outcrops, and farther on, a little waterfall tumbles down a cliff.

Staying close to the creek, the trail rises gently through the meadow, then more steeply through a short stretch of brush and scrub. Near the creek a few Engelmann spruces, subalpine firs and isolated juniper trees try to make a forest. Turn sharply right to go up and around willow thickets, then left onto the talus. For a mile you follow an elusive,

ducked trail which climbs across the rocky slope, drawing slowly away
from Bear Creek. The next 300 foot rise is tough going, but great
views of the craggy red cliffs east of Snowmass Creek make it worthwhile.

Near the top of the cliff, the trail rises gently again, into a grove of
Douglas firs close to the creek, where there are several nice campsites. You continue through alternating forest and meadow areas,
where many hues of wildflowers grow, including Colorado blue columbine, pearly everlasting, fireweed, lupine, mountain bluebells, monkshood, shrubby cinquefoil. and poison hemlock.

A mile past the campsites, you come to the little outlet stream from
the easternmost of the Pierre Lakes, and another campsite. The trail
goes a few yards upstream, then crosses to the south side. From this
crossing the route is a very steep climb up a ridge between the lakes'
outlet stream and Bear Creek. Partway up this ridge the trail more or
less disappears, as hikers take different routes into the lake basin. At
about treeline, turn right and head directly north, traversing at a gentle
grade up and across the slope, back to the outlet stream near a campsite on a bluff overlooking the valley of Bear Creek below. Follow the
stream up another half a mile and find your campsite on the right (east)
side of the stream, at the edge of a tiny meadow mostly surrounded by
small, gnarled spruce.

There is an adequate campsite at each of the two middle-sized
Pierre lakes. The largest and smallest Pierre lakes have no good sites.
From camp, it is but a short walk up to any of the lakes. All are rockbound, with talus slopes extending right down into the water. Huge
Capitol Peak dominates the western skyline, and several smaller peaks
stand out on the encircling ridges. Fishing in the lakes is good. Return
the way you came.

Sandbeach Lake Trail
Length: 9 miles (round trip)
Highest Elevation: 10,283 feet
USGS Quad: Allens Park, Colorado (7½ minute)
Highlights: The original Sandbeach Lake was covered when a dam was
built to create a reservoir in 1902. No longer used as a water source,
present-day Sandbeach Lake has attractions for those with interests in
geology, plants, or animals: the trail climbs and crosses a glacial moraine, wildflowers abound, and a wide variety of birds and animals will
be seen by the observant hiker. Beginners will find this trip challenging, but not overdemanding. More experienced backpackers can look
forward to more rugged explorations and exciting views on the flanks
of the surrounding peaks.
Location: From US Highway 36, just east of Estes Park, Colorado,
drive south on Colorado route 7, 14 miles to the Wild Basin Campground exit. Turn right and drive an eighth of a mile to Copeland Lake.
A parking area, and the unsigned trail head, are near the building at

the northeast corner of the lake.

Description: The trail begins with a short, steep eighth of a mile climb, then rises more gently for half a mile to where a sign announces that you are entering Rocky Mountain National Park. A few yards farther is a trail-use register. Continuing east through a thin forest cover of fir, pine and aspen, enjoy good views of North St. Vrain Creek as it meanders slowly through the marshy meadows in the valley to the left. This lower part of your trip climbs the side of the Copeland moraine, formed of the rock debris dropped at the side of the glacier which carved out this valley. Soon the trail levels out for a short distance, and you come to the junction of the Meeker Park Trail.

From the junction, the trail rises gently, then more steeply, until it meets and crosses Campers Creek on a log bridge. In damp areas here, look for masses of two to three foot high mountain bluebells, and closer to the ground the delicate blossoms of fairy lantern hanging nearly hidden under long, shiny green leaves. Look also for the white, flashing tail feathers of the gray-headed junco and listen for the raucous, jaylike cry of the big Clarks nutcracker.

Leaving Campers Creek, the trail is steep on switchbacks for a short distance, then moderate for a mile to Hunters Creek, which you cross on a long bridge. As you continue to ascend, Douglas-fir trees are scarcer, replaced by subalpine firs. Soon the trail levels out and crosses a marshy area on a corduroy bridge. Then after another short mile, you arrive at Sandbeach Lake, at the very foot of Mt. Orton. The campsites here are clustered together near the northeast end of the lake, in the shelter of Engelmann spruce and subalpine fir trees.

Bluebird Lake, Rocky Mountain Nation Park

Location: Proceed to Copeland Lake as described in the Sandbeach Lake trip. From Copeland Lake, continue west on the dirt road 1½ miles to the Wild Basin Ranger Station and parking area.

Length: 12 miles (round trip)

Highest Elevation: 10,600 feet

Topographic Maps: Allens Park and Isolation Peak, Colorado (7½ minute)

Highlights: This trip high into the heart of the Wild Basin country of Rocky Mountain National Park is one of scenic contrasts, from intimate glimpses of Calypso Cascades and Ouzel Falls to the rocky, alpine grandeur of Bluebird Lake and its surrounding peaks. Varieties of wildflowers are abundant from the lowest to the highest point of the trip, including impressive displays of the state flower, Colorado blue columbine, in the open areas below and above Bluebird Lake.

Description: From the trailhead at the Wild Basin Ranger Station, your route follows a level-to-steep trail along North St. Vrain and Cony Creeks to the junction with the Allens Park-Wild Basin Trail. You cross several small streamlets in the first quarter-mile, then come upon the signed side trail to Copeland Falls on the left.

About 1½ miles farther on, the trail turns south, crosses a bridge over the now-roaring creek, and begins a steep half-mile rise to a trail junction at Calypso Cascades on Cony Creek. Calypso Cascades is named for Calypso bulbosa, the charming fairy-slipper orchid which the lucky flower-lover may find here in large patches.

From the junction, your route now trends northwest, traversing a steep hillside on a gently rising trail for three-quarters of a mile. Then you tackle a short, steep section which brings you to the crossing of Ouzel Creek. A short side trail allows you to view Ouzel Falls. Beyond the falls, the trail bends sharply northeast, then resumes its northwest direction, dropping gently, then rising again. Less than a mile past the falls, turn left onto the Bluebird Lake Trail.

This rather steep trail ascends for a quarter of a mile, then curves west on a gentler grade through a cool forest of Douglas fir, lodgepole pine, and Engelmann spruce. You pass a junction with the trail to Ouzel Lake, then Chickadee Pond and a trail to it. Upward you slog on a rocky trail, crossing several branchlets of an unnamed creek, where a natural garden of moisture-loving wildflowers includes masses of mountain bluebells and monkshood.

From this creek the trail climbs steeply, following another unnamed streamlet with many wildflowers nearby. At the top of this stiff climb, at timberline, you see the dam and the outlet stream of Bluebird Lake. At a sign by Ouzel Creek, the Bluebird Lake camping area is to the left, and the lake itself is half a mile ahead. To reach the campsites, first cross the stream on the log bridge and then follow a trail a short distance downhill.

One could choose, back at the Pine Lakes Trail junction, to turn west and cross the creek. From here you follow the narrow trail that leads upstream. The trail climbs steadily through open aspen woods for half a mile, then meets Bear Creek near a campsite. You veer west as you ascend along the north side of the creek, where tall grasses, cow parsnip, corn lily, and wild rose decorate the entrance into Bear Creek canyon. On the left, Bear Creek flows sturdily at the foot of a cliff-topped talus slope. To the right, a meadow rises gently to some rocky outcrops, and farther on, a little waterfall tumbles down a cliff.

Staying close to the creek, the trail rises gently through the meadow, then more steeply through a short stretch of brush and scrub. Near the creek a few Engelmann spruces, subalpine firs and isolated juniper trees try to make a forest. Turn sharply right to go up and around willow thickets, then left onto the talus. For a mile you follow an elusive, ducked trail which climbs across the rocky slope, drawing slowly away from Bear Creek. The next 300-foot rise is tough going, but great views of the craggy red cliffs east of Snowmass Creek make it worthwhile.

Near the top of the cliff, the trail rises gently again, into a grove of

Douglas firs close to the creek, where there are several nice campsites. You continue through alternating forest and meadow areas, where many hues of wildflowers grow, including Colorado blue columbine, pearly everlasting, fireweed, lupine, mountain bluebells, monkshood, shrubby cinquefoil, and poison hemlock.

A mile past the campsites, you come to the little outlet stream from the easternmost of the Pierre Lakes, and another campsite. The trail goes a few yards upstream, then crosses to the south side. From this crossing the route is a very steep climb up a ridge between the lakes' outlet stream and Bear Creek. Partway up this ridge the trail more or less disappears, as hikers take different routes into the lake basin. At about treeline, turn right and head directly north, traversing at a gentle grade up and across the slope, back to the outlet stream near a campsite on a bluff overlooking the valley of Bear Creek below. Follow the stream up another half a mile and find your campsite on the right (east) side of the stream, at the edge of a tiny meadow mostly surrounded by small, gnarled spruce.

There is an adequate campsite at each of the two middle-sized Pierre lakes. The largest and smallest Pierre lakes have no good sites. From camp, it is but a short walk up to any of the lakes. All are rockbound, with talus slopes extending right down into the water. Huge Capitol Peak dominates the western skyline, and several smaller peaks stand out on the encircling ridges. Fishing in the lakes is good. Return the way you came.

Sandbeach Lake Trail

Length: 9 miles (round trip)
Highest Elevation: 10,283 feet
USGS Quad: Allen's Park Colorado (7½ minute)
Highlights: The original Sandbeach Lake was covered when a dam was built to create a reservoir in 1902. No longer used as a water source, present-day Sandbeach Lake has attractions for those with interests in geology, plants. or animals: the trail climbs and crosses a glacial moraine, wildflowers abound, and a wide variety of birds and animals will be seen by the observant hiker. Beginners will find this trip challenging, but not overdemanding. More experienced backpackers can look forward to more rugged explorations and exciting views on the flanks of the surrounding peaks.
Location: From US Highway 36, just east of Estes Park, Colorado, drive south on Colorado route 7, 14 miles to the Wild Basin Campground exit. Turn right and drive an eighth of a mile to Copeland Lake. A parking area, and the unsigned trail head, are near the building at the northeast corner of the lake.
Description: The trail begins with a short, steep eighth of a mile climb, then rises more gently for half a mile to where a sign announces that you are entering Rocky Mountain National Park. A few yards farther is a trail-use register. Continuing east through a thin forest cover of fir,

pine and aspen, enjoy good views of North St. Vrain Creek as it mean‗ders slowly through the marshy meadows in the valley to the left. This lower part of your trip climbs the side of the Copeland moraine, formed of the rock debris dropped at the side of the glacier which carved out this valley. Soon the trail levels out for a short distance, and you come to the junction of the Meeker Park Trail.

From the junction, the trail rises gently, then more steeply, until it meets and crosses Campers Creek on a log bridge. In damp areas here, look for masses of two-to-three-foot-high mountain bluebells, and closer to the ground the delicate blossoms of fairy lantern hanging nearly hidden under long, shiny green leaves. Look also for the white, flashing tail feathers of the gray-headed junco and listen for the raucous, jaylike cry of the big Clarks nutcracker.

Leaving Campers Creek, the trail is steep on switchbacks for a short distance, then moderate for a mile to Hunters Creek, which you cross on a long bridge. As you continue to ascend, Douglas-fir trees are scarcer, replaced by subalpine firs. Soon the trail levels out and crosses a marshy area on a corduroy bridge. Then after another short mile, you arrive at Sandbeach Lake, at the very foot of Mt. Orton. The campsites here are clustered together near the northeast end of the lake, in the shelter of Engelmann spruce and subalpine fir trees.

Bluebird Lake, Rocky Mountain Nation Park

Location: Proceed to Copeland Lake as described in the Sandbeach Lake trip. From Copeland Lake, continue west on the dirt road 1½ miles to the Wild Basin Ranger Station and parking area.
Length: 12 miles (round trip)
Highest Elevation: 10,600 feet
Topographic Maps: Allen's Park and Isolation Peak, Colorado (7½ minute)
Highlights: This trip high into the heart of the Wild Basin country of Rocky Mountain National Park is one of scenic contrasts, from intimate glimpses of Calypso Cascades and Ouzel Falls to the rocky, alpine grandeur of Bluebird Lake and its surrounding peaks. Varieties of wildflowers are abundant from the lowest to the highest point of the trip, including impressive displays of the state flower, Colorado blue columbine, in the open areas below and above Bluebird Lake.
Description: From the trailhead at the Wild Basin Ranger Station, your route follows a level-to-steep trail along North St. Vrain and Cony Creeks to the junction with the Allens Park-Wild Basin Trail. You cross several small streamlets in the first quarter-mile, then come upon the signed side trail to Copeland Falls on the left.

About 1½ miles farther on, the trail turns south, crosses a bridge over the now-roaring creek, and begins a steep half mile rise to a trail junction at Calypso Cascades on Cony Creek. Calypso Cascades is named for Calypso Bulbosa , the charming fairy-slipper orchid which the lucky flower-lover may find here in large patches.

From the junction, your route now trends northwest, traversing a steep hillside on a gently rising trail for three-quarters of a mile. Then you tackle a short, steep section which brings you to the crossing of Ouzel Creek. A short side trail allows you to view Ouzel Falls. Beyond the falls, the trail bends sharply northeast, then resumes its northwest direction, dropping gently, then rising again. Less than a mile past the falls, turn left onto the Bluebird Lake Trail.

This rather steep trail ascends for a quarter of a mile, then curves west on a gentler grade through a cool forest of Douglas fir, lodgepole pine. and Engelmann spruce. You pass a junction with the trail to Ouzel Lake, then Chickadee Pond and a trail to it. Upward you slog on a rocky trail, crossing several branchlets of an unnamed creek, where a natural garden of moisture-loving wildflowers includes masses of mountain bluebells and monkshood.

From this creek the trail climbs steeply, following another unnamed streamlet with many wildflowers nearby. At the top of this stiff climb, at timberline, you see the dam and the outlet stream of Bluebird Lake. At a sign by Ouzel Creek, the Bluebird Lake camping area is to the left, and the lake itself is half a mile ahead. To reach the campsites, first cross the stream on the log bridge and then follow a trail a short distance downhill.

Southern California

If we define "southern California" as all of California south of the latitude of San Francisco, we take in a lot of mountains: the Laguna Mountains, the Santa Ana Mountains, the San Bernardino Mountains, the San Gabriel Mountains, the Coast Ranges and many desert ranges. Some of these provide good hiking and backpacking only an hour or two's drive from home for the six million residents of metropolitan Los Angeles.

But the showpiece of the southern California mountains is the High Sierra. The Sierra Nevada is the longest and most extensively trailed mountain range in the United States. With its complex ridge-valley makeup, its lofty eastern escarpment and its mild weather, it is a backpacker's paradise, unequalled in intrinsic beauty and scenic grandeur. The High Sierra, stretching south from Yosemite Park, is the climax and culmination of this beauty and grandeur. Here, the finest scenery and the best camping lie in the back country, accessible only by trail. So it is the trails of the High Sierra that lure hikers not only from Los Angeles and San Francisco but from the whole country, so compelling is the attraction of this marvelous mountain world.

Mosquito Flat to Fish Camp Trail
Length: 32 miles (round trip)

Topographic maps: **Mt. Tom, Mt. Abbot** (15 minute)

Highlights: The exciting eastern Sierra escarpment makes the first part of this trip a memorable experience. The trail to Mono Pass offers sweeping vistas that vie for the traveler's consideration with the intimacy of the campsites that dot the banks of Mono Creek.

Location: Go 24 miles north from Bishop on U.S. 395 and then 11 miles on paved and dirt road to road's end in Mosquito Flat beside Rock Creek.

Description: The magnificent Sierra crest confronts the traveler at the very outset of this trip. From the trail head at Mosquito Flat the wide, rocky-sandy trail starts southwest toward the imposing skyline dominated by Mts. Mills, Abbot and Dade, and Bear Creek Spire. A short distance from the trail head, one has good views of thre green-clad little Lakes Valley, and cannot help but feel a sense of satisfaction that this beautiful valley enjoys protection as part of the John Muir Wilderness. The trail crosses the ridge and, in a short distance, meets the junction of the Little Lakes Valley Trail.

Here your route branches right (west) and ascends steeply over rocky switchbacks. In the course of this switchbacking ascent, the moderate-to-dense forest cover diminishes as you near timberline. Immediately below to the east, the deep blue of Heart and Box Lakes and some of the Hidden Lakes reflects the sky above.

Near the meadowed edge of the outlet stream from Ruby Lake is a junction, where you turn left. One cannot see Ruby Lake, which completely fills its cirque basin, until one is actually at water's edge, but this first breathtaking view of the lake and its towering cirque walls makes the climb worth the effort. Good campsites can be found below the outlet of the lake. Lakeside campsites are exposed and usually windy. When ready, retrace your steps ¼ mile to the Mono Pass Trail. Folowing a general east-to-west course, the trail climbs by long, steady switchbacks up the north wall of the cirque, and after a long steady traverse veers northward by steeper switchbacks to the summit of Mono Pass.

North of the pass the trail descends steadily over granite. It traverses the west side of rockbound Summit Lake, and then descends more steeply to the slopes above Trail Lakes. The westward descent around Trail Lakes turns northward, and the trail drops to the Golden Creek ford. Here, this route re-enters forest cover, and it continues to descend as it passes lateral trails to Pioneer Basin and Fourth Recess Lake. Beyond these junctions, the trail fords the outlet streams from Pioneer Basin.

Mono Rock towers on the left as your route passes the Third Recess trail lateral, and, about a mile farther, the lateral to Hopkins Lakes and Hopkins Pass. For the most part, Mono Creek rushes along briskly, but occasional potholes and level stretches in the stream bed contribute to the good spawning areas that any good Sierra trout stream requires.

Anglers and hikers alike will appreciate the colorful abundance of quaking aspens that line Mono Creek. The best time to capture the aspen color on film is usually late September or early October. This route then passes the Grinnell Lakes lateral, and descends to the good campsites on both sides of the log spanning Mono Creek at Fish Camp.

Pine Creek Roadend to Honeymoon Lake Trail
Length: 11 miles (round trip)
Topographic maps: **Mt. Tom** (15 minute)
Highlights: The steep, winding ascent to Honeymoon Lake offers breathtaking over-the-shoulder views of the Pine Creek watershed, and the Honeymoon Lake campsite views of the Sierra crest make this one of the best choices for a base camp location on the east side of the Sierra.
Location: Go 10 miles northwest from Bishop on U.S. 395 and then 10 miles on paved road to a parking area near a pack station.
Description: The dusty duff trail ascends gently from the pack station through a dense, mixed forest cover and fords several branchlets of an unnamed creek that feeds Pine Creek. These fords are decorated by blossoms of wild rose, dogwood, columbine, tiger lily and Queen Anne's lace. A few yards beyond these fords, the trail emerges from the forest cover, directly opposite the Union Carbide tungsten mill, and then merges with a mining road. Although the slope into the Pine Creek canyon is steep, the road's grade is, for the most part, moderate, and this segment is simply a matter of slog-and-pant. Two welcome streams break the monotony of the climb, and the view is spectacular. Through the Pine Creek valley that slopes away to the northeast, one can look across the Owens River drainage to the volcanic Tableland and White Mountain (14,242') on the skyline.

The road ends just above the clapboard and corrugated shacks marking the Brownstone Mine. There is one advantage to the presence of the mining activities in the canyon—the dramatic contrast between industrial and recreational use of wilderness country. Coincident to this is the contrasting tempos of the lower and upper parts of the valley. One has only to watch the juggernaut flow of the tramway buckets and the antlike scurrying of trucks and people across the valley, to fully appreciate the slow, peaceful pace of the wilderness traveler. From the mine, the trail ascends over talus and scree by short, steep switchbacks. Then, with the steepest part of the ascent behind, the trail fords another unnamed tributary and veers north to join Pine Creek just below Pine Lake. Here, the creek alternates cascades, falls and chutes in a riot of whitewater. The trail fords the stream, and amidst a moderate forest cover arrives at the northeast end of Pine Lake. This medium-sized lake has good campsites along the northeast shore.

The trail to Upper Pine Lake proceeds by skirting the rocky northwest side of Pine Lake and ascending the sometimes marshy section that crosses the seepage flow from Birchim Lake. Leveling out, the trail parallels the outlet stream from Upper Pine Lake (excellent campsites) and arrives at the west side of the làke. From the southwest inlet, the trail ascends moderately, crosses the muddy, boggy, multibranched in-let stream, and presently arrives at the Pine Creek Pass/Italy Pass Trail junction. The route turns right, onto the Italy Pass Trail, and soon ascends to the rockbound shores of Honeymoon Lake (10,440'). This moderate-sized lake has good campsites near the outlet stream, and excellent meadowed sites above the waterfall on the inlet stream on the west side. This lovely lake makes an excellent base camp for side ex-cursions to 40 surrounding lakes in four drainages, or for climbing five nearby peaks that exceed 13,000 feet in elevation.

North Lake to Hutchinson Meadow Trail
Length: 22 miles (round trip)
USGS Quad: **Mt. Goddard, Mt. Tom, Mt. Abbot** (15 minute)
Highlights: Hutchinson Meadow is one of the finest in the High Sierra, and the trail to beside Piute Creek takes the traveler through several miles of wild mountain "lawns" and gardens, where Sierra wildflowers are at their best. Add the views of Mt. Humphreys and the spectacular Glacier Divide, and this trip becomes one of the most scenic in all the Sierra.
Location: Go 16 miles from Bishop on State Highway 168 almost to Lake Sabrina and turn right on a dirt road. After a few hundred feet turn right again and go two miles to a backpackers' parking area just west of North Lake. You must walk the last ½ mile to the trail head be-yond the campground.
Description: Shortly after leaving the trail head, this route enters the John Muir Wilderness and then ascends gently along slopes dotted with meadowy patches, aspen groves and stands of lodgepole pine. In season, traveler will find a wealth of wildflowers in these little meadows and in the sandy patches among the granite slabs, including paint-brush, columbine, tiger lily, spiraea and penstemon. After the trail fords the North Fork of Bishop Creek several times, the ascent becomes moderate. The glaciated canyon is flanked by slab-topped Peak 12707 on the south and rust-colored, 13,225-foot Mt. Emerson on the north. The newcomer to the High Sierra will marvel at how the great granite slabs maintain their precarious perches atop Peak 12707, seeming to be almost vertically above him. But they all topple eventually, due to the action of frost wedging, and add to the piles of talus at the foot of the peak. Approaching Loch Leven Lake, the trail levels off; then it as-cends moderately again, through a cover of sparse lodgepole and whitebark, winds among large, rounded boulders, and skirts a small lake before arriving at the next bench up the canyon, which contains Piute Lake. There are good campsites on the north side.

From Piute Lake, the trail ascends an open, rocky slope to timber-line, and switchbacks up to the last traverse before Piute Pass. At the pass there are grand views west to the canyon of the South Fork San Joaquin River, south to Glacier Divide, and north to Mt. Humphreys, highest peak this far north in the Sierra. The rocky trail descends moderately to Summit Lake, and levels off as it fords a stream and enters the great, high lake bowl called Humphreys Basin, which contains 31 lakes that have golden trout. The sandy trail contours through alpine grasses and then descends to ford the outlet stream of Big and Little Desolation Lakes. There is good fishing in Big Desolation for golden trout to 20 inches, reached by going two miles north on the trail that turns right from our route shortly after this ford. Or the angler may wish to sample the waters of Golden Trout Lake, just south of the trail, for the fair fishing for golden (to 10 inches). About ¼ mile before Golden Trout Lake, the trail forks. The newest trail is to the right. About ¼ mile before Golden Trout Lake, the trail forks. The newer trail is to the right. Entering timber, the route begins a moderate descent on a rocky trail through sparse lodgepole forest which soon becomes moderate.

About four miles from Piute Pass the display of flower-studded green "lawns" begins, and from here to Hutchinson Meadow the traveler is seldom out of sight of these subalpine gardens. The amateur botanist will discern paintbrush, shooting star, fleabane, swamp onion, red mountain heather, buttercup, cinquefoil, penstemon, buckwheat, yarrow milfoil, groundsel and Douglas phlox, along with Labrador tea, Lemon willow and alpine willow. Rollicking Piute Creek is always close at hand, lending its music to complete this scene of mountain beauty. Finally the trail levels out, fords the distributaries of French Canyon Creek, and arrives at the good campsites at Hutchinson Meadow.

Courtright Reservoir to Guest Lake Trail

Location: Drive northeast 42 miles from Clovis (near Fresno) on State Highway 168 and turn right onto the Dinkey Creek Road. Follow it 28 miles to the Courtright/Wishon "Y", from where Courtright Reservoir is 7½ miles north, and there is large parking area at the south end of the reservoir.

Length: 37 miles

USGS Quad: **Blackcap Mountain** (15 minute)

Highlights: Of the three lake basins lying close under towering LeConte Divide, Bench Valley is the least known and least visited. This is surprising in view of the excellent angling available at McGuire Lakes and Guest Lake. The other lakes of this basin are among the most picturesque in the Sierra, and the angler with an inclination to visit stirring subalpine scenery en route should give this trip serious consideration.

Description: From man-made Courtright Reservoir the route crosses the dam and, following a brief section of maintenance road, skirts the granite shoulder of the ridge that lines the east shore of the reservoir. Excellent views to the north of spectacular Maxson Dome greet the traveler crossing the dam, and the view down the Helms Creek gorge just below the spillway is a dizzying one that leaves the traveler feeling as though he were treading the brink of hell's abyss. A few yards down the rocky maintenance road, your trail branches left (north), descending at first through an area of granite slabs, and then leveling out.

The trail descends past the meadowed foot of a long sheet of glacially smoothed granite on the left that sports numerous spectacular glacial erratics, then fords the East Fork of Helms Creek and winds through a dense forest cover of young lodgepoles around the east side of Maxson Meadows. Ascending gently, the trail passes Chamberlain's Camp and the Dusty Meadows jeep road. Just beyond Chamberlain's Camp, the trail ascends steeply by short, dusty switchbacks, and then tops this climb in a beautiful mixed stand of red fir and lodgepole. .After passing the first of two trails to Burnt Corral Meadow, the trail fords an unnamed, intermittently flowing stream, and descends gently to the head of beautiful Long Meadow. Aptly named, this grassland stretches away to the northeast for about a mile, and the route winds through the middle — seldom more than a few yards away from the sluggishly flowing South Fork Post Corral Creek.

The route passes a second Burnt Corral Meadow Trail midway through the meadow, fords South Fork Post Corral Creek, and then leaves the sandy-surfaced trail of the meadow behind as it swings east. Then the route passes a faint trail branching left to a privately owned line cabin and descends gently to the excellent campgrounds at the head of Post Corral Meadows. There are several primitive campgrounds at the head of the meadow, and one packer site. Other sites can be found at the foot of the meadow (ford Post Corral Creek) adjacent to the junction of the Hell-for-Sure Pass Trail.

From the campsites, the trail passes the Hell-for-Sure Pass Trail (branching left), and winds through a densely forested stretch of mixed stands of red fir, lodgepole and silver pine. The general southward progress of the trail changes to an upward slog eastward as the trail ascends a rocky, moderate slope, and finally emerges on an open, manzanita-covered ridge above the North Fork Kings River drainage. This open slope is a fine point from which to view the unfractured granite river chasm to the west and the dramatic U-shaped valley to the southeast.

From this ridge, the trail descends on a traverse over infrequently jointed granite to the banks of the river. Excellent campsites can be found a short distance up or downstream, but one should remember that it is illegal to camp within 100 feet of the stream. Angling for brook, rainbow and some brown trout (to 12 inches) is excellent. Swimming in some of the finest sand-bottomed potholes in the Sierra is available just downstream, and photographers seeking a worthy subject will find Sue Falls about ¼ mile downstream.

From the river's edge, the trail swings left through a dense stand of timber, and fords Fleming Creek just above its confluence with the North Fork Kings River. In these shady timber stands, heavy coats of green moss cover rock and tree alike; bright orange shelf bracts flash like great eyes against the forest green; and sounds seem muted on the carpet of pine needles. But the soft duff trail is soon left behind as the route climbs above the river valley over the granite nose of a ridge, and then descends to a snow-survey cabin nestled in granite slabs at river's edge. The trail then passes the Meadow Brook Trail branching left to Hell-for-Sure Pass and the Nichols Canyon Trail branching right, before fording an unnamed tributary and Meadow Brook. Ascending gently, this trail route winds through moderate-to-dense stands of lodgepole and red fir.

After fording Fall Creek, your route leaves the Blackcap Basin Trail by branching left onto an unmaintained shortcut trail that ascends along the south side of Fall Creek. The route is gentle at first, and easy to follow, but this condition changes as soon as the area of the broad granite walls is reached. Here, the hiker keeps on course by staying close to the creek on the south side. This is a pleasant chore, for the creek forms a lovely silver ribbon as it chutes hundreds of feet across glacially smoothed granite.

Our ascending route meets another trail lateral at the foot of the valley, and joined as one they wind alongside the luxuriantly foliaged banks of Fall Creek. Wildflowers fill the valley floor: shooting star, penstemon, larkspur, monkshood, monkey flower, columbine, wallflower and Indian paintbrush.

After traveling a short distance along the creek, the trail begins a steep ascent of the valley's east wall. Short switchbacks, which soon become rocky and steep, mark this strenuous climb, and the first, water-level view of lower McGuire Lake comes as a welcome and pleasant surprise. The lake's waters appear suddenly only a few feet from the precipitous drop-off, and from this point one can indeed ascertain the true meaning of the term "hanging valley." The route passes several primitive and packer campsites as it rounds the north side of lower and upper McGuire Lakes. Through moderate-to-sparse timber, the trail crosses an easy ridge to the fisherman's lateral that turns off the main trail and leads southeast to Guest Lake. Excellent packer and primitive campsites with unobstructed views of Black Mountain line the north shore of this lovely granite-lined lake, and it is a fine choice as a base camp for excursions to 20 nearby lakes in this basin. At Guest Lake fishing for brook trout (to 12 inches) is good. Fishing in the lakes of the upper Bench Valley Basin varies from good to excellent, and offers the angling sportsman a creel of both brook and rainbow trout.

Wishon Reservoir to Halfmoon Lake Trail
Location: Follow the directions above to the Courtright/Wishon "Y" and from there drive east 2 miles to the Wishon Dam and across the dam to the trailhead parking lot.
Length: 22 miles

Topographic Maps: **Blackcap Mountain** (15 minute)
Highlights: Halfmoon Lake, at the end of an unnamed trail, nestled in a cirque below an unnamed peak, can serve as a hideout for the city-dweller who — temporarily — has had it. On the way to this fine lake, Mooreboys Meadow offers a campsite where the flora and fauna are plentiful and fascinating.
Description: From the east side of the dam, the trail angles northeast up a ridge on steep, dusty switchbacks under a mixed forest cover of pines, firs, cedars and occasional black oaks. As views back down to Wishon become less frequent, the trail crosses a jeep road and passes into deep forest. Two tiny streamlets provide thirst-quenching relief on this strenuous climb, and a continuous band of wildflowers periodically expands into gardens in open spots, enhanced by many species of butterflies in an aerial array of blues, oranges and yellows. You descend from the ridge to Woodchuck Creek (good campsites) where a wade-across ford brings you to the junction of this newer section of trail with the pre-Wishon-Dam Woodchuck Trail. Ascend northward from the creek for a short distance, then veer east, climbing a manaznita-covered ridge under a moderate forest cover.

Past the sometimes muddy confluence of the branches of Woodchuck Creek, the trail passes a lateral leading to Indian Springs and Chuck Pass, then ascends to beautiful Mooreboys Meadow, which is filled with thousands upon thousands of shooting stars and corn lilies. The quiet hiker will be entertained by the antics of the very large marmot colony in the rocky ledge on the right, and photographers may wish to camp at the north end of the meadow, along the creek, to take advantage of the large plant and animal population.

A short distance above the meadow, the trail passes a lateral leading left across the creek and up to Woodchuck Lake. The trail bears right and ascends a ridge to a junction where another lateral goes left, this one passing Chimney and Marsh Lakes on its way to Woodchuck Lake. Another mile brings you to yet a third lateral up to Woodchuck Lake. From this junction you ascend east gently to moderately, and climb the southeast ridge of an unnamed granite dome, where the sparseness of scattered lodgepole and whitebark pines allows broad views in all directions.

The trail then drops steeply to the saddle of Crown Pass, from where the vestiges of an unmaintained trail down Nichols Canyon go left and the Crown Lake/Crown Valley Trail goes right. Past these junctions, you follow the ridge north to a beautiful overlook of Halfmoon Lake before descending steeply down a densely forested lodgepole slope to the north end of the lake. Good campsites are on the north and east sides of this striking lake.

South Lake to Dusy Basin Trail
Location: Go 12 miles southwest from Bishop on State Highway 168 to the South Lake turnoff, and then 7 miles to the South Lake parking

area.

Length: 14 miles

Topographic Maps: **Mt. Goddard** (15 minute)

Highlights: A popular route, the Bishop Pass Trail climbs the scenic course of the South Fork of Bishop Creek. At Bishop Pass, the trail enters King Canyon National Park, but, more significantly, it begins the adventure of the high, barren, granitoid country of Dusy Basin. Grand side-trip possibilities are sufficient reason for planning layover days on this trip.

Description: Starting from the road end about ¼ mile above the South Lake dam, the route ascends through a moderate-to-dense forest cover of lodgepole and fir on a somewhat rocky trail. This ascent traverses the morainal slope on the east side of South Lake, bearing toward Hurd Peak, and then passes the junction with the Treasure Lakes Trail. The trail shifts direction somewhat eastward as it slopes upward along South Fork Bishop Creek, and passes the Bull and Chocolate Lakes Trail. Frequent patches of lupine, forget-me-nots, wallflowers, and swamp onions delight the traveler as he/she fords tributaries and crosses swampy sections. The trail then fords South Fork Bishop Creek and switchbacks up to the islet-dotted north end of Long Lake. After recrossing South Fork Bishop Creek, it undulates along the east side of beautiful Long Lake (brook, rainbow, brown, to 17") and passes the Chocolate and Ruwau Lakes Trail. The memorable vistas of the wooded and meadowed shores of Long Lake stay with the visitor as he/she crosses the cascading Ruwau Lake outlet stream and ascends through sporadic subalpine tarn-dotted meadows. Sometimes steep, this steadily ascending trail climbs past spectacular Saddlerock Lake and the unmarked fisherman's trail spur to Bishop Lake.

Beyond Saddlerock Lake, the trail passes timberline and begins a series of steep switchbacks at the head of a spectacular cirque basin. Occasional pockets of snow sometimes blanket the approach to Bishop Pass late into the season, and care should be exercised in the final ascent to the crest. Views from the pass are excellent. From the pass your route descends on a sometimes switchbacking southwestern traverse. This rocky descent contours over rock-bench systems some distance north of the basin's northernmost large lake, fording its inlet stream. Just below this streamford, your route branches left leaving the trail and crossing smooth granite and tundra for a few hundred feet to the good campsites at the west end of this lake. Other good campsites can be found a few yards to the southwest, along the outlet stream.

Cedar Grove to Vidette Meadow Trail

Location: Go 85 miles east from Fresno on State Highway 180 to the road end.

Length: 26 miles (round trip)

Topographic Maps: **Marion Peak, Mt. Pinchot** (15 minute)

Highlights: Climbing 4000 feet, this trip follows an old Indian trade route paralleling Bubbs Creek. Beyond the realm of the day hiker, the trail climbs the path of an old glacier to beautiful Vidette Meadow, a "high country crossroads." Here in the shadow of the spectacular Kearsarge Pinnacles this route meets the famous John Muir Trail.

Description: From the paved road end loop, the wide, sandy trail ascends gently through a mixed forest cover. The murmur of the South Fork Kings River, sometimes near, sometimes far, accompanies the traveler as he/she winds up the gentle ascent and passes the Paradise Valley/Woods Creek Trail (branching north) just before crossing a steel bridge over the South Fork and a series of wooden bridges over the branches of Bubbs Creek. The last bridge crossing marks the beginning of a series of steady switchbacks. This ascent offers fine views back into the dramatic U-shaped South Fork Kings River canyon. Above the switchbacks, at the Sphinx Creek Trail junction, are several fair campsites. Camping here and on the entire Rae Lakes loop is limited to one night in any campsite.

Keeping to the north side of Bubbs Creek, the trail ascends steadily up the canyon, passing a number of fair campsites. The trail fords several unnamed tributaries and then Charlotte Creek. The sparse-to-moderate forest cover reflects the altitude gain, with inclusions of lodgepole and fir and some Jeffrey pine.

Continuing up Bubbs Creek canyon, you can see, on the north wall of the canyon, the cleft of the Charlotte Creek drainage, guarded on the west by Charlotte Dome. The south wall presents several avalanche chutes, which are responsible for the patch of bent and broken trees on the near side of the canyon. After a short, steep stretch of rocky going, the trail goes through fine stands of quaking aspen and black cottonwood to beautiful Junction Meadow.

Beyond the west end of the meadow, your route passes the East Lake/Lake Reflection Trail. At the end of the meadow the trail switchbacks up a dry manzanita slope, sometimes distant from the creek and sometimes right alongisde. The steepest part of the climb ends at the conclusion of the switchbacks, and the trail then proceeds on a moderate ascent to the junction with the John Muir Trail. The route turns right, fords the tiny outlet creek from Bullfrog Lake, and arrives at the good campsites at beautiful Vidette Meadow, scattered along Bubbs Creek.

Onion Valley to Charlotte Lake Trail

Location: Drive west from Independence on U.S. 395 15 miles to the road-end parking lot.

Length: 34 miles (round trip)

Topographic Maps: **Mt. Pinchot, Marion Peak** (15 minute)

Highlights: Employing one of the "easiest" east-side entries, this trip climbs past the friendly lakes making up the headwaters of Independence Creek. The ample opportunities for good angling and the exciting alpine scenery at Charlotte Lake occupy one's weekend time in grand style.

Description: The trail leaves the road a few yards north of the campground and switchbacks up over a dry, manzanita-covered slope. After about one-half mile, the trail enters the John Muir Wilderness and switchbacks steadily again, until after a mile it comes close enough to tumbling Independence Creek that only a few steps are needed to reach the wildflower-lined stream bank and slake one's thirst.

On a more gradual slope our path crosses many runoff rills in early and mid-season. At the top of this gentle grade is Little Pothole Lake, not much for camping, but boasting two beautiful, willow-lined cascades pouring into its south and west bays. After another set of rocky switchbacks, the trail levels off in a slightly ascending groove across a glacial moraine and then reaches small, round Gilbert Lake. Poor-from-overuse campsites dot the shores of this fine swimming lake, and fishing is good in early season. This small lake absorbs much of the day-hiking impact from people camping at Onion Valley, as does Flower Lake, at the top of the next set of switchbacks. Less used and more scenic are Matlock and Slim Lakes, the first reached by a trail that leads south from the east side of Flower Lake, and the second, cross country west from the first. There are many highly used campsites along the north and east sides of shallow Flower Lake.

At Flower Lake the Kearsarge Pass Trail turns north and ascends steeply to a viewpoint overlooking Heart Lake. From this point the trail switchbacks up to another overlook. This time the lake below is the nearly perfect blue oval of Big Pothole Lake. From the switchbacks on, the trail rises above timber (excepting a few hardy whitebark specimens) and then makes two long-legged traverses across an exposed shaley slope to the low saddle of Kearsarge Pass.

The route drops down on the west side of the pass on a traverse that later resolves into the inevitable switchbacks. Passing a spur trail branching left to the Kearsarge Lakes (camping) and Bullfrog Lake (no camping), the route continues westward on a gentle descent into sparse timber. Crossing several small runoff streams in early season, the rocky-sandy trail contours high on the slopes above Bullfrog Lake.

Soon you meet the trail that leads northwest from Bullfrog Lake and follow it past a junction where a shortcut trail leads right to the John Muir Trail. Your route descends gently onto a sandy flat in a broad saddle overlooking Charlotte Lake, where at an "X" junction you take a signed trail that switchbacks down moderately-to-steeply for a short mile to Charlotte Lake. Good campsites line the north shore.

Texas

Texas is noted for the diverse character of its land forms and vegetative zones. Within the state, the hiker can find desert land, rugged mountains, prairies, plains and woods.

Lake Texoma Hiking Trail
Location: Trail head is located in West Juniper Point Recreation Area. Approximately ½ mile inside the recreation area entrance, take the right fork. A little further up, take the left fork. The trail head is just past the second fork.
Length: 22 miles
USGS Quad: Wordonville, 1958 (15 min. series)
Description: The trail is along the south banks and coves of Lake Texoma, providing many scenic overlooks of the lake. The red earthen bluffs carved out by the Red River, contrast sharply to the deep blue lake waters. The trail traverses four park areas which provide camping areas and access points for overnight backpackers.

Many species of vegetation intermingle here, providing an interesting array of flora. The trail is of sufficient length to provide trips of varying duration, and ample access points and camping areas are present. About seven miles of the trail, between Juniper Point Park and Cedar Bayou Park, is more clearly marked and gets heavier usage. The remainder of the trail is in a very primitive condition.
For More Information: Contact the Resident Engineer, U.S. Army Corps of Engineers, Drawer A, Denison, Texas 75020.

Big Bend National Park

Outer Mountain Loop Primitive Trail
Location: Trail head is located in the Chisos Mountains Basin
Length: 33 miles
USGA Quad: The Basin, 1971; Emory Peak, 1971 (7½ min. series)
Description: The Outer Mountain Loop Primitive Trail is located high in the Chisos Mountains. The trail passes through rugged terrain containing interesting and oftentimes unusual scenery. Numerous canyons and jagged peaks provide a dramatic change from the lower desert elevations. A wide variety of plant communities ranging from desert-types to alpine ponderosa pine, douglas fir and Arizona cypress are present.

This loop trail actually encompasses several smaller trails in what is known as the High Chisos Complex of trails. These trails offer panoramic vistas of such notable landmarks as Emory Peak, Elephant Tusk Mountain, the Sierra del Carmens, as well as Cathedral Mountain near Alpine and the mountains in Mexico. Picturesque meadows, beautiful arroyos containing springs and rugged canyons are a part of the trail. Numerous endemic, and oftentimes rare, plant and animal life may be seen.
For More Information: Contact the Park Superintendent; Big Bend National Park, Panther Junction Headquarters, Big Bend National Park, Texas 79834. Phone: 915/477-2251.

Guadalupe Mountain National Park

McKittrick Canyon Trail
Location: Trail head is located at Pim Springs Headquarters

Length: Approximately 15 to 20 miles.

USGA Quad: Guadalupe Peak, 1933 (15 min. series)

Description: The Guadalupe Mountains are rugged, desert mountains contain a biological mixture of Canadian forest types which contrast sharply with the Chihuahuan desert vegetation of the lowlands.

McKittrick Canyon is a complex and fragile ecosystem composed of unique geological formations. Exposed within the canyon is one of the largest fossil limestone reefs in the world, the Capitan Barrier Reef. Springs within the canyon provide sufficient moisture to support a large variety of plant life including ponderosa pine, douglas fir, maple and cacti, sotol and yucca.

The trail suitable for long-distance hiking and backpacking exists only by way of Pine Top Mtn.; the Bowl to McKittrick Canyon. McKittrick Canyon itself is suitable for nature walks and day hikes.

For More Information: Contact the Park Superintendent, Carlsbad Caverns and Guadalupe Mountains National Parks, Carlsbad, New Mexico 88220. Phone: (915) 828-3285.

Sam Houston National Forest

Lone Star Hiking Trail

Location: Western trail head located at the junction of Forest Service Road 149-A and Highway 149, about 3.7 miles east of Richards, Texas. Eastern trailhead is located on Farm Road 2025, a few miles northwest of Cleveland, Texas. Several intermediate trailheads exist.

Length: 100 miles

USGA Quad: Richards, 1962; San Jacinto, 1959; Moore Grove, 1959; Galilee, 1962; Huntsville, 1962; Phelps, 1960; New Waverly, 1960; Oakhurst, 1961; Maynard, 1960; Coldspring, 1960; Camilla, 1960; Westcott, 1958; Cleveland, 1958. (7½ minute series)

Description: The Lone Star Trail traverses the rolling hills and piney woods of Sam Houston National Forest. Numerous streams and creeks as well as the West Forest of the San Jacinto River provide the relief in the topography. The national forest is not one large unit, but is composed of many small tracts of land interspersed by private tracts. The trail follows continuous units of the national forest. Both pines and hardwoods exist in the forest, along with dense undergrowth.

This is the longest overland trail in Texas. Primarily, the trail follows primitive Forest Service roads, tram roads, pipeline rights-of-way, game trails, highways and paths cleared through the understory. A small amount of private property is crossed. Primitive campgrounds are available, as well as the previously established Stubblefield Lake, Double Lake and Big Thicket Scenic Area campgrounds.

For More Information: Contact the Forest Supervisor, National Forests in Texas, P.O. Box 969, Lufkin, Texas 75901. Phone: 713/632-4446.

Pedernales Falls Trail

Location: The trail head is found by taking the first right turn past the

park headquarters building.
Length: 7 miles
USGA Quad: Pedernales Falls, 1967 (7½ min. series)
Description: The trail is located in rugged, hilly terrain along the Pedernales River. Limestone hills are dominated by cedar and live oak. Several creeks have formed small canyons leading to the river. The trail traverses fern-lined creeks and small canyons which contrast sharply with the upland hills. One of these canyons, formed by Bee Creek, contains several pools of crystal clear water and a larger pool known as Arrowhead Pool. Also found in this canyon is a fragile waterfall called Twin Falls. The trail winds along the scenic, bald cypress-lined Pedernales River which contains clear waters flowing over a limestone and gravel bed. Perennially flowing Jones Spring is located along the trail.
For More Information: Contact the Park Superintendent, Pedernales Falls State Park, Route 1 Box 31A, Johnson City, Texas 78636. Phone: 512/868-7304.

Utah

Residents of Salt Lake City and environs are very fortunate in having so many fine hiking trails so close to town. In one hour, a hiker can hit the trail into the Wasatch Mountains, where the proposed Lone Peak Wilderness is likely to be a reality soon. In three hours, the dedicated solitude seeker can be on his way into the Uinta Mountains, with their 244,000 acre High Uintas Primitive Area, where motorcycles, jackhammers and jetports are forbidden, and man is a visitor who does not remain.

The Uinta Mountains bear the marks of recent glaciation, so much so that they provide often-used textbook examples of the landscape features that only glaciers can create. These mountains are also the only major range in the United States that trends east-west. Above their clear lakes and idyllic meadows, peaks rise over 13,000 feet above sea level, culminating in Kings Peak (13,498 feet), highest point in Utah. This is a wilderness area in which to rekindle the basic human spirit that city life is constantly trying to extinguish, and it will attract people from far beyond metropolitan Salt Lake City.

Moon Lake to Kidney Lake Trail
Length: 18 miles (round trip)
Highest Elevation: 10,000 feet
Elevation Gain: 2240 feet
USGS Quad: **Kidney Lake,** Utah (7½ minute)
Highlights: A very pretty walk up Brown Duck Creek culminates in glacially carved Brown Duck Basin. Kidney Lake, the largest of several lakes in the basin, provides ready access to the spectacular views from

Brown Duck Mountain and Tworoose Pass, and the fishing can be quite rewarding.

Location: From Duchesne, Utah, on US 40 turn north onto Utah 87, following signs to Mountain Home and Moon Lake Resort. In about 14 miles, turn left onto an unnumbered route signed "Mountain Home" and "Moon Lake Resort." After Mountain Home, follow a well-graded, all-weather road of alternating stretches of oiled gravel and gravel, for about 15 miles across an Indian reservation. Beware of lumbering trucks. As one enters the Moon Lake Forest Service Campground and the Moon Lake Resort, the pavement resumes. To get to Brown Duck Trail's official trail head, follow signs to the boat ramp (right). Long-term parking is permitted here.

Description: From the trail head, walk north past the trail sign onto the lakeshore. Beyond the far edge of the campground, the trail forks left (west) into the hillside woods. Paintbrush and stonecrop flowers brighten the undergrowth as you follow a wooden rail fence. Quiet, early hikers may surprise some browsing deer, scolding squirrels, frightened rabbits, or friendly chipmunks in this primarily aspen forest. About 1¼ miles from the trail head, you emerge onto a one-lane road and follow the road to the right (north) as it climbs another 1⅓ miles to a turnaround with parking spots (and garbage cans).

The trail leaves the road here, turning right (north) across a small brook. The Primitive Area register is 50 feet up the trail. White and pink wild geraniums and dandelions are prominent, while monkshood and yellow monkey flower color the cool creekside habitats of this lodgepole pine and Englemann spruce forest. Beyond the trail register, you cross gravelly Slate Creek. Soon, a weatherbeaten wooden sign welcomes us to the High Uintas Primitive Area. To the right, far below, is Brown Duck Creek, whose drainage the path follows up to Brown Duck Lake. Descend briefly to a Forest Service livestock gate and notice occasional narrowleaf cottonwoods in this region of transition between the mixed deciduous and coniferous forest of the lower elevations and predominantly lodgepole pine woods you soon enter.

When the trail finally levels off, you are almost at Brown Duck Lake, and all but about 100 feet of the elevation gain to Kidney Lake is behind us. At about mile 6.7, a small wooden sign indicates that Dog Lake is through the forest to the left. Just 50 feet farther is the Ledge Trail-Brown Duck Trail junction. Go left (west) toward Brown Duck Lake, Kidney Lake, and Tworoose Pass. To the right is Clements Lake.

Brown Duck Lake, a popular camping and fishing spot, is 100 yards up our trail. This is a recommended goal for families with limited endurance. Lodgepole pine and Engelmann spruce shade the shores, while mountain elderberry and dandelions are conspicuous among the ground foliage.

The trail to Kidney Lake continues along the top of Brown Duck Lake's dam. Cross the outflow creek by descending into the gully it cut in the rock-and-earth dam, then re-ascend to the dam top to complete the crossing. The path leaves the lake, passing through a meadow with snowcourse markers on nearby trees. Only ¾ mile from the trail junction you come to Island Lake, a second inviting campspot for weary hikers. It is considerably larger than Brown Duck Lake, and also dam-enhanced. Continue, if you choose, toward Kidney Lake, crossing the dam and circum-hiking Island Lake on its north shore. Beyond Island Lake, ford two creeks and enter the **interlaken** glade region—a beautiful, moderately level area with abundant campsites and a large, somewhat marshy, central grassy region, nourished by the stream draining Kidney Lake and feeding Island Lake. The Brown Duck Wilderness Ranger Camp, which houses a ranger-fire warden throughout the summer, is situated here. Less than 2 miles from the trail junction we approach Kidney Lake's long dam. Follow the trail across the dam to copious campsites.

Highline Trailhead to Naturalist Basin and Four Lakes Basin

Location: Utah Route 150 provides the easiest access to the High Uintas Primitive Area. It approaches from the west, convenient to the residents of the metropolitan areas west of the Wasatch Mountains, and from the north (exit I-80 near Evanston, Wyoming). This good blacktop route passes within ½ mile of the Primitive Area boundary. The Highline Trail Head is 2¼ miles north (by road) of the Mirror Lake Resort, on the east side of the highway. It is designated by a large Forest Service sign. Ample off-road parking, horse mangers, hitching racks and car-camping spots are provided at the trail head.

Length: 12 miles (round trip)
Highest Elevation: 11,000 feet
Elevation Gain: 1000 feet
Highlights: A moderately graded trail traverses through typical Uinta Mountain Forest and then climbs into scenic Naturalist Basin, a glacially carved bowl nestled against the main backbone of this mountain range. The basin earned its name from a visit, several years ago, by a group of French naturalists, and many of the lakes there are named after members of that expedition.

Description: The trail takes off from the prominent wooden Primitive Area map at the southeast corner of the parking lot, and enters an obviously horse-trodden trail in a light forest of Engelmann spruce. In only 150 yards, the trail enters the Primitive Area and begins a slightly rocky but very gentle descent.

The quite worn and obvious trail is blazed with an I and it can be easily followed in early season when it's likely to be snow-covered in spots. Bistort, red huckleberry, pennycress and dandelions are common throughout this hike. Corn lily, marsh marigold, paintbrush and bluebells color the banks of this small creek you soon cross. After 1½ miles you reach the first major junction. Mirror Lake is 2 miles right (west) while Naturalist Basin is 4½ miles left (east). Go left, and sign in at the trail register.

Marshy meadows frequently command your view as you stick to the rock-littered forest trail. Soon a faint trail Y's off to the right, and lily-dotted Scudder Lake, the path's destination, is visible to the right. One and a half miles from the junction, a "Mt. Agassiz" sign is followed in 40 feet by the trail fork to Wilder, Wyman, and Packard lakes. This downhill trail is much rougher and rockier than the Highline Trail, and the camping at Wilder Lake is not choice. Stick to the Highline Trail by bearing left. In ¼ mile your path borders a very pretty rock-garden meadow with a brook. Then the trail levels, and forest yields sporadically to meadows of paintbrush, clover, buttercups, violets. and, of course dandelions. When there is any wind at all, the woods are alive with the eerie groan and chatter of swaying, rubbing trees. The grating call of the "camp-robber" jay reminds you to be careful with your food when you finally make camp.

Four and a half miles from the trail head you descend to a creekside junction of the Naturalist Basin Trail and the Highline Trail. Here you are 1½ miles from Jordan and Morat lakes, and somewhat farther from other lakes of Naturalist Basin. Along the Highline Trail, Four Lakes Basin and Pinto Lake are each 4 miles away.

Turn left onto the Naturalist Basin Trail, and climb easily along the edge of a marshy brook. Pennycress, bistort, and glacier lilies are eye-catching as your forest-sheltered path negotiates some open, boggy areas. The terrain dries out as you descend a shelf, and from here on downed trees are likely to obstruct the trail. Scattered boulders on the forest floor are reminders of the not-so-long-ago (geologically) time when glaciers thrived here and carved out the numerous basins of the Uintas. Below us, to the right, you will hear one of Naturalist Basin's main creeks singing us a greeting as it bubbles cheerfully down the hillside. About 5½ miles from the trail head is another signed junction. . It is here you must decide your destination, as the route to Jordan, Leconte, and Shaler lakes diverges from that to Morat and Blue Lakes.

Jordan and Morat Lakes are most heavily used, as they are nearest and they provide good fishing. Blue Lake is above timberline, so firewood is severely limited. Everyman Lake, near Jordan Lake, is too shallow for fish but would make a fine camp for fishermen willing to commute to one of the deeper lakes, or for people who don't wish to be bothered by fishermen. Alternatively, a camp could be made beside any of the unnamed small lakes in the basin, or near the large meadow that lies immediately ahead.

To get to Jordan, Leconte, Shaler, or Everyman Lake, cross the nearby brook immediately on rocks, and follow the initially flat dirt trail along the edge of a beautiful meadow with paintbrush, elephant heads, marsh marigold, bistort, pennycress, and even dwarf laurels. Cassin's finches and pine grosbeaks are not uncommon in this basin dominated by a glacially plucked palisade. All the climbing is saved for the final

200 yards to Jordan Lake, where the trail becomes quite steep, rocky and rough.

To go to Morat and Blue Lakes, continue on this side of the brook, passing immediately through a campsite with horse hitching racks and a toilet. Then start the climb to the lakes' basins.

Naturalist Basin is a delightful place to spend a few days, whether fishing, rambling, loafing, photographing, or even naturalizing. Jaunts to other lakes, especially Blue Lake, should be quite enjoyable.

If, 4½ miles from the trail head, you stay on the Highline Trail, you first cross the brook on a long bridge. A little elevation must be gained so that you can traverse a steep slope, wooded with lodgepole pine, far above a roaring river. You descend to cross Jordan Lake's outflow creek just upstream of its precipitous cascades into the deep valley of the East Fork of the Duchesne. A half mile from the junction, the climb out of this stream's valley is merely preparation for the rocky but easy grade to the signed East Fork—a simple boulder-hop, despite its name. Just a hundred yards beyond the "river", Skinner's Cutoff Trail to Pinto, Rainbow, and Governor Lakes branches to the right (south). A lovely, large meadow, affording good camping around its perimeter, is bisected by Skinner's Cutoff Trail.

The Highline Trail continues ahead to start the climb toward Rocky Sea Pass and Four Lakes Basin. It is a tiring uphill slog, but rewarded by views, and ultimately Four Lakes Basin and camp. In about ¼ mile you pass a nice camping area near a flat marsh-meadow.

About 7½ miles from the trail head, the path forks. The left branch diagonally ascends the talus ridge toward Pigeon Milk Springs and Rocky Sea Pass. To the right (south) Four Lakes Basin is only one mile away. Very soon, signed Olga Lake is patchily visible through trees to our right. The path continues to climb along a bench at the base of a talus slope, and views improve as the forest thins on the approach to the 10,950 foot high point of the trail. A signed trail branch invites you to Rainbow Lake (four miles of level and downhill). Stay left and very soon the grade lessens as the trail turns east, aiming for the southern base of the talus ridge. At the crest, a "Four Lakes Basin" sign identifies the valley below. Its glacially plucked cliffs and flat floor leave no question about the agent that sculpted it.

Joan Lake and Dean Lake (farthest from the trail) are nestled against the plucked cliffs at the head of the glacial valley. Dense, rocky-floored forest confines these lakes on their southeast shores. Camping in this section of the basin is better for smaller parties than for larger, as the rocky till is absent only in small areas. If you prefer meadowy shores with lighter forest and more sun, continue on the trail toward Dale and Daynes Lakes. The approach to Dale follows a well-defined trail that forks off the main trail to the left (east) on the near side of the marshy area between Dale and Daynes. Daynes Lake is left off the main trail near a final "Four Lakes Basin" sign. Large parties might select the Daynes Lake area, as there is more flat, unrocky ground there.

Pacific Northwest Trails

9

The Pacific Northwest is not a well-defined geographic region even though certain portions of it seem to be well established in the minds of the local residents. It is generally accepted that the Pacific Northwest includes at least the western portion of Washington, Oregon and British Columbia.

According to Amos Wood, the boundaries should extend from Mount Shasta in the south to Skagway, Alaska in the north including much of what is in between. His definition includes a region 1400 miles long and 200 miles wide.

The hikes described in this section represent a wide variety of hikes that vary in elevation from sea level to tree line. They include the seashore, the mountains and the flatlands in between.

Alaska

While hiking in southeastern Alaska you will experience an environment similar to the outer coast of British Columbia, namely difficult access, sometimes violent north Pacific Aleutian weather, exposed rugged coastlines and protected lee beaches.

The hiker is dependent on coastwise ferries and floatplanes to get there. You should go with someone who is familiar with the region.

Southeastern Alaska, known as the "panhandle," is mainly a series of islands and channels that project down the western side of British Columbia. Near the coastal towns, most of the terrain begins an ascent the side of the Coast Range. In many places glaciers come down to the water's edge and break off into icebergs. It is a lot easier flying over southeastern Alaska than hiking it.

Chilkoot Trail Skagway, Alaska
Location: To reach the Chilkoot Trail from Seattle, Washington, most hikers travel on one of the Alaska ferries. A typical sailing for the MV **Columbia** is departure at 9:00 pm Friday; stops at Ketchikan, Wrangell, and Petersburg on Sunday; Sitka on Monday; Juneau, Haines, and Skagway. on Tuesday. The Canadian Nation's **Prince George** has a similar schedule out of Vancouver, British Columbia.
Length: 32 miles (one way); allow four to five days one way.
Highest elevation: 3740 feet

Elevation gain: 2140 feet. Open July through September; rugged trail at upper elevations.

Description: In 1897-98 some 30,000 prospectors in their quest for gold against great odds climbed the Chilkoot Pass in order to seek their fortunes in the Klondike gold fields.

In the 1930's a group of citizens from Skagway petitioned the National Park Service for a national park or monument including Skagway, Dyea, and the Chilkoot Pass. In 1959 when Alaska was admitted as a state, the idea was revived. Soon the Canadian Government indicated a desire in cooperating on such a project on that portion of the trail north of the pass. At present shelters have been constructed, footbridges added, and trail markers established. Now U.S. Park Service rangers are assigned to the trail between Dyea and Chilkoot Pass.

Most backpackers make the trip as the gold rush prospectors did from Skagway up over the Chilkoot Pass to Bennett and return by rail. It would be considerably easier to hike it in the reverse direction from Bennett to Skagway. This way you would start at 2100 feet, climb to 3740 feet then coast down to sea level. Upon arrival by Alaska ferry at Skagway the sights can be seen in a hurry. A grocery store has supplies if needed. An 8 mile taxi ride takes you and gear to Dyea where the trailhead is located.

One underway on the trail, a steep climb is encountered for part of the first mile. The trail then levels off high above the Taiya River. Soon it drops to the elevation of the river. For the first 3 miles it goes relatively easy, partly on a muddy logging road to an abandoned sawmill with some storage sheds. At Finnegan's Point, glaciers can be seen to the west making a beautiful vista.

The Canyon City shelter has been established by Alaska's Department of Natural Resources. This shelter has eight bunks and is often the first stop of the trail. Beyond this shelter and off the trail are the ruins of the original Canyon City townsite.

Beyond Canyon City is a steep climb, then down again to the river to Camp Pleasant. Three more easy miles brings one to Sheep Camp shelter which is similar to the previous shelter. This shelter has artifacts and relics inside and out. From here the trail heads up towards the summit. In about two miles the trail is out of the timber and snow banks are encountered.

On the west side of the pass at mile 15½ is a tramway tower and collapsed building and snowfield. The climb here is on rock and quite steep. After a series of ups and downs, the trail drops into a bowl-like area immediately below the final ascent called the Scales. Here are lots of relics, castoffs prior to the last steep climb and Canadian customs weighing in. After a rock climb, the summit is reached through a narrow gap. The commemorative plaque is located short of the summit on the right after a scramble up some rocks. Abandoned canoe kits are seen to the right on a ledge. The view at the summit is rarely clear. Poor visibility and whiteouts are common.

In 1½ miles is Crater Lake. Between Crater Lake and Long Lake the trail goes through a quarter mile long canyon alongside a stream with loose rocks. Be careful here. Happy Camp is just beyond. Deep Lake is another 1½ miles. A footbridge takes the trail to the west side of the river. At mile 23 is a campsite. At mile 23½ is the metal frame of a boat and several pieces of sleighs.

Upon approaching Lake Lindeman, look for the Ranger Station and two cabins at the south end of the lake. In this general area there are a considerable number of relics. It is another seven miles to Bennett. A cemetery and an uncompleted church is near Bennett.

The trail coming from Whitehorse back to Skagway leaves Bennett after a big prospector's lunch is served in the station restaurant of stew, bread, and apple pie — all of which goes with the price of the train ticket. Reservations for the train trip back to Skagway are necessary because of cruise ship day trip bookings. Although you might see only a few hikers on the trail, when it comes to catching the train and that lunch, about 30 or more hikers will converge on the station.

The Chilkoot trail is generally well marked. There are also interpretative markers, sealed frames about two feet by three feet on stands, that contain enlargements of photographs taken during the gold rush with captions written in English and French. Thus along the trail one can readily imagine the actual hardships these prospectors underwent during that historic trek.

British Columbia

British Columbia is the only Canadian province included in this book. The area is dominated by more mountain ranges than Oregon and Washington. Running generally north and south, ranges include the Rocky Mountains forming part of the eastern boundary, the Coast Range in the western section and smaller ranges that include the Selkirks in the south. Its indented Pacific Ocean coastline of 7,000 miles has many inlets and rivers that provide safe harbors for boats and spawning grounds for thousands of salmon.

This province is famous for its striking contrasts. Arctic weather freezes its northern border, while flowers bloom in the winter at Victoria, the southern tip of Vancouver Island.

British Columbia is big. It runs about 750 miles north to south, and about 900 miles east and west — almost one and a half times larger than Texas. Thus very little is known or documented regarding hiking trails for the entire province.

There are excellent campsite and park areas that have been supported by provincial action, and many of those can be used as a base for extensive hiking.

Much backpacking is done in British Columbia along with other activities like fishing and hunting. On the whole, British Columbia appeals not only to the more experienced backpacker, who enjoys a primitive wilderness, but also to the day hiker, who wants to enjoy the rugged scenic beauty.

Queen Charlotte Islands Trail

Location: The Queen Charlottes are about 60 miles out into the Pacific Ocean from Prince Rupert on the British Columbia mainland. Surface vessel and air service is available from Prince Rupert to Masset. There is also surface vessel and air service from Vancouver, British Columbia. From Vancouver, British Columbia, Northland Navigation Co., Ltd. operates two ships from Vancouver to Masset via Prince Rupert. Pacific Western Airlines flies daily except Wednesday to Sandspit on Moresby Island.

Of the four different ways to go, it has been our experience that the best and easiest schedule is to fly from Vancouver, British Columbia to Sandspit and continue by surface transportation to Masset. From the Sandspit airport one takes a bus or taxi six miles to Alliford Bay where a two mile ferry trip across Skidegate Inlet brings you to Skidegate Landing. Nearby to the west is Queen Charlotte City of about 850 people with a hospital, government offices, stores, charter services and transportation connections. Nearby to the east is the Indian reservation of Skidegate Mission where about 300 Haidas reside.

Length: 50 miles (one way); allow four to five days.

Highest elevation: 500 feet, easy, but lengthy sea level beach hike. Open June through September.

Description: Captain John Meares, during his fur trading expedition to the Pacific Northwest in 1778, apparently was the first white explorer to record seeing a stand of carved poles, great wooden images, erected by the Haida Indian Nation. This art is believed to have its orgin on Langara Island at the northwest corner of Queen Charlotte Islands. From here the practice of carving totems spread to other Indian nations. The poles were later reported on the mainland as far north as Yakutat, Alaska, inland up the Skeena River at Kispiox, British Columbia. and south with the Nootkas on Vancouver Island. Although these carvings may have had religious significance initially, they took on great political and social importance. Today in the Queen Charlotte Islands a few poles can be found at Skidegate Mission, Haida. and in some abandoned villages.

Our objective is to hike the beach perimeter of the Naikoon Provincial Park. The park is located in the northeast corner of Graham Island, one of the more inaccessible hiking areas of the Pacific Northwest. This hike starts on North Beach, near the village of Haida, goes out to Rose Spit then south to Tlell. It is a sea level trail, in places adjacent to the beach, elsewhere it is the beach itself. The adjoining land is rolling lowland, partly covered with dense second growth timber, other parts have sparse growth. Much of the area is featureless except for some 25 foot high sand hills.

Daily bus service is available at Queen Charlotte City to Masset which is about 60 miles north. The road runs along the east shore of Graham Island bordering Hecate Strait for about 20 miles to Tlell, the beginning of the Naikoon Provincial Park. Here there is the world famous Tlell River with its superb fishing. The Tlell Provincial Park is located about two miles north, encompassing the river mouth and spit.

Beyond the Tlell River the road turns inward about 12 miles to Port Clemments, on Masset Inlet, a community of about 400 with marine and store services here. In another 15 miles north is Pure Lake Park with picnic and rest facilities.

The final 15 miles brings one to Masset, a village of about 1700 people. Here are marine and transportation services, plus lodging and stores. A short distance north along Masset Harbour is Haida, the Indian Reservation of about 750. This is the headquarters of the Haida Indian Nation, which in its earlier days with its vast transportation network, held great political and economic strength and numbered 8,000 people in some 17 villages.

North Beach extends east from Haida about 28 miles to Rose Spit. Going east from Masset is a road to Tow Hill Provincial Park 16 miles away. Tow Hill is a 500 foot high rock outcropping, a prominent landmark for beach hikers and commercial fishermen, and is readily distinguishable from the low terrain of this portion of Graham Island. It is well worth taking the trail that leads to the top for the vistas and photographs.

Another 10 miles along a drift-filled beach and a beachcombers' heaven brings one to Rose Spit, a low sandy point extending north about two miles and covered with tiny strawberry plants. This spit catches all sorts of drift on both sides from storms of Alaskan origin that occasionally reach 100 miles per hour.

If the weather is favorable and your provisions adequate you can then make the decision to head south down the east coast for the 40 mile trek to Tlell. Miles of relatively protected sand hills with some clay cliffs stretch along a wide flat beach. Here the hiker will beachcomb more glass fishing floats and other strange oriental items than he can carry out. There is the occasional stream to cross, but none is impassable. Wild cattle frequent this northeast region of Graham Island, and may surprise the hiker. Water may be a problem, not from availability but because some streams originate from low inland brackish sources. The readily visible shipwreck Pezuta tells one he is approaching the Tlell River, and the road back to the amenities of Queen Charlotte City.

Clams can be dug at low tide on these beaches assuming there is no red tide closure. Be sure to check with provincial officials in Masset. Also check with Forest Service officials regarding campfires. The hike would be incomplete without fishing some of the streams, so pick up your non-resident license at Masset. Many birds will be seen and eagles are prevalent. Deer are often seen on the beaches.

Northern California

Only a small portion of California is discussed here — most of it the mountainous region within the Klamath National Forest and Marble Mountain Wilderness. Here the potential for hiking is good. The population density of this region is low, so only a few of the state's 21 million people live or vacation here. The climate is dry, and there is very little wind.

There are a variety of trails. Many are former logging roads. Some trails are so faint that, if the destination can't be sighted, it is doubtful where to proceed.

There are spectacular trails in wilderness areas of the Marble Mountains and Trinity Alps. Toward the coast, lush vegetation extends from the flat river valley agricultural lands up into the foothills.

Near the Oregon border, in the region of Pyramid Peak north of Seiad Valley, there are several excellent one-day and overnight hikes. On the Pacific Ocean front there are the beach trails.

Black Butte

Location: To get to Black Butte, drive north on I-5 from Redding, California, past the Shasta Lake recreational area. Dunsmuir, and onto Weed. Soon after Dunsmuir, Mount Shasta appears ahead to the right; however, cone-shaped Black Butte is seen directly ahead. I-5 skirts the base by the width of a pasture field and train tracks. The Butte is almost as impressive as Mount Shasta.

Take the South Weed Boulevard Exit and turn right (east) at the exit stop sign. Continue 1/10 mile to the second stop sign at Tee intersection. Turn right (south) and proceed about ½ mile and turn left (east) past several abandoned buildings. Go about ¼ mile to the Southern Pacific Railroad tracks and turn left. In a short distance take the ramp up to the right, opposite salvage yard, and cross the tracks. Next turn right (south) at a water tank which is painted black. Drive parallel on the east side of the tracks. At 4/10 mile from the water tank go to the left where a side road comes down to the tracks. Keep to the left again where the road forks. Keep to the left a third time. At 2.6 miles from the water tank you will encounter a junction that has power lines crossing diagonally overhead. Turn right and proceed onto this narrow road for about ½ mile to a turnaround passable only by all-terrain-vehicles, preferably bulldozers. Park here. The trail begins at the south edge of the turnaround. There are no markers anywhere.

Length: 2½ miles (one way); allow two hours one way
Highest elevation: 6325 feet
Elevation Gain: 1835 feet. Open June through October
Description: Seldom does the hiker have a built-in volcanic rock con-

ical tripod that is 1800 feet high, set perfectly, in front of a 14,000-foot snowcapped mountain for his picture taking. Black Butte is exactly that. This three pinnacled so-called cinder cone, the site of a former lookout, provides at its peak an ideal place for the hiking-photographer to catch Mount Shasta in her best northeast profile. Because black Butte rises suddenly from the flat valley floor near Weed, California, it is a *climbing* hike.

Black Butte has been properly named. It is a mass of shadows from its many individual rock faces resulting in a dark appearance on the surface even on a sunny day.

The trail begins at the northeast base of the butte, and rises with an even, moderate grade. The first ¼ mile is in the woods, but it suddenly turns to open rocky hillside trail and stays that way to the top. Initially, the trail heads west along the north face and presents an ever increasing number of fine vistas of Mount Shasta. It then follows south on the west face. At about 1000 feet above the valley, the low rumble of a Southern Pacific switch engine and the occasional bleep of its air horn can clearly be heard almost directly below. Immediately adjacent to the railroad is multi-laned I-5 highway with cars crawling along like so many ants on its cream colored ribbon surface—all in marked contrast to the surrounding greenery.

The trail abruptly turns east through the valley of the boulders. After a short distance, there are a series of switchbacks before heading west again above the depression which separates the two principal peaks. With a few more short switchbacks, the top can be seen. Towards the top are fallen telegraph poles and line, remains of the former communication link with the lookout station. A few alpine firs eke out an existance near the top.

The lookout has been removed. However, a small concrete foundation remains on the pinnacle. Strangely enough, the lookout's small necessary auxiliary structure still stands—an extremely rustic cubicle perched precariously to the lee, over huge sloping slabs of rock. There is flat space near the lookout foundation where a few sleeping bags could be stretched out for those who might want to camp overnight.

There is no water on the butte, so a canteen is required.

Oregon

Between 1850 and 1875 it is conservatively estimated that more than 50,000 pioneers came over the Oregon Trail by covered wagon to settle in the lengthy Willamette Valley region. The pleasantly mild climate of the region that was a strong inducement to the pioneers encourages an exceedingly high percentage of the state's two million people, perhaps as many as 200,000, to take to the hills in pursuit of outdoor hiking pleasures. Consequently, the thousands of miles of trails now available throughout the state provide continuing incentives to new generations of hiking enthusiasts.

Oregon has an exciting variety of and striking contrasts in its trails. Within a day's drive, you can hike part of snowcapped Mount Hood, beach hike the edge of the sea to a Pacific Ocean sunset or walk the lava sands of sage brush dotted deserts.

Cape Lookout - hike rocky peninsula that extends into the Pacific.
Length: 2½ miles (one way); allow two hours one way
Highest elevation: 800 feet (at start).
Elevation at Lookout: 500 feet: easy day trip: Open all year around.
Description: This trail is on a high rocky peninsula that extends from shore several miles out into the Pacific Ocean. No other similar viewpoint exists along the Pacific. From this cape viewpoint, the northward migration of grey whales can be seen in the early spring and southward in the fall. Often the whales come within a few hundred yards of this prominence.

Cape Lookout is well named. This massive headland juts seaward like an irresistible rock finger from a coast that on both sides has a wide flat sandy shoreline. This formidable peninsula has steep rocky sides which precipitate directly into the water. Thus there is no beach around this land projection with its fortress-like profile.

The trail is within Cape Lookout State Park. The trailhead begins at a high inland viewpoint and parking area on the coast road which connects Tillamook and Sand Lake. At this starting elevation you see a commanding view of the Pacific Ocean towards the southwest. The trail winds initially through a dense spruce stand along the south side of the peninsula. At about one quarter mile is a commemorative plaque on the right at shoulder level denoting the site of an Army Air Force aircraft accident which took place in 1943. Some of the larger pieces of the wreckage may be seen in the underbrush west of the plaque. The trail here skirts a steep drop to the water 600 feet below.

The trail heads westward and at about the one mile point crosses over to the north side, and to a side trail viewpoint with a northwestern exposure. The trail threads another 1½ miles to the final viewpoint at the southwest corner of the Cape, but is muddy much of the time. From here on a clear day, Tillamook Head can be seen 42 miles to the north and Cape Foulweather 39 miles to the south. A whistler buoy is located about a quarter mile offshore. Occasionally grey whales are seen inside this buoy.

Cape Lookout is perhaps the most scenic headland on the Pacific Coast. It was set aside as a rain forest wilderness and wildlife refuge in 1935. This 2,000 acre state park also includes extensive overnight camping, picnic, and bathing facilities located at beach elevation immediately north of the cape itself.

Location: To get to Cape Lookout from Portland, Oregon, drive west on state route 26 for 26 miles to interchange onto route 6. Here go 13 miles to Glenwood, then 36 miles to Tillamook. Drive west out of Tilla-mook to the Cape Lookout-Cape Meares junction. Turn left and follow Cape Lookout signs for 11 miles. Upon entering the park, take Sand Lake road which diagonals left. This winds up at the top of the head-land for about 2½ miles to an 800-foot elevation summit where a prom-inent sign identifies Cape Trail parking to the right. The trailhead starts from this viewpoint parking area. Bring your camera, binoculars, and water. When viewing the Pacific Ocean from the west end of the trail, enjoy the bird life and grey whales in season. Remember that you are standing on a geographically significant prominence almost exactly on the 45th latitude, named by fur trader Captain John Meares in 1788.

From the felled alders, the trail continues into a grassy clearing, where in summer grow common cowparsnips by the thousands. Conti-nue a short distance past the clearing until you locate a 2-foot high 5-inch square wooden post, originally painted orange but now faded — an official survey point. Turn to the left for a short distance and then to the right. Climb a fairly steep grade to a second almost level aban-doned logging road. At this road, turn left (west) and follow it to an open shale rock bed where you turn right. Proceed uphill to a small ridge and onto the saddle. Turn left on the ridge and follow the guide markings through snags and new growth to the summit. From here on a clear day are beautiful vistas in all directions with conical-shaped Mount Saint Helens, round-domed Mount Adams, and streaked Mount Hood all standing snowcapped to the east.

This trail is not readily visible much of the time because it is almost completely grown over with bracken, thimbleberry, and five-inch diame-ter alder; and apparently has little usage.

Reforestation efforts by the Oregon State Forestry Department and private industry have been most commendable. The deer are back. Rabbit, squirrels, fish have been restocked. Bear and cougar are re-ported.

This hike is a very satisfying day trip. Here is the opportunity to see a new woodland being created Phoenix-like from the ashes of a catas-trophic forest fire. Kings Mountain trail is a living interpretive display for the rebirth of our forest heritage.

Tillamook Head Trail (follow Lewis & Clark to coastal viewpoint)

Location: To get here from Portland, Oregon, drive northwest on State Route 26 for 76 miles joining northbound Highway 101 into Seaside. At the southern edge of town, turn left (west), cross over the Necani-cum River, past the gold course, and again turn left (south) on South Edgemont Road. Drive south about one mile up a gradually rising road to the Ecoloa State Park parking lot and trailhead sign.
Length: 6 miles (one way); allow three hours one way
Highest elevation: 1200 feet
Elevation gain: 1100 feet Open all year around unless posted; easy one-day trip.

Description: The Lewis and Clark expedition to the Pacific Northwest had great national significance to the development of our country. To trace some of their footsteps today is to help understand regional history.

On January 6, 1806, Clark and a party of 12 set out from their winter quarters at Fort Clatsop to visit the advance team on the shores of the Pacific at their salt manufacturing cairn which today can be seen at Seaside, Oregon. Here they hired an Indian guide to help them reach a beached whale to the south because they wanted to acquire some of its meat for food. To get there they had to ascend Tillamook Head.

The original trail up over Tillamook Head was by necessity used by the Indians because there was no beach trail available for several miles. A low inland trail around this rocky prominence might have been twice as long. Thus this direct trail goes up to an elevation of 1200 feet and down again. It was an important coastline route of the Indians.

The 6 mile hike is now included in that part of the 62 miles dedicated Oregon Coast Trail extending from the Columbia River south jetty to Tillamook Bay. The completed trail is planned to cover the entire Oregon coast.

The north end of this hike begins at the Ecola State Park boundary trailhead about two miles south of Seaside, Oregon. The trail begins in thick growth. At about ½ mile one encounters a series of switchbacks to a viewpoint. Here to the north Seaside and its unobstructed stretch of beach can be seen. The trail continues in the forest for about 1½ miles at about the 1000 foot elevation.

Soon at this elevation one approaches an open area with knee-high grass and a 360 degree view. Here at 3½ miles from Seaside is a wood marker post on the ocean side. Immediately to the right and in about 30 feet is the commemorative plaque and a rest bench denoting the spot where Clark extolled the beauty of the broad Pacific. Here one can see the Pacific Ocean and its coastline in a full 360 degree sweep. The view extends past the broad beaches of Seaside and Gearhart to the Coast Mountains at the mouth of the Columbia River 25 miles north, and as far in the opposite direction to the south.

Amos Woods has yet to find in his travels along the Pacific Ocean as commanding a view. Thus in Clark's quest for food he and his party discovered an outstanding vista that few people even today have experienced. Again, only the hiker can enjoy such thrills.

From here going south, the trail enters a dense forest containing numerous huge trees apparently toppled over by some disastrous Pacific Ocean windstorm. Switchbacks are again encountered. At four miles from Seaside is another wood marker post at a road crossing. To the right is the Tillamook Hikers Campground. The trail continues inland through a heavy forest partially logged off. Here the needle strewn trail is protected from ocean winds although the forest is open without underbrush.

At about 5½ miles are two good viewpoints of the ocean and Tilla-mook Rock and its abandoned lighthouse about one mile offshore. These viewpoints are precariously close to vertical coastal cliffs, so be careful. The final portion of the trail is down through enormous wind swept spruce trees some 5 feet through. Indian Beach comes into view; and, once across the trail footbridge, a right turn brings one into the Indian Beach picnic site and parking lot.

Tillamook Head is a coastal mountain graced by precipitous bluffs, heavy and massive coastal forest growth, little underbrush, soaring gulls, and a historic viewpoint. Bring your camera, binoculars, and water.

William L. Finley National Wildlife Refuge Trail

Location: To get to Finley Refuge from Portland, Oregon, drive 69 miles south on Interstate 5 to Albany. Go five miles past Albany to junction of State Route 34. Turn right, or west for nine miles to Corval-lis. Here turn left, or south on Highway 99W. Go south for 10 miles where you are greeted with a large entrance sign on the right. Turn right and follow the road for about 2½ miles to parking area by the ref-uge office and large red barn.

Length: one to seven miles (one way); allow one day. Open January thru October; easy day hike.

Description: In western central Oregon south of Corvalis is the William L. Finley National Wildlife Refuge, an attraction for an individual hiker or family group to see and experience firsthand a Federal conservation resource. Nestled against the eastern foothills of the Coast Range in the broad, famed Willamette Valley with snowcapped peaks of the Cas-cades to the east, this refuge of over 5300 acres is situated on a bird flyway for numerous wintering waterfowl.

At Finley Refuge in addition to ponds and dikes, a system of numer-ous trails has been established. Extensive fields of food crop such as corn, millet, sudan grass, milo. and ryegrass are now grown on the ref-uge to provide the needed winter feed for wildlife. The refuge also serves as an outdoor laboratory for many departments of Oregon State University located only 12 miles north. Bird, mammal. and plant lists are available at the refuge headquarters. Hiking, birding, photography and nature observation activities are encouraged here. A birder could spend several days and not cover the possibilities.

There are a large number of individual primitive trails. They wind through a wide variety of habitats—Oregon oak and maple woodlands, Oregon ash thickets, second growth Douglas fir, brushy hedgerows, marshes, meandering creeks, open meadows, pastures and cultivated fields. In addition, ponds, knolls, buttes, prairies, swamps. and a few access roads make for a continual changing scene. Day hikes of one to seven miles provide opportunities to see extensive wildlife.

There are special viewing locations and intrepretive outdoor dis-plays. The main attraction to this fine preserve is the variety of things to see in the native rural setting.

The refuge is available for day visits only. The nearest campgrounds are at Alsea Falls or Corvallis.

Washington

The Evergreen State is well named since its mild climate, with its even rainfall, keeps the foliage green in most of the western portion of the state throughout the year. From the hiker's standpoint, this half of the state — a region perhaps 200 miles wide and 240 miles long, with its mountain ranges, dense forests, beautiful lakes and hundreds of miles of Pacific Ocean coastline — is a veritable hiking heaven. When the western slopes are overcast with rain, the hiker can head for the sunny eastern slopes of the Cascades. Most of the eastern half of the state is dry plateau land, and much of it is irrigated to produce fruit and agricultural crops.

Carbon River Glacier Trail
Location: To get to the Carbon Glacier from Seattle, Washington, drive south on I-5 towards Tacoma. At about 23 miles, take Mount Rainier Exit 142B and go west for about ¼ mile to stop light. Turn left (south) onto State Route 161S towards Puyallup. In about seven miles, after crossing the Puyallup River, turn left (east) onto State Route 410E towards Yakima. Do not go into the city of Puyallup as the Mount Ranier signs might indicate, for these signs now lead to a different Mount Rainier entrance. When on route 410E Mount Rainier is directly ahead. In the springtime, this broad flat valley near Puyallup is covered with fields of daffodils and tulips. Follow 410E for 14 miles towards Buckley. Watch for logging truck activity on week days. Upon reaching the intersection with State Route 162, turn right (south) for two miles, then bear left on State Route 165 towards Wilkeson. Watch for a bridge with one-way traffic. Past Carbonado, the narrow road hugs the deep gorge of the Carbon River. Shortly, take a left at the Carbon River Entrance sign. The road is gravel for a distance, then paved. Soon you break out into a view of the beautiful river valley. The park entrance is 22 miles from Buckley. Another five miles inside the park boundary, an easily graded gravel road brings one to the Ranger Station. Here check in and get a set of park rules. A short distance ahead is the Ipsut Creek Campground. Park here by the trailhead.
Length: 3½ miles (one way); allow 1½ hours one way
Highest elevation: 4000 feet
Elevation gain: 1700 feet. Best time - July through September; easy trail along Carbon River bed.
Description: One of the privileges of the Pacific Northwest is to admire the glacier fields of its snowcapped mountains. From where the Woods family eats breakfast in their Mercer Island home, they can see Mount

Rainier with its massive glacier system to the southeast—exactly 53 miles away. From its summit and in direct line of their sight is the Carbon River Glacier slowly creeping down the mountainside.

Of all Mount Rainier's 22 glaciers, this one extends the furthest distance away from the summit. Since the edge of the Carbon River Glacier is only 46 miles air line from our home, Amos Woods chose this one for his glacier hike. There are many beautiful glacier vistas on Mount Ranier, most are considerably more photogenic. Numerous other glacier fields are located in the state of Washington in both the Cascade and Olympic Ranges. For the hiker to visit any one of these is to induce an infectious craving to seek out all the others.

The Carbon River Glacier is 3½ miles in from the Ipsut Creek Campground at the extreme northwest corner of the Mount Rainier National Park. From the trailhead, the first ½ mile is on a wide easy trail of even grade, and for the next mile continues to follow the forested valley floor close to the river elevation. At the first trail junction, follow marker directions to the left across the Carbon River. Glacier moraine all across the wide river bed, the milky colored condition of the water, and a blast of icy cold air confirm our upstream objective. Here at the river bed the summit of Mount Rainier can be seen 8 miles away. On the east side of the Carbon River, the trail heads south and steepens with switchbacks. Huge windfalls crisscross the river bed. At the next trail junction, keep to the right. For the next mile, the needle laden trail leads through a quiet forest primeval where trees have moss-covered exposed roots; and slippery log footbridges across streams have helpful side handrails. Soon you come to the junction with the Wonderland Trail which circuits the entire glacier system of Mount Rainier. At this point the trees begin to thin out.

Up the valley the glacier soon comes into view. In another ½ mile on a rock ledge trail the glacier snout is disgustingly dirty, unattractive, and difficult to photograph — unlike the glacier's beginning in its upper reaches. This glacier is well named, for it has a layer of dirt and rock on its upper exposed surface. Even the ice is dirty where it sloughs off in huge chunks. Small streams emerge from under the unsightly icy face giving birth to the Carbon River. A sign warns hikers not to approach the face of the glacier because of danger from breaking ice and boulders which roll down from the top. One only has to sit still beside the trail for a few minutes to see these very things happen.

More views of the glacier can be seen further up the trail. In another two miles, Moraine Park is reached and an additional mile to Mystic Lake takes one to an elevation of 6000 feet after a steep ascent, a gain of 3700 feet from the trailhead.

Ebey's Landing Trail

Location: To get to Ebey's Landing from Seattle, Washington, follow the lake I-5 to the Mukilteo Ferry, then a 26 mile drive to Coupeville. From State Route 20, turn left on Engle Road to Prairie Center. Here take a right onto Ebey Road. To visit the blockhouse in the cemetery, turn right on Cook Road and go up the hill towards the trees. Another left bring you to the cemetery. Returning to Ebey Road drive westerly towards the beach. The Ebey homestead is to the left as you approach the bluff. Before driving down to the beach, stop and visit the memorial marker to the left on the bluff. At the beach level, parking is to the right.

Length: 4 miles (one way); allow 3 hours

Interesting half-day hike, good in any season.

Description: On this hike Pacific Northwest history is mixed with seacoast beauty and ocean trail beachcoming. Ebey's Landing is the locale of the massacre of Colonel Isaac Ebey in August of 1867 during an Indian uprising.

Few hikes can match this for sheer scenic beauty. The trail goes along the top of a sloping salt water bluff which faces the Strait of Juan de Fuca from the westernmost beach of Whidbey Island, Washington. Past the shipping lanes, Vancouver Island is visible to the right while to the left is Port Townsend and the Olympic Mountain Range behind. Ships headed for the Pacific, tugs with barges and Alaska bound cargo fleets are seen while you are hiking this relatively easy trail.

En route to the start of the hike, be sure to enjoy some of the amenities of the neighborhood near Prairie Center. Here in excellent farming country are original homesteads. Visit the blockhouses still standing, the quaint cemetery, and the monument depicting the site of the Indian massacre. This commemorative memorial is also unique in that it was thoughtfully erected here by a private individual, the late Frank Pratt, Jr.

The trail follows a portion of Whidbey Island's western coastline that is also blessed with good beachcoming. Pacific Ocean currents and winds bring floating debris through the Strait of Juan de Fuca directly to this beachline. Driftwood, fishing gear, agates, shells and bottles of oriental origin can be found here any season of the year.

Here is a scenic trail in an isolated untouched region. The hike can be made nicely with two couples and two cars heading the trail in opposite directions. For the northbound leg, park at Ebey's Landing. About 200 yards north, watch for the trail to veer up the side of the bluff to skirt along a cultivated field. The trail then rises to a second 100 foot elevation rise to pass alongside a forest edged with picturesque windswept trees. Here the trail provides a stupendous view. At about the one mile point, you overlook a half mile long long-filled lagoon, several hundred feet below this sloping bank, named Perego's Lake after a Civil War veteran who homesteaded here in 1876.

A completely incongruous growth of small cacti covers the bank above Perego's Lake. If you decide to go down to the lagoon, carefully pick your footing. Do not slide or fall down. The cactus spines break offin short lengths and are not readily removed. On one trip, Amos

Wood and his family took this shortcut to the lagoon, but they do not intend to repeat that adventure. Sheep used to graze here, so there are numerous narrow parallel paths all along this bluff. About ½ mile beyond, the trail diagonals down to the beach.

Continue north along the beach to Partridge Point beach area. Beyond this, the Patridge Point fog horn is seen up on the bluff. Directly east of the fog horn lies abandoned Fort Ebey of former strategic military importance now planned for ultimate restoration as a state park. In about another 200 feet is a small driftwood filled lagoon. At the south end of this lagoon is a side trail that leads up to old Fort Ebey with its gun emplacements and bunkers. A second side trail from the north end of the lagoon leads to Lake Pondilla serenely surrounded with woods.

A short distance north perched precariously at the edge of the beach bluff, remains of World War II concrete coastal fortifications can be seen but are not to be confused with the old abandoned Fort Ebey. Immediately beyond is Libbey Park, an Island County waterfront park and picnic site with adequate parking. Here is parked the car of the southbound couple. They arrived here after driving past Coupeville to the northwest corner of Penn Cove, turning left from State Route 20 onto Libbey Road, and going west to its termination at Libbey Park.

Federated Forest State Park Trail

Location: To get to the Federated Forest from Seattle drive east on I-90. About one mile past Mercer Island, turn south on I-405. Go 7 miles and take Exit 4 in Renton. Join State Route 169 and go left (east) 19 miles to Enumclaw. Here turn left (east) on State Route 164 for about one-half mile and join State Route 410 going east. Drive 17 miles and turn right at the Federated Forest State Park sign. Bring your own lunch.

Length: two miles (one way circuit); allow two hours

Base elevation: 1700 feet easy half-day walk. Open all year around

Description: In Washington the Naches trail, one of the first pioneer trails between the eastern side of the Cascades and the Puget Sound country, passes through the Federation Forest of the Snoqualmie National Forest. Westward migration of settlers necessitated an improvement of the Indian trail between Fort Walla Walla in Eastern Washington and Fort Steilacoom in Western Washington. In 1853 work was begun from the west end toward Naches Pass to widen this trail for wagon travel. In the meantime the westbound Longmire-Biles wagon train of over 100 people had started up the eastern side of the Cascades criss crossing the Naches River toward the pass. On the west side south of Pyramid Peak they had to lower their wagons down a steep 1000 foot drop to the westward flowing Greenwater River and then the White River to become the first party to cross the Washington Cascades.

In 1854 this route was used by another wagon train and the U.S. Army during Indian uprisings. Because of the numerous crossings of the Naches River that were required and the Pyramid area problem, this route fell into disuse after 1884 in favor of lower and easier crossings then available. The original Naches Pass trail still winds through heavily wooded areas and summit meadows affording today's trail hiker identical landscapes as seen by these pioneer wagon train groups, including spectacular views of Mount Rainier.

Tree blazes made in the 1850's are occasionally found along this trail, but only on larger standing trees. It is reported that the military used their own blaze and the one used by General McClelland consisted of an X with two bars below. Most of these blazes are now obliterated by heavy bark growth.

Today part of the Federated Forest State Park west trail follows the original Naches Pass pioneer covered wagon road and evidence of this road is still visible. Because this is a relatively short hike within a developed State Park, it appeals to many senior citizen and garden groups.

The trails within this park are level and easily walked. No special gear is required. This forest area is at foothill elevation, 20 miles north of Mount Rainier in the heart of the Cascades alongside the White River.

An impressive interpretive center is located here within the 612 acres of virgin timber. Of special note to those interested in the flora across the State of Washington are exhibits of the coast forest zone, mountain forest zone, sub-alpine zone, alpine zone, yellow pine forest zone, bunchgrass zone and sagebrush zone. Also featured are living displays which contain representatives samples of plant life found in the first five of the zones listed.

Lost Creek Ridge Trail

Location: To get to the Lost Creek Ridge trail from Seattle, Washington, drive north on I-5 about 30 miles to Everett. Take exit 194 and Route 2 east for three miles and turn left on Route 204 toward Granite Falls. In 2½ miles turn left (north) on Route 92 at stop light. After 1½ miles turn right (east). Mount Pilchuck looms directly ahead. At the town of Granite Falls proceed ahead, after four-way stop, three short blocks to second stop sign. Turn left here on South Alder Way past high school on right towards Verlot.

Upon entering Mount Baker National Forest, the Verlot Ranger Station is in about ½ mile. Stop at the Ranger Station to check snow conditions and obtain a permit for overnight camping. Road is paved for the next 20 miles east of Verlot to Barlow Pass. Here turn left (north) onto Darrington-Monte Cristo road for about seven miles, past the North Fork Guard Station on the right to Sloan Creek road, number 308, also on the right. As indicated, the trail is 3½ miles in and on the left.

Length: 5 miles (one way); allow four hours one way
Highest elevation: 5550 feet

Elevation gain: 3550 feet. Strenuous hike with considerable elevation gain. Open late summer depending on winter snow.

Description: The purpose in suggesting this hike is to present an opportunity to climb to a vantage point on Lost Creek Ridge in order to see and photograph a striking profile of Sloan Peak. Few mountains are as unique or as photogenic as 7790 Sloan Peak with its characteristic monk's hood appearance. Two additional dividends for this trail are: first, to view 10,540 foot snow-covered Glacier Peak to the northeast; and second, to visit Round Lake to the north, conditions permitting.

Because of the elevation, location and lengthy seasonal snow cover, you should check ahead with the Forest Service relative to snow conditions at the summit. From the crest of Lost Creek Ridge trail, the side trail to Round Lake leads down steep slopes to the lake, but is hazardous in snow. This side trail does not not melt out until late summer.

Many people enjoy this hike as a day trip for the outstanding vistas it affords. For overnight backpackers, the trail continues on to Kennedy Hot Springs with its warm bath, and finishes on the White Chuck River road. Taking this route requires being met at that end several days hence, a 19 mile hike from one road to the other.

Lost Creek Ridge trail is within the Mount Baker National Forest 30 miles east of the Verlot Ranger station, or about 15 miles southwest of Darrington. This trail is the access to the Glacier Peak Wilderness. The Cascade Crest Trail passes between Sloan Peak and Glacier Peak.

The trail begins on the Sloan Creek road, number 308, about 3½ miles east of its junction with the Darrington-Monte Cristo road. At the left is parking and a trail sign. After about ½ mile of easy trail, it rises steeply with continuous switchbacks through open woods. In three miles it rises 2425 feet to Bingley Gap. Along this portion of the trail are open views of Sloan Peak. From Bingley Gap the trail continues another two miles along the ridge to a saddle where Round Lake viewed to the left (north). The short ¼ mile side trip into Round Lake is recommended only when the snow has melted. East of the saddle are good vistas of Solan Peak and Glacier Peak. Here is where your telephone camera lens comes in handy.

In August there may still be snow on the ridge. In overcast conditions, be prepared for chilly weather and cold winds. When planning this hike, try for a sunny day. Then your black and white and color pictures of photogenic Sloan Peak, taken either in the morning or afternoon, will be among your very favorites of the Washington Cascades.

This trail provides a variety of closed and open woods, open meadows, a crest ridge view of mountain peaks and good picture taking. The 3550 foot climb in five miles is well worth the effort, especially if you bring both cameras. Pictures of Sloan Peak will impress your friends.

Ozette Lake Trail - visit the Pacific Coast's outstanding archeological dig

Location: To get to Ozette Lake from downtown Seattle, take the 45-minute ferry trip across Elliott Bay and Puget Sound to Winslow, Bainbridge Island. Follow State Route 305 across the island and the Agate Pass bridge joining State Route 3 then 104 when crossing the Hood Canal Floating Toll Bridge. Join State Route 101 past Sequim to Port Angeles, a total distance of 78 miles so far. Here take State Route 112 to Sekiu, another 49 miles. About 3 miles past Sekiu turn left (south) onto the well marked road to Ozette Lake, a distance of 21 miles. When approaching the lake, bear right. The Ozette Lake Ranger Station and parking lot are at the end of the road.

Length: 9 miles triangular circuit, allow one day

Highest elevation: 100 feet

Elevation loss: 100 feet; easy day hike or overnight backpack. Oper all year round

Description: This Olympic National Park coast trail is shaped like an equilateral triangle with each side being about three miles long. The first tip of the triangle is at the trailhead near the Ozette Lake Ranger Station. A second tip is at Sand Point on a secluded Pacific Ocean beach. The third tip is also along the ocean shoreline at Cape Alava and marks the location of the Ozette Village dig, one of the most if not the most significant archeological finds in all of North America.

Campsites are available at Cape Alava. There are also seasonal guided tours of this site of an early Indian village that was covered by mudslides and hermetically sealed for 500 years. The dig has been worked since the late 1960s under the direction of Washington State University experts.

Over 40,000 artifacts have been recovered and catalogued. All this resembles the opening of a time capsule containing the culture of the Ozette Indian tribe. Many of the artifacts will be stored at Neah Bay at the new museum and cultural center, cared for by descendants of the Ozette People.

The hiker of this trip has several options: a day hike into the dig, an overnight at Sand Point, or a beach hike south from Sand Point and back for an easy second overnight.

Both trails, the Indian Village Nature trail to Cape Alava and the Sand Point trail, start from the trailhead at Ozette Lake. Both go through typical quiet oceanside forest on improved trails, parts of which are cedar plank walkways raised above the wet marshy areas. The trails are usually maintained in excellent shape. Waterproof footwear is a must, especially in damp weather.